THE COMING CHRIST
and
THE COMING CHURCH

THE COMING CHRIST

and

THE COMING CHURCH

EDMUND SCHLINK

Professor of Dogmatics
University of Heidelberg

FORTRESS PRESS

PHILADELPHIA

This is basically a translation from *Der kommende Christus und die kirchlichen Traditionen*, published by Vandenhoeck & Ruprecht in Gottingen, 1961.
A number of items are reproduced by permission from existing English translations, sometimes with slight emendations.
Owing to editorial difficulties resulting in delay of publication, the final major essay 'Ökumenische Konzilien einst und heute' has been replaced by 'Themes of the Second Vatican Council'.
Quotations from scripture are generally from the Revised Standard Version, copyright 1946 and 1952 by the Division of Christian Education of the National Council of the Churches of Christ in the United States of America and are used by permission.

First published in Great Britain by
Oliver and Boyd Ltd., Edinburgh and London, 1967

AMERICAN EDITION
First published, 1968

Printed in Great Britain by
R. & R. Clark, Ltd., Edinburgh

CONTENTS

INTRODUCTION

THE TASK

IN OUR DAY we have become deeply ashamed of the ever increasing divisions which have accompanied the historical development of Christendom. An irresistible desire for unity has come to life in all Churches. It is mainly manifested by a longing for communion in the Lord's Supper and for joint service in witnessing for Christ to the world. The most urgent appeal for unity has been made by the 'Younger Churches', which no longer wish to see the Christian message, which is preached to the pagan world, being refuted by Christian disunity. In Europe this appeal has received its deepest response among the laity and Christian youth, who are constantly exposed to the threat of nihilism.

This desire for unity is checked by the established traditions of divided parts of Christendom. These may be forms of worship which have arisen through history, the formulations of dogmas or a rigid ecclesiastical administration with particular regard to Church orders. In essential points these differences are not only seen as variety, but as contradictions. Moreover this diversity is intensified by the important influence of non-theological factors of an anthropological, cultural and political nature, which cannot be transplanted into all parts of the Christian world. As a result of the differences between the Churches, the concepts of the desired unity are by no means identical. Even in joint prayer we do not pray for the same thing. In view of this fact many people have come to the conclusion that the most that can be achieved is to bring the various parts of Christendom nearer to each other. This would lead to a varying degree of co-operation in mutual service for one another and for the world. And because of our lack of unity, we should begin by working together in social and charitable affairs.

There can be no doubt whatever that Christ demands nothing less than the unity of Christendom in faith and confession, in intercommunion and in the mutual recognition of

Church orders. Here the enthusiasm of the younger generation, in its eagerness for full unity, is justified over against the resignation of many of the older generation. Christ desires to manifest Himself through Christian unity on earth as the one Lord, to whom the universe is subject and by whose victory on the cross the hostility between men was overcome and peace established. Moreover, He does not merely wish for unity but He has created it. In other words, unity is not only His will, but, in Him, it is already realized. The Church which he created is one at all times and in all places. Her unity may be denied or distorted by man but it can never be lost. Thus it is not our task to create the unity of the Church but to make visible the unity which is given by Christ and to remove everything which obscures it.

But how can this be achieved? We must recognize that the existing traditions among the Churches cannot be passed over lightly. For every Christian has received the Gospel message through the tradition of a particular Church and was incorporated by baptism into the one Church (which is the Body of Christ) within a particular tradition. This is valid irrespective of whether he holds a particular view of tradition or not or even whether he reflects upon the tradition of the Church or understands himself as being a contemporary of the early Christians. Anyone who tried to ignore this fact would never overcome the existing divisions but rather increase them. Our task is not to ignore the existing traditions, but to open them up for each other. One can only wish that the theologians of the divided Churches would devote themselves to this theological task with the same eagerness and passion as the enthusiasts for unity demonstrate in passing over traditions. Therefore in our present situation, in which Christendom is looking for unity, we should distinguish between two stages in ecumenical discussion. Firstly we must look beyond the borders of the Church in which we received our faith in Christ and in which we know ourselves to be members of the one, holy, catholic and apostolic Church by our baptism and our participation in the body and blood of Christ. And we should also look in hope and love for the signs and the reality of the same Church in those parts of Christendom which are separated from us. And only when the one Church has been clearly recognized there, are we entitled to commence conversation with a view to union. If we were to take the second step before the first, it would become a failure, even though it might at first seem to be successful. Taken as a whole, Christianity now finds itself in the beginning of the first stage of the ecumenical discussion. The experience of unity, which breaks through divisions, demands theological clarification or else it will lead to confusion and disappointment. But how can divided traditions discover one another at this initial stage of discussion?

It is not sufficient to compare another tradition with one's own, and to identify what it has in common with one's own. We must rather look back to the historical foundation laid by the Apostles upon which the Holy Spirit builds the Church and to which all parts of Christendom appeal in one way or another. As far as it is possible we must try to understand the different traditions as the transmission and development of the apostolic witness to Christ, and of the apostolic admonitions and ordinances, while at the same time making allowance for their dependence on history. This requires both a critical examination of one's own tradition to see how far the apostolic tradition has been preserved and developed or how far it has been obscured and distorted.

Looking back to the apostolic witness to Christ we are at the same time directed forward to the coming of Jesus Christ, which has been proclaimed by the Apostles. Jesus Christ is not only the Church's historical foundation, but her present and coming Lord. The nature of the Church traditions and their relationship to each other would be misunderstood, if we were to content ourselves with looking back to the Church's historical origin and development. Jesus Christ will judge all these traditions; for he is the judge of the world and of the Church. Traditions can only mutually enrich each other, when we realize that they are only provisional themselves—even more, that the Church itself is provisional. Within most traditions, however, ecclesiology is taught in peculiar isolation from eschatology.

This search for the Church outside the limits of one's own tradition must not be confined to those parts of Christendom which are already closely related, as e.g. the Lutheran and the Reformed or the Orthodox and the Old Catholic Churches.

Our vision of the one Church must rather embrace the whole of Christendom, and we must dare to begin conversations with Churches which on first inspection seem far removed. Only within the wide horizon of the whole of Christendom will the discovery of the individual traditions take place in a way which will also give impetus towards unity in other Churches. For the Reformation Churches this implies that they do not take ecumenical discussions seriously unless they are prepared to enter upon discussions with the Orthodox and with the Roman Church.

If we look at the present situation of Christendom realistically, it is obvious that even the task of the first stage of ecumenical encounter is vast and difficult despite the desire for unity which has arisen in our time. Everybody who participates in ecumenical conversations is aware of the temptation to become sceptical, to withdraw to the existing traditions of his own Church or to accept the view of enthusiasts who content themselves with the invisible unity of the Church. But God's Spirit is already active in opening up the divided parts of Christendom for each other. He draws our attention to those elements within the various traditions which are derived from the apostolic tradition and belong to the living Christ. And the Spirit begins to present these elements as a common gift for all Christians. A fullness of unity has already started to shine through the dividing barriers between the Churches, even though we cannot yet grasp it in concepts or demonstrate it in our teaching. This emerging unity, however, presses for visible embodiment.

All the contributions in this book are derived from the conversations between divided Churches in which I have taken part during the past years both within the World Council of Churches and in meetings with theologians of the Roman and the Russian Orthodox Church. I have deliberately restricted myself to selecting those contributions which are concerned with the problems of the first stage of ecumenical discussion, and in particular to those which are concerned with the clarification of the methical problems involved in these discussions. Most of the contributions are papers which were read at ecumenical conferences. Since the presentation in each case is influenced by the audience of Church representatives to whom it was addressed, the form of a paper has normally been retained without change, although this leads to repetitions in certain cases. After all, the form of giving lectures and reading papers is particularly appropriate for the present stage of the ecumenical discussion.

Although the different chapters result from very different situations and from encounters with representatives of very different Churches, they still present a systematic unity. 'The coming Christ and the traditions of the Churches' is the theme which has increasingly suggested itself to me during these conversations. But this title must not be misunderstood as implying an examination of the differing concepts of tradition within the different Churches nor as an attempt to provide systematic exposition of the concept of tradition. This could only be done within the larger context of a treatment of the problems concerning the canon of Scripture, of dogma and biblical and dogmatic hermeneutics. Finally, it would only be possible within the consideration of ecclesiology as a whole. We are not primarily concerned with any theoretical definition of tradition; our concern is rather the mutual understanding and enrichment of existing traditions within separated Christendom. Normally, however, the traditions themselves and the Church's ways of understanding of her tradition do not coincide. For this reason the problem of tradition has become the most confused problem in interconfessional theological debate. Here it should be approached simply from the point of view of factual differences.

PART I

CONSIDERATIONS OF METHOD

I. THE TASK AND THE DANGER OF THE WORLD COUNCIL OF CHURCHES[1]

I

THE World Council of Churches is probably the most paradoxical organization in the history of the Church up to now. This is clear in the report of the first section of the World Conference of Churches of Amsterdam in 1948.[2] But it becomes quite explicit in the extremely well considered and precisely worded declaration made, in 1950 at Toronto, about the self-understanding of the WCC.[3]

The constitution and 'basis' which was accepted at Amsterdam defines the WCC as 'fellowship of churches, which recognize our Lord Jesus Christ as God and Saviour'. The Toronto declaration adds to this: 'The Basis of the World Council is the acknowledgement of the central fact that "other foundation can no man lay than that is laid, even Jesus Christ" '.[4] And yet the basis of the WCC is no common creed, since the interpretation of the declaration is left to every Church. Moreover it is perfectly possible for any Church to regard other Churches within the WCC as lacking the true confession, i.e. as being heretical.

The member Churches of the WCC believe that the Church is one. This belief has been even more firmly expressed in the declaration: 'Our unity in Christ is not a theme for aspiration,

[1] This address was delivered to an ecumenical working conference at Berlin–Spandau on October 13th, 1954. Trsl. G. Overlach and D. B. Simmonds.

[2] Official Report of the First Assembly of the WCC, Amsterdam, 1948 (cf. my critical report about the preparatory work of the first section in *Th.L.Z.* 1948, p. 614ff.).

[3] The Church, the Churches and the WCC, London, 1950 (cf. Peter Brunner, 'Pneumatischer Realismus' in *Ev.-Luth. Kirchenzeitung* 1951, p. 120ff.).

[4] Ibid. IV, 1.

it is an experienced fact' (Oxford 1937,[1] cf. the solemn declaration of unity in Edinburgh 1937[2]). By the 'mighty work of His Holy Spirit . . . we have been drawn together to discover that, notwithstanding our divisions, we are one in Jesus Christ'. 'It is our common concern for that church which draws us together and in that concern we discover our unity in relation to her Lord and Head' (Amsterdam[3]). And yet the WCC does not conceive of itself as the Una Sancta.[4] It is not the 'koinonia' of the Churches as we find it in the NT, nor a council of Churches as in the Early Church. For intercommunion is lacking as well as the mutual recognition of the Churches represented as belonging to the true Church.

'The member Churches recognize that the membership of the Church of Christ is more inclusive than the membership of their own church body'—they 'recognize in other Churches elements of the true Church' (Toronto declaration[5]). But in the WCC there is no agreement as to what these elements of the true Church are, and whereby they may be perceived.

The WCC sends messages to its member Churches and beyond them to the whole of Christendom and the world. These messages are a call to repentance and a proclamation of the dominion of Jesus Christ. They are both an assurance and a challenge. Thus the WCC effectively executes the essential functions of Church government. At the same time it must be remembered that 'it cannot legislate or act for its member churches' (Toronto declaration[6]). None of the Churches is obliged to make known to its congregations any message which was agreed upon by the World Council of Churches even if the decision was unanimous.

'A further practical implication of common membership of the WCC is that the member churches should recognize their solidarity with each other, render assistance to each other in cases of need, and refrain from such actions as are incompatible with brotherly relationships' (Toronto declaration[7]).

---

[1] 'The Churches Survey their Task', the Report of the Oxford Conference on Church, Community and State, 1937, London, p. 58.
[2] *The Second World Conference on Faith and Order*, Edinburgh, 1937, ed. Leonard Hodgson, p. 205ff.
[3] Official Report, p. 51.   [4] Toronto declaration, III, 1.
[5] Ibid. IV, 3 and 5.   [6] Ibid. III, 1.   [7] Ibid. IV, 7.

But the implications of this statement are not drawn out. For instance, it does not necessarily require the giving up of anathemas against another member Church.

We might continue in this direction. But it is obvious that these contradictions are far-reaching enough to provide a constant threat to the existence of the WCC. The WCC can only exist with these paradoxes as long as it does not make them a permanent fixture, but must move on towards the 'eschaton', in vigilant and clear awareness of the anomaly or rather the shame and disgrace of the present divided state of Christendom. The WCC must press on towards the Coming of Christ who will gather and judge his flock. Of course it is possible to understand these contradictions as an ecclesiological parallel to the 'simul peccator justus' of the reformers. But this is no static formula, but an expression of eschatological dialectics. Its purpose is not to sanction sin, but to disclose its reality ('peccator in re') and to assure the sinner of the saving righteousness of Christ, which is imputed to the sinner ('justus in spe'). Thus the contradictions of the WCC, which we have mentioned, do not allow us to rest content with its present state. In other words, the WCC can only live with these contradictions as long as it progresses towards the unification of its member Churches. For the Churches shall wait for their Lord and Judge as the one Church, and not as individual divided Churches. If the WCC does not continue on its way to further union, but comes to a standstill, it will be destroyed by its own paradoxes. It will cease to be worthy of trust, and become a mockery before the world, and the shame of divided Christendom in the sight of God and of the world would be greater than if the WCC had never been formed.

II

The Ecumenical Movement has undoubtedly made encouraging progress during the short period of its existence:

1. The divided Churches have discovered each other afresh and have drawn closer to each other. Ignorance has been largely overcome and the Churches have become acquainted with one another. Indeed we have discovered brethren in Christ where we had previously not expected to find them.

2. Common worship, in which the representatives of

different Churches have shared, has had its significant influence on ecumenical conferences. We have mutually received the assurance of the Gospel. We have prayed together. Some of the existing limitations regarding intercommunion have been overcome, and even where this was not possible we have learnt to participate in the communion of another Church by prayer and meditation and in spiritual reception of the Body of Christ.

3. This new awareness of our brethren has resulted in comprehensive and sacrificial works of charity which possibly represent the most extensive and certainly the most unusual assistance which has been given in the history of the Church. For help has been given to different Churches and confessions. The only criterion was their need, the name of Christ and love.

4. Beyond Inter-Church Aid, a powerful impulse was given by the discovery of a common social and political responsibility. The WCC does not merely negotiate or make resolutions to help Christians in need, but it has also made the rights of the oppressed the subject of important negotiations, decisions and actions.

5. Beyond dealing with the practical questions involved in initiating the movement for 'Life and Work' in 1925 at Stockholm, the WCC has become a place for basic scholarly theological study of the whole problems concerned with the Church and the world.[1] A good opportunity has been given to advance beyond problems concerning such matters as secular authority, the theological basis of law, the responsibility of society and the meaning of work, etc., which have already been dealt with in a promising way. It should also be possible to reach further results which might be accepted by all the different Churches, and which might give new impulses to their life.

All this work is fully under way.

III

In comparison with this, progress in the ecclesiological task itself is very small. Already at Lausanne in 1927 it was declared, 'God wills unity. . . . However we may justify the beginnings of disunion, we lament its continuance and henceforth must

[1] Cf. e.g. 'From the Bible to the Modern World', Two Conference Reports, ed. by the Study Department of the WCC 1947. Also the Treysa Conference in 1950 on 'Gerechtigkeit in biblischer Sicht', Geneva, 1950.

labour, in penitence and faith, to build up our broken walls.'
'God's Spirit has been in the midst of us' (during the conference). . . . 'We can never be the same again.'[1] Beyond this the
conferences of Oxford and Edinburgh have borne witness to
our common experience of the Church's unity in Christ.
Amsterdam, however, did not make much progress beyond this
in its insights and statements about the Church. The progress
at Amsterdam consisted merely in the production of the legal
constitution of the WCC, which replaced the previous ecumenical movement with its living fellowship of ecumenically-
minded individuals by a legally organized co-operation of the
Churches.

Of course we must not underestimate the significance of
the fact that the different Churches have come to know each
other afresh and have learnt to see each other in a new light,
with the result that they have gained better understanding of
their points of agreement and disagreement. In addition to this,
more common ground has been recognized in a new, surprising
and unforgettable way. This is the result of a methodical
comparison of the confessions, a procedure which was so highly
refined at Amsterdam that not only agreements and disagreements, but also 'the agreements within our differences' as
well as the 'differences within our agreements' were to be
investigated and presented. This method was largely employed
in the preparatory work for the Faith and Order conference at
Lund in 1952.[2]

The method, however, is purely formal. It could be equally
well applied in comparing Christianity with Judaism or even
in comparing Christianity with pagan religions. It is primarily
statistical. But such a formal and comparative procedure does
not demand any changes or sacrifices from the Churches
involved. On the contrary, it implies a fixed, unalterable
structure of the Churches, which must be compared with each
other. After all, every Church is entitled by the constitution

---

[1] 'Faith and Order', Proceedings of the World Conference, Lausanne,
1927, p. 460.
[2] Cf. esp. the three important volumes *The Nature of the Church*, *Intercommunion* and *Ways of Worship*, SCM Press, London, 1952. (Since 1952
the comparative method has been progressively replaced by new efforts in
biblical studies in the work of 'Faith and Order'.)

of the WCC to remain as it is. And even though this method at first sight led to the surprising and delightful discovery of considerable agreement, it must also (because of the increasing exactness of its application) lead to a clearer perception of the seriousness of the differences, which had been underestimated in the enthusiastic early days of the ecumenical movement. This is clearly revealed by the exposition of 'Our Deepest Difference' in section I of the Amsterdam report.[1] I am convinced that we have reached a natural limit of the method hitherto employed in our work for 'faith and order' and that we cannot make any further progress by using a method which does not demand any sacrifices from those who are involved. In fact this can only lead us into ever increasing difficulties.

The present position which has been reached in the movement towards unity within the WCC is in accordance with this statistical method. Some important moves have been made in bringing Churches together and a few unions have indeed been achieved since the ecumenical movement began. For example, we may note the union of Churches in South India and the union of the Church of Christ in Japan. In Europe the Anglican Church has reached agreements on intercommunion with the Lutheran Churches of Sweden and Finland and the Old Catholic Church. Furthermore we may observe the federation of the German Reformed Churches in the Evangelical Church in Germany. Further approaches and unions are under way.[2] But in all these cases it is a matter of agreements between neighbour Churches. The major communions—even apart from the Roman Church—remain unchanged alongside each other.

IV

In this situation the WCC is exposed to the danger of an insufficient understanding of its ecclesiological task.

[1] Cf. esp. the three important volumes *The Nature of the Church, Intercommunion* and *Ways of Worship*, SCM Press, London, 1952. (Since 1952 the comparative method has been progressively replaced by new efforts in biblical studies in the work of 'Faith and Order'.) p. 51.

[2] Cf. Oliver Tomkins, *The Church in the Purpose of God*, Faith and Order Commission Papers No. 3, 1950. (About the present stage of negotiations for union, which have increased considerably since 1951, see 'Survey of Church union Negotiations 1957–59', *Ecumenical Review*, Vol. XII, 1960, p. 231.)

Is not our common *faith* in the unity of the Church sufficient for unity? This faith has in fact been witnessed to time and again by the divided Churches on the World Conferences. But such a limited view would imply a docetic ecclesiology and false spiritualism. For the Body of Christ is always a visible fellowship in the Word, the Sacraments and Orders.

Is not the diversity of the Churches the organic development of the abundance of Christ's Body according to the Pauline multiplicity of spiritual gifts? This kind of organic thinking was once advocated by Schleiermacher and the scholars of the Romantic period.[1] But can we speak of fruitful diversity as long as it is not rooted in unity? The Church is constituted as the one Body of Christ by our participation in the Body of Christ in the Sacrament. Wherever full communion is lacking, we must not speak of a blessed diversity, but of division, disorder, disgrace and shame.

Or is the ecclesiological problem solved by reiterating that one's own Church is the Una Sancta and that it is simply a matter of calling upon the members of other Churches to join this Church? It is no longer possible to make such a retreat since all the Churches represented in the Ecumenical Council have recognized that there are members of the Body of Christ outside their own boundaries.

Or should we avoid all these dangers of resignation, of easy satisfaction and laziness by an actualism which simply by-passes and destroys the interconfessional problems instead of solving them? We know the catchwords: No Church confession but real confession! No Church dogma but real teaching! No Church Orders but real service! No liturgy but real witness! etc. But such a superficial attempt to break down all barriers would be contrary to both the practice and the earliest witness of the catholic Church, as has been demonstrated by modern New Testament research. There is no doubt that this ecumenical actualism—the twin brother of existentialism—would not lead to Church unity but would result in another denomination. It would not help us positively since its results, even if it were to succeed in pulling down all barriers, would be to turn the Church into a mass of people. This would correspond to the

[1] Cf. L. Lambinet, *Das Wesen des katholisch-protestantischen Zwiespaltes*, Einsiedeln-Köln, 1946, p. 61ff.

present growth of mass-societies and would result in a kind of 'Church mash'.

V

How then should the doctrine of the Church be approached in ecumenical work?

1. We shall have to concentrate our joint efforts in a more intensive and comprehensive study of the Bible. And the Churches will have to conduct their joint exegetical research with a new openness and determinedly radical approach to the original biblical witness. The biblical-theological contributors to the Amsterdam conference were too much bound by their traditional and confessional modes of thought. Sometimes it seemed as if the Bible was primarily used in order to justify the present nature of various Churches in the ecumenical movement. Meanwhile, however, exegetical scholarship has employed methods in its historical and linguistic research which have led to results which have, as yet, been given insufficient consideration in ecumenical discussion though they could prove to be fruitful. This also applies to the differences which have been recognized in the nature of the witness borne by the various New Testament writings. These differences were the result of the advance of the Gospel into constantly changing historical situations. The fact that these differences were not only tolerated by the Early Church but were perpetuated[1] by her in her definition of the NT canon provides ecumenical work with important and promising possibilities in dealing with these differences. This task is facilitated by the common recognition of Scripture as the supreme norm by all the Churches in the WCC, despite differences in the definition of the relation of Scripture to tradition. The Roman Catholic Church, on the other hand, has demonstrated its lack of respect for the apostolic tradition in its most recent Mariological dogma.[2]

[1] Unfortunately E. Käsemann has overlooked this. In answering the question 'Is the NT canon a basis for Church unity?' he feels bound to answer 'No'. *Ev. Theol.* 1951, p. 13ff. Cf. also *Exegetische Versuche und Besinnungen*, I, 1960, p. 214ff.

[2] Cf. *Evangelisches Gutachten zur Dogmatisierung der leiblichen Himmelfahrt Mariens*[1], München, 1951, and the instructive summary of the critical reports of the various Churches concerning the new dogma by Friedrich Heiler in *Ökumenische Einheit*, 1951.

2. We must be much more conscious of the presuppositions which everyone brings with him in ecumenical work.

a) This is, first of all, true of the dogmatic presuppositions which are frequently identified with biblical truths. This hinders a new readiness to listen to the biblical message.

b) It is also true of the philosophical presuppositions which are operative in the dogmatic formulations of the different Churches. There are dogmatic differences which are merely differences in philosophical terminology without involving disagreements in the truth which is asserted. Here a much more comprehensive work of scholarly translation must be performed than has generally been the case up to now.

c) We must also consider the anthropological presuppositions inherent in the different thought-forms, the varying individual constitutions and the basic forms of the Subject–Object Relationship, etc. These basic anthropological structures, which vary considerably from person to person, are transcended by revelation, but at the same time they are employed in Christian witness.[1] They are not eliminated, but their differing forms remain operative in the formulation of doctrinal statements by individual believers or Churches. Here, too, a difficult task of translation must be done.

d) We must pay more attention to the political and social factors, which have decisively influenced our divisions and which still exert a powerful influence of which we are not fully aware.

e) This is true of unconscious presuppositions in the widest sense. 'Forgotten factors' (Dodd)[2] of this kind may be, for example, allegiance to great men and events in the history of a Church, which are natural elements in a self-complacent pride of one's own tradition.

3. The history of the Churches, and especially the origin of schism, needs to be given a critical reconsideration by common research and by applying all those factors which have just been mentioned. The history of the Churches has seldom

---

[1] A more detailed account of this is to be found in my book, *Der Mensch in der Verkündigung der Kirche*, München, 1936, pp. 20ff., 209ff., 283ff.

[2] A letter concerning unavowed motives in the Ecumenical Discussion, *Ecumenical Review*, 1949, Vol. II, p. 52 ff. Cf. Tomkins, *The Church in the Purpose of God*, p. 108ff.

been given sufficient consideration in ecumenical work. Some people confined their attention to the present situation of the Churches and sought to gain immediate unity by jumping over historical differences. This tendency is to be found not only in American but also in 'pietistic' and rationalist thinking. Others made a biassed selection from Church history in order to justify their own Church or confession. Here again Church history was not taken seriously. Yet every schism has a 'traumatic' effect on the Churches who continue to live on in separation. One may attempt to suppress this trauma from one's consciousness, but this only results in increased disturbance. The sickness of Church disunity can only be aggravated by disregarding the historical facts concerning its origin. The only proper course of action would be to face these facts openly. We must look again for the demarcation line between the Gospel and human impenitence and self-confidence in history.

4. In all this, we must remember that Christology is the most important problem—since it is the presupposition to every single question of order. In previous ecumenical work this has been insufficiently realized,[1] despite the fact that the WCC has a christological basis. Although this basis sets limits,[2] it may still be variously interpreted.[3] It says nothing about the life of Jesus Christ, i.e. about His cross and resurrection, nor does it refer to His incarnation, exaltation and second coming. Also the 'for us' element of His person is not explicitly expressed, even though the words 'our God and Saviour' exclude a false metaphysical understanding. The conferences which have been held in these last few years have shown that the member Churches of the WCC have much more common ground than

[1] Cf. the important christological symposium 'Mysterium Christi', Berlin, 1931, which was the outcome of ecumenical co-operation between English and German theologians.
[2] For instance, it is incompatible with early liberalism (cf. the discussion in the Schweizerische Theologische Umschau). But also Bultmann has pointed out that this basis is hardly compatible with his NT theology. ("Das christologische Bekenntnis des Ökumenischen Rates," *Ev. Theol.* 1951, p. 1ff., and *Glauben und Verstehen* II, p. 264ff. E.T. *Essays*, SCM, 1955, p. 273ff.)
[3] For instance, although it is Trinitarian, it might still be understood as implying patripassianism.

might be expected from its basis. There are indeed great possibilities of declaring our common faith in Christ in common statements of witness and doctrine. Efforts in this direction ought to take into account the fact that the great variety of christological statements in the NT has only partly made its weight felt in the history of dogma.

VI

Any German co-operation in these tasks should not neglect the important support which is given by the Augsburg Confession which is the doctrinal foundation for most churches within the Evangelical Church in Germany—even including some Reformed Churches.

On the other hand the articles on the Church in the Augsburg Confession oblige us to point out that the Church's unity is essentially a unity of faith which requires agreement in the preaching of the Gospel and in the administration of the Sacraments. At the beginning of the Ecumenical Movement there were times when this consideration was found to be inconvenient. Now, however, all Churches have realized that the place of truth must be guaranteed, and this is an essential condition for the participation of the Reformation Churches in the WCC.

On the other hand it is obvious that the Augsburg Confession in its definite allegiance to the doctrine of the Gospel, gives us considerable freedom in our search for brethren in other Churches. This freedom can hardly be found in any other Church which is bound by dogmatic principles. For since the Church is taught as being 'the assembly of all believers among whom the Gospel is purely preached and the Sacraments are rightly administered', the whole emphasis is laid on the reality of the present action of Jesus Christ in Word and Sacrament. Even if a Church possesses the purest confession, the finest liturgy and the best system of orders, this is no substitute for the actual preaching of the Gospel and the administration of the Sacraments according to Christ's command. Thus the conception of the Church in the Augsburg Confession continually calls in question the Churches of this confession. At the same time this conception points to the fact that the unity of the Church is not necessarily bound up with a common system of orders, worship and discipline, nor even with the acceptance of the same confessional documents and Biblical canon.[1] Only the same aspostolic Gospel must be preached and the same Sacraments administered according to Christ's command! The Lutheran confessional documents are not to be understood as a mark of the Church, neither do we find in them any demarcation of the canon of Scripture. The present and active Jesus Christ is one and all. His voice has to be listened to wherever it calls. And wherever the voice of the good shepherd can be heard, there also is the Church.

VII

In spite of all this we must never forget that even a definite goal and perfect methods cannot bring about or replace the indispensable presupposition for any further approach towards a final union of divided Churches, which is a change of heart. Neither the most careful and scientific work, nor the most clever diplomacy, nor friendly persuasion nor threat and menace can produce this change. It is the work of the Holy Spirit alone. But the working of the Holy Spirit is not a miracle, for which we have to wait as for a fateful event. For we know that God desires to give us the Holy Spirit. All other petitions are conditional petitions ('not as I will, but as Thou wilt'), but our prayer for the sending down of the Holy Spirit is God's unconditional will. We also know that the Holy Spirit bears witness to Christ and comes through our witness to Christ. The inspiration of the Scriptures does not only mean that the Scriptures themselves are inspired, but also that the Word of Scripture actively inspires us. Thus the Holy Spirit is not unknown to us and we know his reality and the way he operates. Therefore we are called to strive for the Spiritual Gifts. This insight that only God's Spirit can change our hearts does not entitle us to be idle or to adopt an easy self-righteousness in our theological thinking, but demands constant and intense prayer and an increasing study of the Scriptures. If we avoid this and simply harp on the unity of the Church, God will humble us by His judgement and unite us as He did in situations during the Second World War.

Unlike the World Conference at Lausanne the WCC which

[1] See p. 109ff. in the German text.

was constituted at Amsterdam has rightly refused to set up one or more ideal images of the united Church and left the mode of union to the Lord of the Church and to the working of His Spirit. Nevertheless the following conditions seem to be indispensable:

1. We must be humbly prepared to share our best gifts of God's grace—past and present—with all the Churches separated from ours. It is an essential part of love to be ready to give ourselves to our neighbours for Christ's sake.

2. We must realize that we have misused God's gifts. We must acknowledge our guilt, our ingratitude, our want and our poverty. In our disruption we lack abundance. Our repentance consists in being ashamed of the scandal and guilt of our divisions. In this repentance all security is taken from Christians, and the bulwarks of hardened self-sufficient piety are broken down in God's presence.

3. We must passionately look for our brethren in other Churches and be prepared to discover the gifts of grace, which God has given to them, and desire participation in them. This is the joyful expectancy of those who wait for the voice of the good shepherd within the other Churches. It is the complete readiness to commit oneself to the work of the risen Christ, wherever it is done.

4. Whenever a union between divided Churches is achieved none of those Churches can remain the same. Union does necessarily imply a sacrifice of one's own possession, a surrender of habits and securities which were previously taken for granted. And yet such a sacrifice does not imply loss. For it is joy in the reception of greater gifts of greater value. We have already received many of these riches in the Ecumenical Movement. Much more is yet to be received.

II. THE STRUCTURE OF DOGMATIC STATE-MENTS AS AN ECUMENICAL PROBLEM[1]

AT ANY ecumenical gathering it may be observed that members of divided Churches find it much easier to pray and witness together than to formulate common dogmatic statements. In other words the members of one Church have little difficulty in appropriating for themselves the prayers and preaching of another Church. This preaching, which both strengthens and admonishes them, is perceived as applying to themselves. On the other hand, they find it much more difficult to accept as binding the dogmatic statements of another Church. This observation can neither be brushed aside simply by pointing out the edifying character of prayer and preaching, nor by maintaining that, in this case, emotional factors such as the experience of fellowship, exclude the application of strict theological standards which are normally applied to dogmatic statements. Nobody can deny that such emotional factors are influential at ecumenical conferences. But this does not invalidate our initial observation—an observation which has been frequently made and will be made time and time again, especially by Christians who give the same serious consideration to every utterance they make through prayer or preaching as to their dogmatic statements. The striking fact is that it is possible to speak with one voice in prayer or preaching about such matters as Christology, Anthropology, Soteriology or Ecclesiology, while it is impossible or very difficult to make common dogmatic statements about the same questions. This raises the question—what happens when one transfers the theological meaning of statements expressed in prayer and preaching into the category of dogmatic statements? What is the distinctive structure of a dogmatic statement over against the structure of prayer and preaching, and how do these differences affect the meaning of dogmatic statements?

[1] Trsl. by G. Overlach and D. B. Simmonds.

1. The Dogmatic Statement as a Basic Form of Theological Statement

The Gospel, as the message of the death and resurrection of Jesus, is the presupposition of the following considerations. The Gospel is not only the report of the man Jesus and his historical fate, nor is it simply the words of assurance 'died and risen for you', but it is also the Word through which the risen Christ performs His saving work as the saving Lord. The Gospel is not solely the message of God's action in delivering Him to death and raising Him from the dead. Nor is it merely the assurance of God's love, which was revealed in this action; but through the Gospel God Himself deals with the sinner in His love, reveals his sinfulness, makes the sinner righteous and recreates him. The Gospel accomplishes whatever it promises. It is the power of God which not only demands faith, but also creates it.

The divine message of the Gospel cannot be preached consistently without the believer's response. The Gospel is the power of God which will continue to act through the believers. To refuse to respond in faith would automatically involve the loss of faith itself. What is the response which is demanded of believers?

There is a twofold response of faith from those whom God first loved: the loving address to God and love towards one's neighbour. The response to the call of the Gospel is prayer to God and witness before men. Neither of the responses can be separated from the other, although they are not directed towards the same 'Thou', although, indeed, the 'Thou' addressed is as different as the heaven is from the earth, or as light is from darkness. Our love to God cannot be separated from our love to our neighbour, nor can the love to our neighbour exist without the love to God. 'If any one says, "I love God", and hates his brother, he is a liar' (I John iv. 20). It is equally impossible to separate our prayer to God from our witness before men. Although the persons addressed are entirely different, one address cannot exist without the other. This intimate connexion between prayer and witness can be seen most clearly in the primary act of responsive faith, namely in confession. For in confession prayer and witness coincide in a single statement.

i. *The Basic Forms of Theological Statements*

In order to discuss the structure of dogmatic statements it is essential in the first place to bring to mind the different forms of responses of faith and to pay special attention to their different personal[1] structure. In this connexion we must confine ourselves to singling out systematically the most elementary basic forms from the abundance of types of 'responses of faith' contained in the Old and New Testaments.

a) *Prayer* is the response to the Gospel in which the divine 'Thou' addresses us. In this response the believer takes possession of the saving act which is proclaimed and enacted through the Gospel as being effective for himself. Prayer is based on God's action in dealing with the sinner and confirms this action before God. This is properly done before God when the believer confesses himself as an unworthy creature and thanks God for His saving act, and basing his claim upon it, implores for God's action. In the Old Testament psalter God's constitutive act of saving Israel is praised over and over again. God is given thanks for this saving act and by basing her appeal on it and on God's revealed name Israel calls for further action on behalf of the nation and its members. Similarly the Christian community of the New Testament showed its response to the saving act of God in Christ by constantly giving thanks and taking hold of this saving act with praise and an imploring use of Jesus' name. Thus the believer responds to God by praying to Him as the 'father of our Lord Jesus Christ' (e.g. II Cor. i. 3), and by calling upon Him 'in the name of Jesus' (cf. John xiv. 13f. and xvi. 23ff.), 'through Jesus Christ our Lord' (Rom. vii. 25) and 'in Christ Jesus' (Ign. Rom. ii. 2). For 'it is Christ Jesus, who died, yes, who was raised from the dead, who is at the right hand of God, who indeed intercedes for us' (Rom. viii. 34). This is to recognize that the act of salvation is not merely a past event, but was performed once and for all time and is thus simultaneously past and present. Jesus not only died and rose, but as the one who died and is risen, is the present Lord, who intercedes for us. If we pray we take the love of God seriously,

---

[1] TRANSLATORS' NOTE—'personal' here and throughout this essay is the translation for the German 'personal', which indicates that personal categories or relationships are somehow implied in the word it qualifies.

which he showed to us at the Cross, putting our trust in the God who is love and counting upon God's love which is new every day and which also takes the future under its wing.

Prayer is both the address of the divine 'Thou' and the expression of the human 'I'. This 'I' is a necessary part of both prayers of thanksgiving and prayers of petition. It cannot, of course, be separated from the 'we' of the congregation (for example, in the Lord's Prayer it is only to be found in the 'we'). Nevertheless the 'I' within the fellowship of the praying congregation is the individual man who is unique in history and cannot be substituted in his encounter with God, who has reached out towards him personally. Thus our gratitude does not simply consist in giving thanks for the saving act which happened once nor merely in our thankfulness for the redemptive act performed for the Church, but in all this it includes a thankful appreciation that the work of salvation was done *for me* in spite of my sin. The same holds good for the prayer of petition: the 'I' is inextricably tied to the 'we' of the Church and extends to all those who are in need of intercession. But in all this *my* guilt, *my* temptation and *my* need are at stake. Thus a dialogue takes place between God and man in his hearing of the Word and in his response of prayer. In this dialogue man becomes through God's address the 'I' that can praise God as 'Thou', and can question him, pray to him and even assault him.

b) Among the many types of prayer, *doxology* has a special place regarding its personal structure:

In doxology the believer does not ask for anything for himself, nor does he ask God to act for other people. He simply worships God. The first three petitions of the Lord's Prayer request the coming of the Kingdom, while the doxology of the congregation simply acknowledges: 'for thine is the kingdom, the power and the glory for ever and ever'. Doxology is basically concerned with praising and acknowledging the divine reality. Thus it is possible to address God in the second person, as, for example, in the doxology in the Lord's Prayer. But, as a rule, in doxology God is addressed in the third person, i.e. God is not addressed as 'Thou' but as 'He'. If we translate: 'Glory to God in the highest . . .' (Luke II. 14) or 'to him be

c

glory forever' (Rom. xi. 36), this does not mean that God receives through the doxology the attributes 'glory', etc., which He did not previously possess. Rather the doxology 'gives' to God that 'glory' which is already His. In other words, it praises the glory which God has and 'is' whether man honours Him or not. Doxology is the reflection of the eternal divine majesty in human praise.[1]

Doxology is based on God's redeeming act. The believer glorifies God for His action towards mankind and the world. This is quite clear in the OT psalms of praise. Because God who reigns on high has shown mercy by His redemptive action in history towards those who were of no account, He is extolled as the Lord, who continually stoops down in mercy from on high, but beyond this He *is* eternally exalted in majesty and at the same time merciful, gracious, kind and condescending. Adoration is rooted in the acknowledgement of God's action in history. It is, properly speaking, the theo-logical development of thankfulness for God's action, whenever this gratitude is translated into a song of praise for the eternal God Himself. 'That descriptive praise arises out of reporting praise' does not imply that God's action in history is portrayed in 'descriptive praise' itself. On the contrary we should recognize, despite the

[1] Doxological expression did not first come into existence as a result of the advance of the Gospel into the hellenistic world, but it was in existence long before this time in the OT. Here again it is not confined to scattered individual assertions, but occurs as a basic form of personal and communal life. Thus Claus Westermann in carrying on the form-critical analyses of psalms begun by Gunkel and Begrich has distinguished between two 'basic types': 'the reporting and the descriptive psalm of praise. They have in common the same basic characteristic of exalting God. In the one case he is praised for a unique act of intervention; in the other he is praised for the abundance of his being and activity' (*Das Loben Gottes in den Psalmen*, 1953, p. 14). Descriptive praise is not the confession of the redeemed, but reflects upon 'the sovereign activity of the great God at all times and at all places and extols him for them all' (p. 22). Thus it does not confine itself to God's action in history in which He stooped down from His majesty on high to visit His people and the individual believer. On the contrary, it praises the nature of the divine action, which is always to have mercy upon sinners from on high and glorifies God's eternal majesty, omnipotence and grace. 'In the structure of these psalms we can observe the tendency to praise God's divinity in its fullness' (p. 97). This basic form of adoring praise has found its most abundant expression within the scriptures of the NT in the prayers of the heavenly liturgy of the Apocalypse.

inseparable inner connexion between them, that we are dealing with two different 'types' of psalms of praise (Claus Westermann).[1] These forms of praise follow from the distinction between giving thanks for God's action and adoring this divine nature and being. The NT doxologies are likewise evoked by God's redemptive act, that is by the saving act in Christ which is complete and perfect despite the expectation of the parousia. Thus the congregation on earth may here and now join in the triumphal songs of the perfected saints, who rejoice in the consummation of God's kingdom and in the overthrow of all powers hostile to God, praising God and the Lamb. Since God's redeeming acts are the basis of doxology, they are frequently to be found in the words of NT doxologies. But they are not indispensable in the text of any doxology, and even when they are expressly referred to in a doxology they do not constitute more than the occasion and cause for the doxology and thus they are not determinative for the content of the doxology (cf. e.g. Rev. IV. 11; XIX. 1ff.). Doxology, in the last resort, is directed towards God Himself. It is directed towards God, because of what He has done for us men and for the world. It is concerned with God who is distinct from His activity and who performs His deeds with the freedom belonging to the almighty and loving Lord. God existed before He acted and will continue to exist, He is the first and the last, the beginning and the end. Doxology is not only concerned with God's activity in history, but with God Himself, in His own eternal reality. 'Holy, holy, holy is the Lord of hosts; the whole earth is full of His glory' (Is. VI. 3). This statement is valid, whether the earth magnifies Jahveh or not. 'Holy, holy, holy, is the Lord God Almighty, who was and is and is to come!' (Rev. IV. 8). 'To the king of ages, immortal, invisible, the only God, be honor and glory for ever and ever' (I. Tim. I. 17). 'Amen! Blessing and glory and wisdom and thanksgiving and honour and power and might be to our God for ever and ever' (Rev. VII. 12). In these and many similar utterances the intention is to acknowledge God as God, who from everlasting to everlasting is the same holy, mighty, glorious and wise God both before His redemptive acts and after. Consequently in the development of doxology we can observe the appearance of statements about God's

[1] Ibid. p. 96; cf. p. 20ff. and p. 83ff.

existence, essence and properties, whose purpose is to exalt His eternal unchangeableness which comprehends all history. The same holds true of the praise of Jesus Christ, who is extolled not only as the crucified and risen one, but also as the eternal one who embraces all time, is pre-existent, and with the Father remains the first and the last, the beginning and the end.

If in the doxology the divine 'Thou' gives way to the 'he' the 'I' of man who utters the doxology is bound to disappear as well. Nevertheless the 'we' and 'our' do occur at times as also the 'Thou' (cf. e.g. Rev. XIX. 1). But generally the 'I' of the worshipper withdraws into the background. In doxology he neither asks for anything for himself, nor does he give thanks for God's dealings with him. He does not pay attention to himself as the person who is offering praise. Neither the 'I' of the worshipper nor his act of worshipping is explicitly mentioned in the words of the doxology. Thus both the individual human 'I' as well as the 'we' of the congregation lose their prominence, though without vanishing altogether. The basic form of doxology is not, 'God, I praise Thee', but 'Let God be praised'. It is not, 'God, I glorify Thee', but 'God is glorious'. Although doxology is man's response to God's dealings with him, man keeps silence about himself. God Himself is the one and only subject in doxology. Hence doxological statements appear to be supremely objective. Yet the absence of the 'I' from the text of many doxologies does not imply an uncommitted lack of concern, but indicates utmost devotion. For although the 'I' of the worshipper does not occur in the text, it is contained in the actual performance of worship. The 'I' is sacrificed in doxology. Thus doxology is always sacrifice of praise.

c) *Witness* is the response to the Gospel which is directed to the 'you' of our fellow-men. Witness is indeed another response to the Gospel, since the believer testifies to his fellow-men to the same act of salvation which God both proclaimed to and effected for him. Thus the response to the 'good news' is further 'good news'. The Gospel which has been received can never remain the private property of the believer. The Gospel is the urgent Word, storming into the world, by which the exalted Christ takes possession of the world which God has committed to him. Christ takes every Christian into the service of his victorious calling and his urgent salvation and sends him forth as a witness. Like prayer, witness is performed in various ways. It may be borne in a prepared address, in conversation, in the congregation, in missionary advance, or it may take the form of an assurance or a demand. All these forms of witness have one thing in common. They are based on God's action in Christ, that is, they are carried out in the name of Christ. If witness is borne in the name of Christ, we can be certain that the exalted Christ will acknowledge it, and manifest His presence in it, since He chooses to speak and to act through human witness.

In witness God is not addressed as 'Thou'. Notwithstanding the acknowledgement of His active penetration into the world through witness, He is spoken of in the third person. The 'Thou' of witness is our fellow-man in his inexchangeable historical reality. The same saving act which God has wrought in the believer, has to be proclaimed to our fellow-man in the light of his own sin, his difficulties, his real subjection to political, ideological (weltanschaulich) and religious powers in his own conceptual world and language. The Gospel should be set forth within a historical development that penetrates the whole world. And it will permeate the world by seeking and finding the concrete historical 'Thou' of every individual man and every particular nation.

In directing our attention towards the concrete 'Thou', the 'I' of the witness is generally also expressed. This is partly true in the sense that, in the last resort, it is the believing person himself who bears witness. Seen in this light it is apparent that the 'I' is also expressed in the doxology, although the mere text does not give any indication of the person who utters it. In witness, however, unlike doxology the 'I' of the believing person is explicitly expressed. For it proclaims God's action not only as a past event, but as the event which happened once and for all and which determines the present and is actively at work as God's activity in the present. Whenever the 'I' of faith appears in witness, it indicates that a witness is speaking, who does not merely reproduce something he once heard, but who stands up for the truth of what he heard and proclaims the salvation which he himself has experienced.

d) Among the many forms of testimony which we bear to

our fellow-men, *doctrine* holds a special place regarding its personal structure.[1]

There is no uniform concept of didache in the scriptures of the NT. When the Synoptists describe Jesus' words in single and summary statements both as teaching and preaching, they are using these terms as synonyms. This corresponds to the relation of Jesus to Moses and the law, which is characterized by the fact that Jesus is both interpreting and at the same time superseding the old and setting up the new.[2] 'Teaching' and 'preaching' are to be found as interchangeable terms elsewhere in the NT scriptures as well. Sometimes their combination must be understood as a hendiadys (i.e. as two ways of saying the same thing). Paul differentiates between various types of statements, with which believers address their fellow-men on the basis of God's saving acts. Thus in Rom. xii. 6ff. he distinguishes between 'prophecy', 'teaching' and 'exhortation'. In I Cor. xii. 8ff. we find 'utterance of wisdom', 'utterance of knowledge', 'prophecy', 'various kinds of tongues' and 'the interpretation of tongues'. Further in I Cor. xiv. 26ff. we find 'hymn', 'lesson', 'revelation', 'tongue' and 'interpretation'. These are not only different statements of faith, but different spiritual gifts, different spheres of service, which have been given to different members of the Church to carry out. They are partly so specifically related to particular people, that he does not merely regard these spheres of service as functional, but as personal—and consequently refers to 'prophets', 'teachers', etc. (I Cor. xii. 29; cf. also Acts xiii. 1 and Eph. iv. 11). What does Paul mean by teaching, in contradistinction to prophecy, which is the actual and dynamic revealing, strengthening and guiding Word of the Spirit of the present and effective Christ. 'Didache' is not only the moral teaching,[3]

---

[1] TRANSLATORS' NOTE—Doctrine, didache, teaching and instruction will be used to translate the German 'Lehre', which covers all these terms. Where it occurs, we have attempted to choose the most appropriate translation, but sharp distinctions must not be drawn. For 'Lehre' was deliberately employed to cover all these aspects, and in particular to stress the continuity of the development of NT didache into later doctrine.

[2] Concerning the appearance of Jesus' proclamation as teaching against the external background of Jewish teaching see Rengstorf, Art. *Th.W.B.N.T.*, Vol. ii, p. 141ff.

[3] Cf. e.g. M. Dibelius, *Die Formgeschichte des Evangeliums* [2], 1933, p. 241;

which is added to the proclamation of salvation, neither is it the mediation of moral standards. This is contradicted by Gal. I. 12, where the Gospel is identified with the content of 'didache'. Besides, moral precepts, which must be obeyed, are also transmitted by prophecy as distinct from 'didache'. On the other hand the Pauline concept of 'didache' cannot be interpreted as a later addition, which is based on the 'kerygma'. From this point of view the 'didache' (which is rooted in the 'kerygma' of the saving act experienced by faith), is simply the exposition of the new self-understanding which is opened for the believer through this saving act: 'God's revelation . . . is the basis of knowledge and doctrine, insofar as it bestows the possibility of a new understanding of oneself' (R. Bultmann).[1]

'Didache for Paul' is theology 'as the conscious and methodical exposition of the knowledge which is received by faith'.[2] Against this, it is important to note the close connexion, which existed for Paul, between 'didache' and its transmission as has been shown by H. Greeven.[3] 'Didache' is chiefly concerned with the transmission of fixed pieces of the Church's tradition. This includes the tradition of our Lord's sayings, reports of Jesus' deeds, and His passion as well as the appearances of the risen Lord. In addition it is concerned with the transmission of kerygmatic, confessional, hymnic and other fixed types of formulations and alongside with this ethical rules as well.[4] Thus prophecy and teaching represent the 'vertical and the horizontal components' in the witness of the Church, and are therefore 'strictly related to each other': 'Prophecy without "didache" degenerates into enthusiasm (Schwärmerei), teaching without prophecy is petrified into law'.[5] All this implies that 'didache' is more than the subsequent exposition of the saving act that takes place

'The mediators of this moral teaching were obviously the teachers who are for the most part frequently mentioned in the early Christian literature'.

[1] Kirche und Lehre in NT, *Glaube und Verstehen* (I), 1933, p. 178.

[2] Ibid. p. 186.

[3] "Propheten, Lehrer, Vorsteher bei Paulus," *Z.N.W.*, Vol. 44, 1952/53 —cf. the detailed argument on pp. 20ff.

[4] Cf. ibid. Thus the 'standard of teaching', to which the baptized were made subject (Rom. VI. 17), was probably an instruction about the very facts concerning the crucifixion, death, burial and resurrection, into which the sinner has been baptized (cf. p. 20f.).

[5] Ibid. p. 29.

through the message. Indeed, Paul constantly justifies his message by appealing to statements of doctrinal tradition. Accordingly in this decisive respect it is his message which appears to be the exposition of 'didache'. And it is this message based on 'didache' which meets man in his actual situation. Hence Paul understands both the direct address of the prophetic word and the function of teaching as operations of the Spirit. The risen Lord does not merely work through Paul's own words which demand obedience, but also through the tradition and with it through teaching. In his enumerations of the gifts of the Spirit Paul never opposes 'kerygma' to 'didache'. The same 'kerygma' is rather proclaimed in a variety of ways and it is this variety which bears witness to the final redemptive action of God in Christ and makes it a present reality. Viewed in this light, doctrine will be treated as one particular form of witness among others. In this context we should note that Christian doctrine from the very first was not confined to the transmission of received tradition. The fragments of tradition are interpreted as well, especially in their relation to the scriptures of the OT. But an explanatory exposition of a phrase, such as 'according to the scriptures', which occurs in I Cor. xv. 3ff. (a fragment of tradition which is quoted by Paul to support his argumentation) has a different character in this doctrinal context than the exposition of the transmitted saving act which takes place in preaching and pastoral care.

Doctrinal statements are not merely designed to protect the faith, but they are also intended to bring about its revival and propagation. But they do not touch the individual human 'you' in its actual historical situation with the same directness as does preaching. Doctrine does not confront the individual, the Church or even the world in its actual condition of corruption and rebellion in the same way as does the prophetic word with its pointed message of judgement, justification and exhortation. Doctrine is also concerned with man, but it addresses him less directly. For it simply passes on and explains what God did for men and through men, in history, what He did for His people, what He did to Jesus and through Him and what He did to each and every man whom Jesus met and finally what He did to His Apostles and through them. Even though the express 'Thou' and 'you' of those addressed by the teacher have a less prominent place in words of instruction, and are displaced by the tradition of historical facts which other men have experienced and are transmitted in the context of God's saving history (Heilsgeschichte) (as can be seen in the connexion between New and Old Testaments), this tradition is nevertheless quite different from historical (historisch) reporting in our modern sense. It is a statement of faith and its constant purpose is to create faith. As teaching about the great deeds of God it is the indispensable basis for the progress of witness in the world in its many forms. Thus far, teaching is not divorced from witness. For both the history of the synoptic tradition as well as the history of fragments of early tradition in the NT letters show that even in the transmission of particular historical facts and sayings we find frequently—though quite unconscious—a turning to the situation in the world, which has led to changes in stress, omissions and explanatory additions. Nevertheless teaching is different from a direct call to repentance, an assurance or a claim. Its way of addressing man remains peculiarly indirect and it always requires explanation through the prophetic word and through preaching and pastoral care.

In teaching, the 'I'—like the 'Thou' of our fellow-man—is also less prominent than in direct missionary preaching or conversation. Moreover the origin of a tradition is generally more important than its transmitter who in most cases remains anonymous. In his teaching the believer does not in the first place bear witness to the saving act which is now being realized for him and the Church. Teaching is especially concerned with preserving the identity of the message throughout the changing historical situations and in holding firmly to the message of the historical witnesses. In other words, teaching is concerned with the historic, once-and-for-all redemptive act of God in Christ, as the basis of all the manifold responses made by faith—even if this divine action is explained in its relation to what God did to His covenant people in the OT, or what He does for His creation.

Thus both doxological utterances and didactic formulas of teaching appear peculiarly 'objective', though in different ways. Common to both is that the 'I' of the speaker and the actual historical situation out of which he speaks remain in the background and that neither is necessarily explicitly referred to in the text of the statement. The same is true of the 'Thou' to whom teaching is addressed and even more so of our fellow-men in whose presence the doxology is sung. Thus addressing God in the third person is common to both. Yet the actual 'I' is not absent in these two forms of expressions of faith. For it is actual historical persons who produce these statements. In this case, however, the existential character of the statements is constituted by the fact that the actual person engaged in the service of teaching commits himself to God's eternal glory and joins in the praise of God's historical saving work—and as a sacrifice of praise he becomes instrumental in its further spread.

We should not, however, fail to see the differences between teaching and doxology. Teaching is concerned with men; doxology is directed towards God. It recounts God's deeds, which He performed in history, and beyond it, bears witness to the creation in the beginning and the future consummation. In doxology, on the other hand, it is ultimately God Himself who is glorified as Lord in His eternal holiness, omnipotence, love and wisdom. He does not only attain lordship as a result of His deeds, but has performed His great deeds according to the glorious freedom of His love and will continue to perform them. We have seen then that doxology is based on God's great acts and accordingly upon witness and teaching.

e) In *confession*[1] there is a unique concentration of all responses of faith. Confession reproduces so plainly the Gospel which it has received that no shadow of doubt can arise that it is the same act of salvation, and the same Lord proclaimed by the Gospel, who is here acknowledged in faith. This assumes the shortest possible form in ascribing to the man Jesus one or more of his titles of honour, that is by confession as Christ, Son of God or Lord. In this shortest form the crucifixion and resurrection are not explicitly mentioned. Yet they are contained even in these credal statements, since the resurrection of the crucified is the presupposition of the recognition of His honour.

---

[1] TRANSLATORS' NOTE—Confession, credal statement, creed and 'the creeds' will be used to translate the German 'Bekenntnis', which covers all these terms. Where it occurs, we have attempted to choose the nearest English equivalent, but it must be borne in mind that the translation in every case does not convey the full meaning of 'Bekenntnis'. In our translation 'confession' must never be confused with the 'confessional'.

But even if the death and resurrection of Jesus are actually expressed in a credal statement, it never confines itself to these facts as such. In addition to this titles are employed as a witness to the crucified and risen Lord, who is present in the church and in whose presence the confession is made. Credal statements soon developed beyond this into statements concerning Jesus' second coming, the incarnation of the Son of God, about God the Father and the Holy Spirit. From there they increased during the history of the Church, successively producing a multitude of alternative forms and subtleties from its original basic pattern.

In reciting the creed the Christian places himself at the disposal of the present Lord. But although the worshipper is aware of His presence, he does not usually address Christ directly in the creed. He does not say, 'Thou art the Lord', but refers to Him in the third person, 'Jesus Christ is Lord'. The reduced importance of the 'Thou' corresponds to the fact that in the creed Jesus is not generally addressed as 'my Lord'. The creed does of course imply the subordination of my person to this Lord and the acceptance of my person by Him. But in the creed Jesus Christ is acknowledged as *my* Lord simply by virtue of his recognition as *the* Lord, whom God has placed over all. Just in depriving himself of all concepts of a personal encounter between God and man (you and yours, thou and thine, I and mine) while acknowledging the all-embracing re-demptive act of God in Christ, the believer bears witness to the saving act performed on his behalf.

Confession is made before men. Indeed the need to address our fellow-men is essential to it. For in confession, the individual believer joins the confession of the congregation. Baptism for instance demands at least the presence of the baptizing agent, who accepts the profession and who thereupon receives into the congregation by baptism. Thus members of the congregation participate in the act of confession as witnesses. Moreover confession has to be made before non-Christians, even before enemies and persecutors. Consequently the Church and the world both have their place in confession, because confession in-volves the acknowledgement of the subjection of all things to Christ the Lord of the Church. But in spite of this relation to the men around us they are not directly addressed by the confession.

The 'Thou' is lacking; indeed, generally they are not even mentioned in the creed.

The creed can only be said by a believer. This may be seen in its opening phrase, 'I believe . . .'. Yet we do not find any statement *about* the act of faith in the text of the earliest creeds. For everything is concentrated upon the Lord to whom our faith is directed. Thus the 'I' is not indispensable to a credal statement. It may be contained in the 'we' of the confessing Church, 'We believe . . .'; it may even disappear completely, 'Christ is risen, Christ is the Lord'. The creed is of course essentially *my* own confession. It signifies *my* own dedication to Christ the Lord. And yet this self-commitment in the creed is so complete, that there is no further mention of this act of self-dedication in the creed. In the creed the subject to whom confession is made is so exclusively the Lord, that the 'I' of the confessing person disappears from the credal statement. But this also implies that the 'I' may be assured of its preservation in the 'we' of the Church and consequently in the Lord who is the subject of the creed.

Every structural element in the creed contains within it a limitation. Our submission to Christ implies the renunciation of those powers which were dominating us so far. At the same time it requires participation in the Church's creed as well as separation from the creeds of other communities. And this self-dedication in faith includes the confession of one's own guilt, a turning away from one's own past. All these negations are in fact contained in every creed, but they do not necessarily occur in the text of every creed. In the initial act of confession, the negation is included in the totality of the affirmation without being explicitly expressed.

In the creed, doxology and didache, prayer and witness are uniquely combined. Like prayer, the creed is dedicated and offered up to God, even though God is not addressed as 'Thou' in it. Although our fellow-men are not addressed as 'you', they are present, and therefore the creed is a witness to them. Without being merely doctrine the creed participates in the manner in which doctrine reflects upon God's final act of salvation without directly applying it to the actual historical man. The creed is not simply doxology. Nevertheless it partakes of the structure of doxology, which exalts God and His Christ in their glorious sovereignty over all history. The different basic forms of the responses of faith are merged and reduced in the creed to an unparalleled concentration of expression. To all appearances there is no encounter between 'I' and 'Thou', and yet this is precisely the response which well becomes God our Lord and Saviour who through the Gospel alone met the sinner in free grace. This concentration on facts in the creed denotes the objectivity of a legal act. It is the 'yes' of the believer to the legal act, which God has wrought on the cross for the sake of the world. It is the affirmation of the covenant God instituted in Christ's death.

f) These different elementary forms of response to the Gospel are brought together in the ways in which the congregation and every individual Christian express themselves. This 'belonging together' is not merely factually true of the NT scriptures, but is a fundamental principle. Even if the gift of prophecy is committed to one Christian, and the gifts of teaching, wisdom or a hymn are given to different individuals, this far-reaching differentiation of responses does not exclude, but rather presupposes, the response of faith in confession, prayer and witness which every Christian owes to God. The total response to the Gospel can only be expressed by means of all the basic forms, for only so can a fitting response be made to God. After all, God is no mere object of perception and statement like other objects, which we can perceive, investigate, comprehend and define. On the contrary, he meets us in the Gospel as the Lord who has a claim on us and bestows grace upon us. Because of this He wills to be honoured as the Lord in the fullness of His glory by the whole man, that is by man in all his personal relations: in the total turning of man to God, in the renunciation of the world and in his turning back to the world under God's direction. Because of this the explanation of the elementary forms of theological statements is not only of phenomenological interest, but it has normative significance. And since it is not possible to express the same idea in every single form, because the totality of basic forms is required to express the whole response of faith, this clarification is also relevant regarding the content of this response.

If the response of faith were confined to only one of the basic forms this would not merely imply morphological impoverishment, but also a curtailment of the content and beyond that disobedience to God, because it would involve a refusal to acknowledge fully his saving act and the eternal divine fullness revealed by it. The resulting isolation and absolutizing of any one elementary form would inevitably lead to the distortion of its meaning, which could only be legitimately expressed while it was still used within the whole context of the responses of faith. Doxology without petitionary prayer does not remain true doxology; didache without personal assurance ceases to be true teaching; witness without prayer is no longer borne in the name of Christ; and confession without prayer and witness soon falls into decay. Where God is only recognized as 'He' and no longer appealed to as 'Thou' He is no longer honoured as the Father. Where the saving act in history is taught without declaring its significance to our fellow-men as a present saving action, God's work is no longer proclaimed as the eschatological work of redemption.

All these basic forms of the response of faith are expressly concerned with God, whether He is worshipped, proclaimed or glorified, or whether all these expressions are concentrated in confession. Because of this, statements of faith in all these basic forms may be called 'theological statements'. We cannot confine the term 'theological statement' to carefully reflected statements over against expressions of faith. These primary expressions of faith are, as they stand, theological statements, and it is of fundamental importance to bear in mind that these basic statements of faith are the presupposition for all theological statements. Consequently, a theological statement as such is not automatically a statement 'about' God, but is primarily address to God, proclamation in God's name, confession and committal to Him and worship. Only when all these aspects are taken together can a theological statement be 'doctrine of God'.

g) Finally, we must take into consideration the fact that each of the five basic personal forms of theological statement may undergo morphological changes according to whether they are made *free and personal* or *formulated and prescribed*. Fixed forms are, above all, crystallized through the process of teaching, through confession and thanksgiving. Formulas of this kind may then be employed in preaching and be termed 'kerygmatic formulas'. In particular cases it is hardly possible to distinguish between kerygmatic, credal, liturgical and didactic formulae because all of them are responses to the redeeming act proclaimed by the Gospel. Kerygmatic phrases may accordingly be incorporated into creeds and hymns just as credal and liturgical formulas may be included in proclamation. Again all formulas are the subject of tradition handed on by teaching. But petitionary prayers and sermons (especially in missionary work) have significantly fewer traditional formulas than didache, confession and doxology. After all, in petitionary prayer the actual historical situation is brought before God, while in preaching, witness protrudes itself into this historical situation. Important differences in the personal structure of theological statements are the varying degrees of fixation which the basic responses of faith have acquired (whether it be in confession or preaching, in petitionary prayer or doxology). Differences are also caused by the varying extent to which liturgically fixed statements have superseded or even suppressed free expression. Moreover the valid sphere of influence claimed for any such formula may be very great. It is one thing to claim one formally fixed statement as valid for a local congregation. It is quite another thing to demand the recognition of this same statement by all the Churches in one country or by the whole of Christendom. Structural shifts of this kind are not merely of phenomenological interest but are of fundamental importance. For through any enlargement of its sphere of validity, the element of reality is reduced both in the response of faith and in the personal surrender to God's redeeming action. Both ordered and free modes of response are related to each other in the same way as the believer is related to the Christian community in his assent to the Gospel. He is within this fellowship as the unique individual whom God has loved and exposed as a sinner. Only if the Church provides for the right balance between ordered and free expression will she remain one and the same throughout the ages. For her identity consists in the active thrust of her living witness into new areas in the world. In this connexion it is important to note that in the New Testament there is no single formula, common to all the early traditions, which records and proclaims the death and the resurrection of Jesus. In spite of the impressive unanimity of the New Testament accounts of the unique redemptive action of God in Christ, and despite the ever-increasing number of formal statements which have been discovered in recent times, there is no single common Christological formula.

ii. *The Structural Problems of Dogmatic Statements*

If we continue our investigation by asking for the place of the dogmatic statement within the many basic forms of theological statement, it must be remembered that the term 'dogmatic statement' has a dual meaning. (a) Firstly it may be understood as an article of dogma itself, that is, as a formulation which has been made or has found its reception in a particular Church and is recognized as binding for all her utterances and work. (b) Secondly, it may be understood as a dogmatic statement which confirms and interprets the existing dogma. Or it may go beyond this in making statements which may in some cases be received and employed by the Church as preparatory work for the definition of further dogmas (cf. the genesis of some of the documents of the Reformation). This latter understanding of dogmatic statements is much wider than the first, just as the history of theology is much broader than the history of dogma. Obviously both are closely connected and overlap considerably. In what follows we are primarily concerned with the dogmatic statement in its wider sense. Accordingly, we shall only briefly point out a few important changes which have taken place in dogma, in order, subsequently, to deal more extensively with structural shifts in dogmatic statements.

The root of dogma is the confession of Christ. Irrespective of the question as to when and in what sense the term dogma found its way into the Church through its use in confessional documents,[1] it is obvious that the past and present function of dogma has its origin in the credal statements of early Christendom. Owing to the peculiar concentration of all responses of faith in confession, one should not sharply distinguish between the confessional, hymnal, doxological, kerygmatic and didactic elements in any investigation of the origin of dogma. On no

---

[1] A. Deneffe, 'Dogma, Wort und Begriff', *Scholastik* VI, 1931, pp. 318ff. and 505ff.

account is it legitimate to exclude the last two elements. In the Apostles' and Nicene Creeds (Nicaeno-constantinopolitanum) dogma is still expressed in their confessional structure. In both these symbols of the Early Church, doxology and instruction, prayer and witness are united. They are professed in the combination of all the responses of faith—whether by the candidate for baptism or by the worshipping congregation. This basic credal form has not been retained in the history of dogma. On the contrary, single structural elements contained in the creeds as initial acts of faith began to become autonomous and to be differentiated into various forms of dogma.

We can see a shift of structure in the introductory words of the Chalcedonian Definition. It does not begin with 'we believe' (as in the Nicene Creed) but with the words, 'we teach, that it ought to be confessed'. Admittedly the Christological statements in the Chalcedonian Creed are clearly doxological in character, but the introductory phrases indicate that this creed is not a liturgical confession but is doctrine about proper confession. The shift in credal structure from confession to doctrinal teaching was particularly successful in the West where this change took place with such consistency that the doxological element disappeared both in the opening phrases as well as in the body of doctrinal definitions.

A further structural change may be seen in the Athanasian Creed. The great bulk of its statements, especially those concerning the properties of the Trinity, still have a distinctly hymnal ring. But its introductory formula is no longer related to the act of liturgical confession—'Whosoever will be saved: before all things it is necessary that he hold the Catholic Faith. Which Faith except every one do keep whole and undefiled: without doubt he shall perish everlastingly. And the Catholic Faith is this: That we worship . . .'. In this creed we also find a shift from the act of confession to doctrine about proper confession. Moreover, the tendency to fission, implicitly contained in every creed, becomes explicit here for the first time, though this can only be seen in the introduction and conclusion. The continued development of attempts to explain this tendency to fission led to the formulation of negative statements which consisted of dogmatic definitions of erroneous doctrine. By this process dogmas arose which consisted

D

exclusively of negative statements, as may be seen in the anathe-matization of unacceptable doctrinal statements. This change reduced both the creed's doxological character as well as its positive element of witness. Witness to the world is substituted by separation from the world. The Athanasian Creed has hardly ever been used in worship. Moreover, if anathemas are made a definite part of the liturgy, as in the festival of Ortho-doxy in the Eastern Church, then these credal statements no longer combine all types of Christian response within their structure. The Augsburg Confession was, without doubt, made in God's presence, yet it was not directed to God but to the Emperor and his contemporaries. Thus the element of worship and doxology which was included in the original acts of con-fession, is completely absent from this confession of faith. This explains why the Reformation Confessions were not used in worship but remained operative as 'confessional documents'. We may further observe how, in the course of its interpretation, its didactic character ceased to be determined by its relation to preaching. This may be seen in the exposition of the Augsburg Confession in the Formula of Concord. Instead of this, preaching itself became progressively understood as doctrinal instruction.

In addition to such structural changes in dogma—as the former examples have illustrated—one further fact of impor-tance must be noted. After the rise of the Imperial Church in the 4th century, dogmatic unity was progressively realized by the general acceptance of one formula which was officially imposed, whereas the general practice in the first centuries had been to give mutual recognition to the various confessional formulations which were in use in different congregations or territorial churches.

The creed is the morphological starting-point for dogma in the same way as teaching was the first step towards dog-matics. For the moment we shall neither concern ourselves with the historical question of what terms have been applied to the Church's teaching, nor with the question when teaching was first called 'dogmatics'. As far as we know this did not take place until the 17th century. Here again we shall confine our investigation to its structural aspects.

In the life of the Early Church, doctrine was expounded as a part of catechetical instruction. This type of instruction was closely connected with exhortation and admonition which included a call to repentance and confession and to be baptized. In fact, it became continually transformed into the structure of testimony (e.g. the edifying catechetical instruction given by Cyrill of Jerusalem). The development of teaching, however, could not be confined to baptismal instruction. Debate with philosophy and heresy demanded its further development—even for those who had already been baptized, in order to warn, enlighten and strengthen them (in this connexion, the Catechetical School at Alexandria did not confine itself to the instruction of catechumens only). Above all, preparatory instruction for those about to be given positions of responsibility in the Church was not covered by baptismal instruction. Here teaching is no longer directly connected with living witness nor with the actual call to repentance and faith, nor even with Baptism or the Lord's Supper. All this now becomes the subject of instruction. Instruction no longer remains teaching about the redeeming act, which must be proclaimed in definite witness to every man, but it becomes teaching about preaching, repentance and faith, etc. Thus instruction does not remain as tradition and the exposition of its statements, but it becomes teaching about tradition.

The development of doctrine throughout history has caused a tremendous expansion of its contents and hence of the material which must be studied. This becomes increasingly true as our separation in time from the Apostles becomes greater.

The teacher cannot restrict himself to passing on what he himself has heard directly. He must rely upon the original apostolic teaching and message as the valid basis of all later teaching. This must be applied as the critical norm to all that he has heard during his lifetime. Teaching must not be restricted to one particular stream of tradition contained within the entire Christian message (for example, it must not be solely Pauline or Johannine). It must be based on the apostolic teaching and message in its entirety. In other words, the whole message must be incorporated into teaching and doctrine. Because God's act of salvation in Jesus Christ was a historical event, the testimony of the historical eyewitnesses of Jesus' life, death and resurrection will always be of fundamental importance for the Church.

Moreover teaching cannot be restricted to statements made by a particular teacher at a particular time in his personal encounter with unbelief, heresy and violence. It must also take into consideration all the dogmatic decisions which the Church has made in the course of her history in order to defend herself from various heresies and external threats. For it is only when we have understood the ever-changing forms of the onslaught which heresy has made upon the Gospel throughout history, that we are able to discern the real nature of heresy. And only if we are informed about the history of the dogmatic decisions made by the Church, we can clarify our understanding of the role of dogmatic decisions today. Thus the abiding character of the Church's teaching will always be manifested. The function of dogmatics includes the treatment of all the statements made by the Church during her history—whether they be recognized or disputed, consistent or inconsistent, pseudo-Christian or anti-Christian.

Furthermore, teaching must not confine its attention to biblical or dogmatic statements or to the world's rival theories. It must interpret dogmatic decisions in the context of the entire theological work of those who made them. Now dogmatics includes within its scope not only the history of dogma, but also the whole range of the history of theology. If we bear in mind that the creed is the concentration of all responses of faith, and is the root of dogma, we shall not merely be concerned with dogmatic scholarship as the study of theological teaching (whether it be biblical or exegetical, historical or dogmatic in nature), but also with the whole range of Christian response made within the Church. Dogmatic scholarship is obliged to consider the rich diversity of Christian responses, whether in proclamation, in demanding, in thanksgiving, in assurance, in prayer or in doxology. In other words, it must examine the history of preaching and liturgy and examine the problems which face us in our prayer and witness. During the course of history the quantity of teaching material has grown enormously. Yet this expansion must be seen as a whole and not as the growth of disconnected fragments. This development was not, however, merely the inevitable result of the Church's history, but it was the result of inner compulsion. For dogmatic scholarship is concerned with the unique redeeming act of God as the only valid and present reality throughout all changes of time and place. In the midst of all the different assaults and temptations of this world, the task of teaching is to bear true witness to Christ crucified, whom God has made both Lord of the faithful and of the universe. Dogmatic thinking is centred around this same Jesus Christ, in whom God's first and last acts in the 'old' and new creation are revealed. Because of the great variety of material which dogmatics has to deal with, it is related to the wholeness and fullness of the Church—which despite the great variety of her prayer, her forms of witness and her creeds, remains one at all times and in all places. Since every credal statement implicitly or explicitly implies the rejection of a different formula, the task of dogmatics in seeking to unify the variety of the responses of faith evoked by God's saving activity, must include an attempted delineation of the Church's limits. Every effort to determine where the Church ceases to exist is essentially an attempt at avoiding wrong demarcations which would inevitably lead to a mistaken or distorted understanding of the fullness of the Body of Christ. The problem of seeing the unity of the Church amidst the multiplicity, variety and irreconcilability of the different responses of faith is an essential function of dogmatics. Thus it must ask—in what sense and to what extent may this diversity be seen as unity? Dogmatics does not only teach the individual but also the Church how to respond to God. Again, it is not merely concerned with the response of one congregation at a particular time and place, but also with the response which must be made to God by the Church at all times and in all places.

The development of teaching into what we now call dogmatics has caused structural changes which have affected its contents. They are not caused by a neglect of the concept of the unity and universality of the Church which was always of fundamental importance for doctrine. Nor are they caused by the assimilation of the vast and steadily increasing material which has been produced through the advance of biblical exegesis, and through the history of the Church or her dogma. These changes which have taken place in the relation between doctrinal statements and other elementary forms of theological statements are of far-reaching significance.

a) In the course of its development doctrine has not been restricted to its specific function of explaining the great acts of God, but it has made the other types of responses of faith subjects of its teaching and has even incorporated them into its own special structure. Here doctrine does not serve the same function as catechetical instruction whose purpose is to lead people towards repentance, faith, prayer and witness. Instead it becomes doctrine about faith, repentance, prayer and witness, and is thus in danger of dissolving all these various types of theological statements into teaching (which is undoubtedly of fundamental importance for all the responses of faith, but which should itself remain subservient to them). It is the function of doctrine to give a systematic and objective presentation of the tradition of Jesus' sayings and deeds (for example, the institution of the Lord's Supper) and of his death and resurrection. It must also give an account of confessional, kerygmatic and other formulas, apostolic injunctions and other elements of Early Christian tradition connected with the Old Testament and its interpretation throughout the Church's history. In addition to this, doctrine makes equally objective statements about everything which is expressed and realized in the acts of prayer, witness or doxology. But these statements undergo a change of meaning in being objectified into didactic form. Prayer to God becomes talking about God and about man at prayer. Witness to one's neighbour in God's name gives way to statements about God and about the preacher and listener. Furthermore, in doctrine the act of personal encounter is objectified with the result that the historical nature of this encounter is replaced by general statements. Kerygmatic assurance, apostolic exhortation, prayer and thanksgiving, creeds and hymns are used as didactic material from which theoretical and timeless doctrinal statements are extracted. And these responses of faith are themselves turned into such timeless statements.

Thus the teacher runs the great risk of forgetting his own position as a man who is addressed by the assurance and challenge of the Gospel. He is in danger of withdrawing himself from the encounter with God who meets him in the Word and of seeking a neutral position from which this encounter between God and man may be observed, described and be cast into didactic formulas. But if man tries to maintain such an attitude in theological thought in which he imagines that it is possible to survey the revealing God and human existence as two distinct entities, considerable changes will occur in the presentation of theological problems. Attention moves away from the experience of salvation which comes through the Gospel and is concentrated on giving a theoretical definition of the relationship between the divine and human contributions in redemption. It raises the theoretical problem of weighing up the contributions of divine grace and the human will or of discerning the differing roles played by divine and human causality in salvation. One's attention is also diverted from the threat of judgement and the demands of God's Word to the purely hypothetical question of whether man is capable of fulfilling this demand. Our concern is diverted from the fact of our rebellion against God and what we have received by the obedience of faith and is directed to the possibilities of man in general. And yet the believer has received so much that he must acknowledge that even his faith is a gift of the Holy Spirit. There is a difference between faith which is attained by wrestling and groaning and clinging to the Gospel, and faith which is taught as a series of facts, such as that the sinner is saved by the Gospel and by wrestling and clinging to it, etc. Again it is one thing for the believer to confess that he has been saved by the Gospel alone but quite another to teach that God's grace operates irresistibly. Similarly it is one thing to preach 'thou shalt love God' but quite a different matter to teach that 'man is able to love God'. The appeal 'have faith' is not a doctrinal statement about man's ability to believe. The Pauline injunction 'work out your own salvation with fear and trembling; for God is at work in you, both to will and to work his good pleasure' (Phil. II. 12) has a proper place as an admonition and word of comfort to the faithful. But as a sentence of theoretical doctrine, it contains an irreconcilable contradiction. There is no doubt that some of the most important and persistent dogmatic problems which have arisen in Western Christendom first came into existence through structural changes in theological statements.

Doxological statements undergo similar transformations when they are converted into teaching and then employed as doctrinal statements—though doxology seems particularly suited to such treatment because of its peculiarly objective character. Thus statements about God's being, His essence and His properties which are employed in worship become metaphysical doctrinal formulations about God. Consequently the special nature of doxological statements is overlooked. The statements of doxology are ultimate and man cannot go beyond them. They are a mode of expression in which the worshipper brings himself, his words and the consistency of his thought as a sacrifice of praise to God. But as soon as these ultimate statements are employed as doctrinal formulas they assume the form of basic premises, from which logical deductions can be made which in turn are used as parts of a theoretical system. Doctrinal and doxological statements appear to have the same degree of objectivity since they both refer to God in the third person and they both ignore the subject who gives utterance to them. But this must not blind us to the fact that both forms have a different 'Sitz im Lebem', as well as a different function in the Church. Neither structure may be projected or reduced into the other without bringing about changes of meaning as well. The most radical effect of such a structural shift may be seen in the history of the doctrine of predestination. Instead of a thankful recognition of the abundance of God's grace (which alone can save), and instead of God's eternal loving decree, we are confronted with the problem of determinism, in the face of whose awful logic, the voice of doxology is put to silence. This is what happens when expressions of doxology are isolated and incorporated into the structure of theoretical instruction.

If the teacher extends the elementary form of instruction to the specific acts and contents of other basic forms of theological statements, he is in serious danger of forgetting his own position as one who hears, believes, confesses, worships and bears witness. For only when he is in this position doctrinal statements may be made as one of the many different forms of statements of faith. The teacher is tempted to choose a place of observation and reflection from which he tries to survey God's message of judgement and grace, His Word of demand and bestowal (corresponding to the Law and the Gospel), and recognize them as a rational unity. But as long as we are in this world, God's word comes to us in two ways, though the unity of this twofold address cannot be apprehended by us. It is not at our disposal as an object of our knowledge, but we can only grasp it (time and again) in faith—by acknowledging the divine judgement which we have deserved, and turning to Christ, who was judged in our place. We can only take every opportunity to hear the Gospel and receive the Lord's Supper, and at the same time place our reliance upon God's saving grace received in baptism. Likewise the teacher of dogmatics is in danger of leaving those who are on the way to meet the Coming Christ, who will replace faith by sight. Instead he is liable to teach as if he were a perfected saint no longer bound by the dialectic existence of the faithful on earth. Moreover in his misuse of doxological statements as theoretical instruction, the teacher is tempted to leave the company of those who are recognized by God in this world. He is in danger of placing himself above divine revelation and of choosing a position of contemplation and reflection from which he is able to make speculative deductions about God's deeds from his divine nature.

b) These structural changes in doctrine do not automatically stifle the other responses of faith. They may still receive clear expression in the life of the Church alongside her all-embracing doctrine. But this inevitably leads to tensions between doctrine, which has appropriated or even dissolved other basic theological statements, and the practical outworking of these responses of faith in Church worship and individual piety. For there is a difference between the actual response and a theological statement about this response. Thus we may understand the rise of mystical and ascetic literature as an attempt at making up the deficiencies of scholastic theology. Likewise, we may see in Pietism an attempt to make up the shortcomings in the old protestant orthodoxy. The existentialism of Kirkegaard may be regarded as a protest against the mildly speculative dogmatic teaching which prevailed in Denmark during his lifetime. In addition to this, doctrine as a basic form may attain such dominance over the other basic forms of theological statement, that their function is changed or completely disregarded in the life and thought of the Church. Preaching would be transformed into doctrine and didactic lectures, and Christian witness to one's fellow-men would become theological discussion, and Church hymns would be replaced by didactic poetry. Such phases can be discerned in the history of most Churches. The more one-sided these trends are, the greater the reaction will be on the part of the other basic responses of faith. This could result in deep cleavages between doctrine and preaching, between doctrine and prayer or even between doctrine and the whole of Church life.

c) On the other hand, one of the other basic forms of response may attain absolute supremacy. This would have an important influence upon teaching.

If the free expression of personal prayer, the experience of answered prayer and of being led by the Spirit dominate the believer's consciousness, doctrine is in danger of becoming a mere description of religious experience.

Whenever doxological utterance dominates the believer's thought, doctrine becomes transformed into metaphysical ontology. At the same time the historical nature of God's activity fades into the background. For either nothing is said about man, who keeps silent about himself in doxology, or alternatively the ontological structure of theological statements is applied to mankind and the world.

Whenever liturgical and sacramental practice dominate the life of the Church, doctrine is reduced to an introduction into the mysteries. It becomes a meditation upon and interpretation of the liturgical formulas.[1] Here liturgical formulas usurp the place of dogmatic decisions.

Even the elementary forms of witness, that is, the actual, historical and revealing Word which confronts man in his own particular situation, may attain such dominance that the other basic types of statement are suppressed, and their effectiveness in theological thought restricted. Thus, when the basic form of personal encounter is isolated and given predominance, statements about God which transcend the actual act of revelation become suspect. In fact, statements about God's existence, essence and properties would seem to be impossible. Whenever the actuality of witness is radically stressed, the acts of God in history become less and less important because undue attention is given to the divine message which is given here and now. Thus 'Heilsgeschichte' (God's saving history) is dissolved

[1] Concerning the changes in the understanding of 'mystagogische Theologie' cf. F. Kattenbusch, R.E. [3], Vol. XIII, p. 612ff.

into the actuality of present personal encounter. The result is that the possibility of making dogmatic statements of permanent validity is denied on principle.

All structural problems of doctrine are not merely formal, but have a bearing on the meaning of dogmatic statements. They deserve consideration, even if, at first sight, the same statements are made in different basic forms. And if one of these basic forms is made the predominant response of faith in isolation to all the others, it would act as an alien philosophical pattern (whether metaphysical and ontological or historical and existential), which results in a hardening of the system. This would suppress the abundance of the responses of faith demanded by God and would corrupt doctrine. It is no mere accident that some of the most consistent and one-sided theological systems have been detached from the Christian faith and have continued to exist as philosophical systems. The relationship between Scholasticism and the Enlightenment and between Kierkegaard and Existential Philosophy may serve as examples of this process. Dogmatic teaching has always pointed out the limits of doctrine, even when it was most highly developed. Prior to the early Protestant Dogmaticians, the medieval School-men had already stressed that Church doctrine is practical rather than theoretical. Moreover, doctrine is the theology of those who are still en route, but have not yet reached their goal (*theologia viatorum* in contradistinction to *theologia comprehensorum*). It is a perception of faith, not of sight. Again they stressed that the doctrine of the Church is only concerned with the perception of those realities which God has graciously revealed. But it does not pretend to understand the knowledge which God has of His own being (*theologia ektypos* as opposed to *theologia archetypos*). All these former distinctions have their validity. But nowadays one will have to consider more carefully where the limits of doctrine are reached. And here we must consider the structure of dogmatic statements within the sum of the responses of faith.

2. Dogmatic Statements and the Basic Forms of Human Perception

We began by considering the 'basic forms of theological statements' and discerned in them the elementary modes of response to the Gospel which God expects from the individual believer and the Church. Up to now we have only considered such structural problems in dogmatic statements as are caused by the relationship of these basic forms to each other. But apart from this, there are structural problems of theological doctrine which have a completely different origin. These are not the result of the divine message and the variety of responses demanded by it; they are the result of the natural differences within mankind as confronted with the Gospel. There are a variety of religious, philosophical and ideological presuppositions which are responsible for the different existing concepts of God, of the world and of man himself, which precede man's confrontation with the Gospel. Our experience of the world, our historical situation and our social ties all influence our presuppositions in different ways. The languages in which we express these presuppositions are also different. Nevertheless we cannot limit our attention to the diversity of human understanding, but need to consider man as a whole. The variety of our presuppositions is the result of different experiences of our environment, differences of tradition, language and historical situation. It is also the outcome of different basic modes of perception, which are bound up with man's differing psychosomatic constitutions.

Every man perceives his own reality and that of his environment in basic modes of perception which are specifically different from those of others. These basic forms of perception can neither be learned nor forgotten like a catalogue of facts. They are intrinsic to his individual existence, and he apprehends in them. Thus we may speak of basic human forms of perception. Any attempt to derive the diversity of religious, philosophical and ideological concepts from these basic forms of perception would be misguided. This diversity is rather the result of the interaction of individual decisions, personal experiences and inherited assumptions. But in all these factors the basic modes of human perception are operative, and consequently they must be borne in mind in our consideration of dogmatic statements.

i. *The Basic Forms of Human Perception*

These forms are not acquired by conscious decision. They are not chosen as one might choose the application of this or that method. Generally man is quite unaware of the basic pattern in which he perceives. They are intrinsic to his apprehension and they operate in his thinking in much the same way as the peculiarities of his psychosomatic constitution affect his existence as a whole. In this connexion, the concept 'form of perception' must not be limited to ways of discrimination, deduction or of forming of concepts. It also includes the basic patterns of behaviour in general and of man's behaviour in relation to himself and his environment. These forms of perception cannot be separated from the fundamental types of the Subject–Object Relationship[1] and existential awareness.[2] These too are not chosen. It is not a matter of adopting an attitude to anything or of adjusting oneself to someone in the sense of an active decision, but rather of a given relationship within which decisions are made. Moreover these forms of perception must not be confused with grammatical or syntactical modes of expression or with stylistic forms in various languages. Nor may they be confused with the formal differences which occur when the same language is used by different people. Although the basic forms of perception can only be investigated on the basis of semantics, these perceptive forms are more fundamental for man than the language he speaks. This is true, because language can be appropriated and employed as an external form to a much greater extent than is possible for these modes of perception.[3] Just because the

[1] Subject–Object Relationship will be consistently used to translate 'Ich-Gegenstandbewußtsein' = consciousness of the relationship between the subject and object. Thus the idea of 'consciousness' must be understood in the English translation. TRANSLATORS' NOTE.

[2] = 'Existenzbewußtsein', which means literally 'consciousness of existence'. TRANSLATORS' NOTE.

[3] In recent times these problems of morphology have been investigated and presented from various points of view. Special mention should be made of the works of E. Cassirer, *Philosophie der symbolischen Formen* (Bd. I–III, 1923, 25 and 29, Index 1931); K. Jaspers, *Philosophie der Weltanschauungen* (1925), *Philosophische Logik* (Bd. I, 1947, especially p. 302ff.); H. Leisegang, *Denkformen* (1928), and J. Gebser, *Ursprung und Gegenwart* (Bd. I, 1949, Bd. II, 1953). These investigations of the elementary modes of perception were not, however, confined to the interpretation of historical texts. They have also been carried through with the methods of Experimental Psychology. The investigations of E. Jaensch (*Der Aufbau der Wahrnehmungswelt und die Grundlagen der menschlichen Erkenntnis*, Bd. I (2)), who discovered the Eidetic

individual cannot help thinking in his own particular basic forms they are of fundamental importance in the examination of the structural problems of theological statements.

a) *The basic forms of the Subject–Object Relationship.* We need not attempt to answer the question of whether the 'object' confronting the Subject is a person, a thing, a community, a part or a whole. Here we are solely concerned with the question —how all these objects, which are distinguished from the Subject, are perceived as 'objects'. As a result of the comparative investigation of the Subject–Object Relationship, we discovered that objects are, by no means, experienced as unrelated external things. On the contrary, we can observe in this relationship significant structural differences.

aa) The world of objects so penetrates the consciousness of the individual that he is no longer separated from the world. In fact, he becomes partially 'fused' with it. Thus he is no longer an unrelated object, but has the experience of being dissolved into the world. In this situation, the subject is closely connected with the object in fact that even his life becomes drawn into the affairs of the world. And this results in the near identification of (the) subject and object. Lévy-Bruhl[1] has called this form of consciousness of the Subject–Object Relationship the 'participation mystique', and E. Cassirer has termed this relationship 'Konkrescenz und Koinzidenz' (growing together and coincidence).[2] The Subject commits himself to and participates in the Object—he even

Phenomena, and his followers (cf. in particular H. Weber, Experimentellstrukturpsychologische Untersuchungen über das Denken und Denktypen', *Zeitschr. f. Psychol.*, Bd. 116, 1930), who have shown that the basic patterns of thought are intrinsically connected with the psychosomatic unity of the individual. The existence of different basic forms of human perception is proved by scientific experiments, even though the typological classification and systematic co-ordination of these different structures is still debated in some points. With regard to the following survey I refer to my book *Der Mensch in der Verkündigung der Kirche* (1936, pp. 20–111). In it the modes of thought are discussed in a different systematic context with more precise argumentation and a better indication of relevant literature. I have selected the most important results in this investigation in order to present them afresh in a new context.

[1] *Das Denken der Naturvölker*, German edition, (2) 1926.

[2] This is not a mode of perception belonging to primitive peoples alone. It can also be found in civilized nations among adults as well as children.

finds his life in it. But this process is not the result of a decision or an attitude which was consciously adopted. It does not even necessarily involve a consciousness of the relationship, as would be required if the unrelated Subject first had to establish a relationship of kinship with the Object.

bb) On the other hand, the consciousness of the Subject–Object Relationship may be determined by the Subject, who embraces his environment by his process of perception and moulds it or even partly assimilates it. Here the individual does not apprehend by surrendering himself to the Object, but he reaches out to the Object and incorporates it into the sphere of his own self-experience. Thus 'synaesthesia' and metaphors do not merely give a coherent interpretation, but they impress qualities and relationships upon the world around us which cannot be apprehended by a perceptive form which is characterized by the Subject–Object dichotomy. This impressing of qualities upon objects is not a conscious act of transformation, but is the automatic result of apprehension which occurs in this basic form of the Subject–Object Relationship whereby the world is animated by the Subject. A transformation of the Object also takes place in the process of 'mystical participation'. And both transformations will appear to be equally suspect and faulty when the perception which takes place occurs in the form of the Subject–Object dichotomy. But the basic forms of the Subject's surrender to the Object and the environment on the one hand and the Subject's incorporation of the Object and the environment into himself on the other, each present themselves in entirely different ways to our environmental experience. And these basic modes of assimilation are themselves combined with completely different forms of existential awareness.

cc) Perception which takes place in the basic form of a sharp separation between the Subject and his environment— that is, in the awareness of being confronted by an unrelated external object—is not nearly as common as has been generally assumed in Western thought. The basic perceptive form of the Subject–Object dichotomy is but one among many. In this form the observation and identification of objects is strictly separated from moulding them or participating in them. It is at this point that the problem of the Subject–Object Relationship first arises. We are faced with the problem of eliminating our own subjectivity and its accompanying sources of error which threaten our objectivity. Thus, in addition to the difficult task of objective perception, we are involved in the problem of attempting to interpret the Object by the Subject and to understand its significance for the subject.

b) *Basic forms of Existential Awareness.* The different basic forms of the Subject–Object Relationship contain differences in the consciousness of self-experience. If the Subject is dissolved into his environment, he is much less conscious of himself as when his position is one of strict separation from the world. Moreover, the individual may experience himself, either as a single whole, or as split in two (without implying that this self-experience is schizophrenic). He may experience himself as in lasting continuity or in self-change or even self-estrangement. The basic forms of existential awareness do not here denote different degrees of consciousness, but differences in the 'situation' of self-experience within the whole range of psychic processes. The individual does not experience himself in isolation from his capacity to apprehend, to feel, to think and to will, etc. Even less does he experience himself as the abstract transcendental 'I' of the critique of reason which is common to all men, but he becomes aware of himself *within* the other psychic functions. Again, we find deeply rooted differences in the psychosomatic unity of the individual which are determined by the different functions which control the psychic life of man. And it is in these basic functions that man becomes aware of his existence. And these different psychic functions have consequences for one's individual way of thinking. Here again, we are concerned with basic human patterns which are not consciously chosen by the individual.

aa) Some people realize their existence by committing themselves to the reality of their environment and in participating in its affairs. In this case, it is possible to speak of existing in the function of perception—and thus in 'seeing' in its broadest sense (not only in its visual sense). But this statement itself transcends the kind of existential awareness under discussion since it objectifies it by external psychological observation and subsumes it under various psychological functions. However, it is important to note that here man does not experience himself in isolation to objects, nor in any act which

is directed towards an object, nor even in an artificial Subject–
Object Relationship, but he experiences himself in the affairs
of his environment. Here the individual is 'like a vacuum in
which objects of perception interact upon one another and
their significance is unfolded' (H. Weber).[1] Thus man does not
only exist in perceiving things but in the things perceived. In
this basic form of existence there is no deliberate, progressive
and regulative thought-process which predominates, nor does
the individual exist in such a mode of thought. Instead,
thinking accompanies perception—it is more a continuation of
perception than a means of attaining self-development by
existential decision.

bb) If we do not limit the meaning of the term 'feelings'
to sensory or sensual experiences, nor to emotions of desire or
aversion, but, on the basis of Max Scheler's theory of 'feeling-
strata', allow it to include purely spiritual and intellectual
feelings (e.g. one's self-awareness, or the experience of one's
personality), it is possible to distinguish another basic form of
existence which is dominated by feeling. Here feeling is not
simply an incidental accompaniment of perceptions, thought-
processes or decisions of the will, etc., but it is determinative for
the constitution of the individual, and is the existential basis
which underlies all perceptions, valuations, developments,
deductions and actions. It also determines what we overlook,
devaluate or leave to one side. In this situation man does not
exist in perceiving or in thinking or in acting, but these functions are simply the outcome of a deeper existential awareness.
This is operative in the complexity of emotional life which is
partly forced into consciousness and partly already expressed
as intuitions and impulses. Consequently, in this basic form,
thinking is not essential for man's existence since it is not the
psychic function in which he really exists, or in which he
experiences his actual self. Also intuitive thinking which wells
up from the depths of feeling, is not deliberate thinking, in the
sense of making a personal decision—of choosing a goal or
selecting a method. Admittedly, deliberate thinking is no less
present within this basic structure than within others, but it is
of secondary importance. Progressive and deliberate thinking

[1] Ibid. p. 68.

E

simply grows out of complex and unexplained intuitions which are subsequently analysed, arranged and explained in order that their consequences may be made explicit.

cc) Again, yet other people exist mainly in their decisions to act, or in a life of action that is in decisions of the will and in the motor sensations connected with them. In this they experience themselves as themselves. The other spiritual and intellectual functions are co-ordinated or even subordinated to this existential experience. Of course no decision of the will, nor any action takes place without prior thought, but here thought is the means, and action is the end. In this basic form thinking is not the essential mode of existence but subservient to it. Even if it precedes action and has a conscious aim so that it produces results, man does not really exist in the knowledge derived from his thought but in the action which results from it.

dd) Wherever men exist in thinking this mode of existence is independent of every object of thought, whether it be related to empirical perception or to the realization of emotional intuitions or to actions. Even abstract thinking has the quality of fundamental reality in this case. Also a dialectic progression beyond abstract antitheses to further abstract theses and antitheses is an elementary mode of living, in which some individuals find the fulfilment of their existence. Thinking in this case is not added to an existence dominated by feeling. Nor is it simply a means to a life of action. Rather the environment and even feelings are cause and material for the real existence in thought, while action is only putting the intellectual act of existential decision into practice. This kind of existential awareness is also a basic form of human existence. But it cannot always be taken for granted, nor be created as is sometimes assumed in Systematic Theology.

c) *Basic forms of concrete and abstract thought.* In everyone's thought we find concrete as well as abstract elements. This fact is not invalidated by the discovery by Thought-Psychology (Denkpsychologie) that, in principle, it is possible to think of or even convey or represent every object by means of theoretical concepts without the use of visual aids. Empirical psychology, however, has demonstrated that the distribution of abstract and concrete elements varies considerably from person to person.

In addition to this, it has been shown that different forms within these concrete and abstract elements predominate in different individuals. These different forms in turn determine the objects of perception. In this connexion, 'concrete thought' must not be restricted to the objects which can be seen (visually), since it comprehends the imaginative range of all the sense organs. For instance, it is possible to speak of a 'sound-picture' (Klangbild). These differences must not be overlooked, even if abstract thought plays an important role in thought which is determined by concrete elements. Here again we are concerned with the basic forms which form part of the individual man in his entirety. They are not only modes of thought but are also the forms which determine his entire range of perception. These forms are themselves conditioned by man's physical constitution. It is no more possible to separate the concrete or abstract elements in man's basic forms of perception from his constitutional wholeness than to separate Sense-Psychology from Sense-Physiology.

aa) The basic form of concrete thought is mainly characterized by the predominance of mental images in it. They do not only occur as occasional elements (as such they are probably never completely absent from any kind of thinking), but as a basic form of objective preception. In this case thinking develops in its movement to and from mental images in a special way. In exceptional cases the concrete element in thinking is even more distinctly operative than in mental images. This is true of the so-called visionary phenomena which are frequently experienced by children, and sometimes by adults. They are to be distinguished from mental images because although they are not perceptions, they give the impression that the object they portray is physically present. These visionary images may convey knowledge in a special way. For they not only influence the person who sees them, but also enable him subsequently to discern particular features of the visual phenomena which were not apprehended in the moment of perception. Mental images make less impression and are more changeable than these eidetic phenomena, though they are not as versatile or flexible as abstract thought, because they are more objectively fixed. Within the basic form of concrete thinking we can observe the prevalence of certain kinds of mental and perceptive images which are caused by differences in human constitution. This is caused by the predominance of different senses, and here we must distinguish between the visual, acoustic and motor character of mental images.

bb) On the other hand in the basic form of abstract thinking, 'pure thoughts' predominate. In this perceptive form even physical objects and hence the objects of previous perceptions are intellectually represented. This intellectual representation makes abstract and deliberate thought much easier. Within this basic form some may pay more attention to the abstract objects which are present to their consciousness, while others may be more concerned with the relationship of these mental objects to each other. In some extreme instances of formal abstract thought these objects are reduced to mere causes or examples of relationships which have a greater degree of reality than the objects themselves.

cc) Apart from this we must make allowance for basic forms, which fall somewhere between the extremes of concrete and abstract thought. One example for the transition from concrete to abstract thinking may be seen in the determination of thought by verbal images or concepts of feelings. These are derived from actual experience, but the element of concreteness in them only has the function of symbolically illustrating abstract thought. With this qualification, it may be said that such thought is indirectly concrete. It is important to note that thinking may also be determined by geometrical figures. These have their origin in concrete forms, but here they are employed as patterns of thought in general. Such figures as a triangle or a circle may be of enormous systematic significance if they dominate the progression of thought and the organization of facts.

d) *The basic forms of thought-progression.* Some forms of thought-progression are determined by the specific subject of consideration—for example, mathematics, physics, biology and anthropology. But here we are concerned with those movements of thought which are recognized as basic forms of human perception, because they are pre-eminently represented by certain men who persistently apply their particular type of thought-progression to all kinds of objects of perception. These types of thought-progression are not conditioned by the peculiarities of the objects, though they do not escape perception as objects. On the contrary, they have an influence upon the choice of objects of perception. Experimental Thought-Psychology has shown that our thinking does not really proceed according to the rules of logic. It is rather a moving current in which deliberate progressive thought and sudden associations, intuitions, etc., are variously intertwined with one another. There is a difference between thought-progression and its subsequent inductive and deductive arrangement and verbal expression. The current of thought only partly follows one course consciously. Apart from this, it proceeds with sudden intuitions without logical deductions, or by thought-association with its interruption of thought, imagination and concepts of feeling, etc. Here we shall confine our investigation to thought-progression in the strict sense of the process of deliberate thinking—which seeks to be convincing by means of a rational succession of thoughts or even tries to prove things by argument. K. Jaspers has described such structural differences by the term 'technique of thinking'.[1] But this term is misleading, because it is not essentially a matter of technique which anyone can learn and apply. Leisegang has termed these differences 'thought-forms'.[2] But here we should note that the problem of thought-forms is not confined to the form of deliberate conscious thinking. Even though Leisegang has spoken in this connexion of different types of logic, it still amounts to a confusion of Logic and mental and 'Thought-Psychology'. We should rather interpret the different forms of thought-progression as various forms of the same problem of identity within the one and only logical system.

aa) In the circular pattern of thought the movement of thought proceeds 'in the coordination of a concept A with a concept B, the latter is repeated and connected with A again: Thus the thought which feels its way alongside these concepts returns to its origin: ABBA. This basic form may be extended by the introduction of any number of terms in the following order: AB BC CD DE etc. till N NA' (Leisegang).[3] In this movement of thought beginning and end, argument and conclusion, cause and effect cannot be clearly distinguished,

[1] *Psychologie der Weltanschauungen*, ibid. p. 76 passim.
[2] *Denkformen*, ibid. p. 4 passim.   [3] Ibid. p. 61f.

although the train of thought begins at a certain point and proceeds by logical and coherent reasoning. But it returns in a peculiar way. Concepts are mutually connected in such a way, that a deduction from a premise is itself used as a premise for further deductions, whose conclusions coincide with the original premise. The argument does not only proceed from cause to effect, but also from the effect to the cause. Thinking of this kind is not characterized by uninterrupted progress towards a goal, but by the inclusive mutual connexion of concepts and conclusions in a circular movement, which returns to its origin. Circular thinking corresponds to a contemplative movement round the object of perception—whether this is concrete or abstract—and the mutual connexion of features constitutes the truth about the object perceived. Even opposites are comprehended by this circular movement and are woven into the context. In this thought-form the reversibility of the relationship between concepts is experienced as convincing.

bb) In the teleological thought-form, on the other hand, the movement does not return, but proceeds irreversibly. Contradictions are not harmonized by joint arrangement on a circle, but are overcome by common alignment towards a goal (not by retrospective connexions, but by progress in time). Both in circular and in progressive thought the primary concern is not to establish direct causal dependence, but in contradistinction to circular thought a single line of progression is essential in the latter form of thought.

cc) We must distinguish a third type of thought-progression from the preceding two, which proceeds by ascent and descent within syllogistic hierarchical systems of classification. 'The relations between concepts are apprehended in the form of a pyramid. Concepts are related to each other as a continuous series of species and sub-species' (K. Jaspers).[1] Thinking systematizes the context and the plurality of concepts by classifying them into different categories and then by reducing them to a few general concepts, which are in turn used as the basis for reclassifying the individual concepts. Conclusions are convincing if they succeed in arranging objects within a system. This thought-form is characterized by analysis and causal

[1] *Psychologie der Weltanschauungen*, p. 77.

deductions. Contradictions are excluded, if they cannot be harmonized into a system. We are familiar with this thought-form through the development of classical Western logic.

Here we shall not try to co-ordinate the four types of thought-forms which have been discussed, that is those of (1) 'Subject–Object Relationship', (2) 'existential awareness', (1) 'concrete and abstract thinking' and (4) 'thought-progression'. Nor shall we try to draft a typology of human perception in its entirety by co-ordinating the corresponding forms.[1] We shall deliberately leave these four types of basic forms as they are. For we are concerned with the real man, not with the construction of a further typology, which could be added to the existing rival typologies and theories of human constitution. It is not our purpose to establish relationships between the different basic forms on the one hand and various races or various stages in the history of human development on the other. These forms can be found both in historical succession and in coexisting nations and individuals. This treatment of these four aspects and the differentiations within them does not pretend to be a comprehensive systematization of the basic forms of human perception. We have simply confined ourselves to pointing out the existence of these basic forms.

In refraining from constructing a comprehensive system of anthropological basic forms we see more clearly that these different forms are very significant presuppositions for the differing expression of systematic thinking. Each of the basic forms mentioned provides the basis for a distinct system of self-understanding and of perceiving the world. None of these forms are to be understood as mere forms which do not affect their contents. These perceptive forms and similarly the sense-organs are of tremendous importance in determining those things which thinking man chooses from the abundance of living reality within and around himself. It is obvious that the basic forms of perception, which have been demonstrated, may lead to distinct religious, philosophical and ideological (weltan-schaulich) theories and systems if they are consistently applied and developed. 'System' in this context must be understood

---

[1] Connexions of this kind obviously exist between those forms, which have been discussed under aa) in all four types of thought-forms.

not only as a 'shell' containing ideas, but also as a method of systematic thinking (as in the method of transcending (Transzendieren) of K. Jaspers, though in this case 'thought-shells' are explicitly rejected).

ii. *Structural Problems of Theological Apprehension*

We must further ask—what happens to these basic forms of human perception when man is confronted by the Gospel, by which God in His love judges and saves him? What happens when man surrenders himself in faith to Christ as his Lord?

a) The Gospel does not only encounter man as a mere specimen of humanity, but it impinges upon the individual man in his historical uniqueness and psychosomatic wholeness. God removes man from his isolation in which he secludes himself from God and his fellow-man. He exposes him as a member of this sinful race and transfers him into the fellowship of the People of God, the new humanity. But he reveals every man in his own sinfulness, redeems him from his bondage and gives to each one special gifts of grace. The Gospel also meets every man in the individual constitution of his basic forms of perception and in his resulting relationship to the world. It meets him in the actual 'situation' of his existence in order to open up a new life for him. The Gospel penetrates into the innermost being and heart of every man.

b) When a man is seized by the Gospel, his foundations are shaken. The basic patterns in which he hoped to secure his life are disrupted. The things he takes for granted—his existential awareness and the protective 'shell' of his knowledge and his control of his environment—are shattered. His religious and ideological systems which are rooted in his basic forms of perception are refuted.

As far as the basic forms of the Subject–Object Relationship are concerned, it is obvious that man cannot apprehend God's dealings with him either by being dissolved into God or by pressing God into a self-made system. Nor can he apprehend God in the basic form of the Subject–Object dichotomy. A complete dissolution into God is rendered impossible by the Gospel as the message of the historical man Jesus Christ. For only by our faith in Him as the historical mediator do we have communion with God. The representations of the divine image which are made on the basis of human self-experience are destroyed by God when He confronts us in the Gospel as the absolute Lord. It is equally impossible for the believer to continue living in the form of the Subject–Object dichotomy, because in Jesus Christ God has become man (one of us) and has poured His Spirit into our hearts. Thus the believer is in Christ and yet Christ remains distinct from him. And thus Christ meets us in the witness and in the need of our fellowmen, though He is still their Lord. Thus the Spirit in our hearts cries out in our groanings 'Abba, dear Father'. At the same time He is the Lord and the Creator to whom we pray 'Come, Holy Spirit'. Neither transcendence nor immanence is valid when kept in isolation. Both of these aspects are present in God's dealing with man.

Similarly the basic forms of existential awareness are unable to comprehend the self-understanding which is opened up for the believer through the Gospel. Every existing conception is questioned and destroyed by the Gospel. Our past and present trespasses against God are disclosed. Forgotten and repressed guilt is brought into consciousness and what has become cold burns again. God holds us personally responsible for our actions and reveals us, not only as men who have committed sins, but as sinners (by nature) who have forfeited their lives. And it is precisely these sinners whom God addresses in the Gospel with the words, 'You are my beloved, you are my son'. By faith in the Gospel the sinner recognizes himself as justified by God in Christ and as one who has been declared and made righteous. In the light of this faith he also recognizes himself as the man who has been kept and guided by God, the Creator, through judgement and blessings even before he first believed in Him. The Gospel thus calls man to a much deeper self-awareness. But this is not the decisive factor, for there are various degrees of existential awareness outside the sphere of faith. The special character of Christian self-understanding, to put it bluntly, is not a self-understanding at all. Undoubtedly the believer recognizes himself as a sinner. Sin is essentially and exclusively his own deed. His self-understanding as a creature, on the other hand, and above all his self-understanding as a righteous man consists in recognizing the deeds of God the Creator and Redeemer, who created him and sustains him and who justifies him day by day through the Gospel and gives him new life. We do not perceive our righteousness within ourselves, although it is given to us. We can only recognize it in Christ, whom God made our righteousness and who gives himself to us through the Gospel. Our righteousness is hidden from our self-examination by imperfections and even more so by our sin. We do not even recognize the life within ourselves, although we are transferred into life, we can only perceive it in Jesus Christ. He is the new man, the beginning of the new creature. He is our life. We can only seek and find our life by faith in Him, never by the experience of ourselves. 'Set your minds on things that are above, not on things that are on earth. For you have died and your life is hid with Christ in God' (Col. III. 2f.). Thus the believer 'has' life, yet this life is not his own, but the life of Christ. 'I have been crucified with Christ; it is no longer I who live, but Christ who lives in me' (Gal. II. 20). By recognizing himself as justified and living the believer does not see himself, but the redeeming act of God in Christ which was done for him. Thus in one sense it is true that man in the act of faith steps outside himself. Consequently Paul sharply distinguishes faith from all the ways in which man presumes to possess and/or secure his existence, whether it be by his will and actions, his experience of the world or his wisdom.

The basic forms of concrete and abstract thought are also dethroned by the Gospel. God's act of redemption in Christ, which is proclaimed and enacted by the Gospel, is both concrete and abstract at the same time. Moreover it may be said to be concrete and abstract in such a special way, that the perception of this divine act can be characterized neither as concrete nor as abstract. Again the concept of concrete thought must not be restricted to the visual sphere, but it must include the whole range of things which can be perceived or imagined. As a man in history Jesus could be seen, heard and touched, yet He could not be recognized as Christ, the Son of God and as the Lord by these senses. For it is the knowledge of faith, which acknowledges the historical man Jesus as Christ and Son of God in spite of his insignificance and obvious lowliness and despite the disparity between his claim to absolute authority and his defeat on the cross. Although he appeared before his disciples as the risen Lord, the saying remains true, 'Blessed are those who have not seen and yet believe' (John xx. 29). We hear the Gospel, but do not receive its grace by hearing, but by faith. We taste bread and wine in the Lord's Supper, but we do not receive remission for our sins and new life through the body and blood of Christ simply by our taste, but by faith. The redeeming act of God is thus abstractly perceived. And yet this knowledge by faith does not exclude seeing, listening and tasting nor does it exclude concrete thought or the possibility of imagination in the broadest sense. For by faith the believer clings to the Word he has heard and to the food he can taste. He recognizes both the human word, which proclaims the good news, as the Word of God and the bread and wine in the Lord's Supper as the vivifying body and blood of Christ. By faith he clings to the historical Jesus and apprehends His majesty precisely in His human lowliness and His victory in His defeat on the cross. As soon as we see the incarnate by faith, the saying comes true 'we saw his glory' (John i. 14). This glory can be apprehended neither by concrete nor by abstract thought.

Each of the natural basic forms of mental images, thought pictures, diagrams or abstract concepts, etc., is disrupted by the Gospel in a unique way. Thus in none of the basic forms can *one* concept, *one* relationship, *one* mental image or *one* picture alone grasp God's redeeming action in Christ. In the 'I ams' of St. John's Gospel we meet a concentration of images, in which Christ bears witness to Himself as man's redeemer. These images are neither identical nor complementary, but they mutually divest each other of their wordly concreteness.[1] The legal metaphors in the Pauline Epistles have the same central significance as the word-pictures in St. John's Gospel. Whether they are derived from private, contractual, penal or cultic law they are all designed to describe God's redemption in Christ. Paul is not basically concerned with the details of the legal proceedings nor with the persons involved in them but with the relationship between these persons. Consequently his metaphors are extremely abstract. In Paul's letters we find a concentration on the types of relationships which are implicit

---

[1] Cf. John x. 7ff. and 12ff., where Christ is described as the door and the shepherd at the same time. These descriptions would be mutually exclusive if taken literally.

in such concepts as redemption, atonement, justification, cultic expiation, etc. These types are neither identical nor complementary. Instead they conflict with each other when they are understood in their legal stringency. Moreover each of these types of relationship is broken up by the proclamation of the Gospel, since neither the debtor nor the man who stands bail for him pays the ransom, but the creditor, God Himself. Rivals do not make peace with one another, but God reconciles to Himself those who rebel against Him. The guilty, and not the guiltless, are acquitted on account of the condemnation of the innocent, etc. Concrete as well as abstract thinking, if it is touched by the Gospel, reaches a point where its natural assumptions are destroyed. The redemptive act of God cannot be apprehended by either form of thinking. If we were to adhere rigidly to these thought-forms, the act of salvation would appear nonsensical. But the believer, as he listens to the Gospel, is confronted by the whole Christ through each of these images or types as well as through their totality.

The basic forms of thought-progression and their specific ways of reasoning and identification are also broken up. Teleological thought is frustrated because God in His free grace in Christ breaks into the teleological systems of this world and abolishes them. Christ's Second Coming is the goal of God's saving plan which involves the destruction of human thinking, planning and doing. The believer's expectation consists both in waiting for the consummation, and for the Judgement. He thinks teleologically by sacrificing his own teleological thinking to the Lord, the time or hour of whose coming he does not know. Circular thinking is disintegrated, because the Gospel demonstrates the contrasts between light and darkness, sin and grace, life and death, God and world, this aeon and the next. Thus it is no longer possible to understand them as polarities within a closed circular system nor as constantly complementary elements. Instead they are involved in an eschatological struggle, where the victory has already been won, but will only become visible in the end. The thought-form of a pyramid with its hierarchical system of subordination does not succeed in comprehending the relationship between God and world, because God meets the world in Christ as the wholly other Lord—wholly other not only in His omnipotence, but also because He, the Most High, has come down to us in Christ as the humblest of all.

c) The basic forms of perception and their systematic consequences are broken through, when they are confronted with the Gospel. Yet the believer's mode of apprehension does not lose its form entirely. The Christian continues to perceive in his particular thought-form, which is now dislocated and disarranged. For even in this dislocation of a particular form, what remains has still a definite structure, namely the structure of the dislocated form. Theological thinking does not, after all, cease to be the thinking of real men. The Gospel in both judgement and redemption confronts man in his own psycho-somatic constitution with its corresponding basic forms of perception. The Gospel also takes this same man into its service and demands his response of faith in the forms confession, prayer and witness. Man bears witness to other men of God's redemption in the uniqueness and entirety of his psychosomatic existence. The natural gifts of the individual are not destroyed, but God employs them as they are offered up to Him in the response of faith. Every man must confess his sins in his actual situation by repenting of his particular sins and by turning from them. Likewise he is a witness in his creaturely existence and in his own basic perceptive forms. Naturally he is no longer secure nor self-sufficient in them. He can use his disrupted basic forms neither to shelter himself from God's coming nor to grasp God's redemptive act. Thus he also bears witness in the actual forms of his perception. These basic forms of human perception, though widened, disrupted and broken through, show a strange perseverance.[1] In the disrupted forms of the Subject–Object Relationship God's redeeming action is proclaimed. In the disrupted forms of existential awareness faith is distinguished from the previous self-understanding, while in the disrupted forms of concrete and abstract thought and of thought-progression God's incarnation and historical deeds are

[1] We take this fact into account in giving Christian instruction to children by assuming the concreteness of their thought and the absence of the full awareness of the split between subject and object. Likewise in missionary preaching we are aiming at the awaking of faith and witness against the background of their actual non-European thought patterns. This persistence of basic thought-forms can be demonstrated by scientific psychological research into conversion accounts.

proclaimed. Thus the differences between the NT Scriptures are not only differences of concepts or of historical polemic conditions, but also differences in the thought-forms of their authors.[1] These differences must be borne in mind in any comparison of statements from dissimilar contexts. Dissimilar statements which are made in different basic forms of perception may have the same meaning, while identical statements may have different meanings.

d) It must be admitted that basic anthropological forms may maintain and harden their position in theological thought and expression by resisting their disruption and dislocation. In any case, this disruption is never completely achieved. This will only happen when our faith is superseded by sight in the eternal glory. 'For now we see in a mirror dimly, but then face to face. Now I know in part, but then I shall understand fully, even as I have been fully understood' (I Cor. XIII. 12). But if the believer in his eschatological progress towards the future dissolution of his perception becomes dazzled by his new sight, or if he stands still and secures the possession of his own faith, the basic anthropological forms will again start to limit and adulterate the apprehension of God's redeeming acts. And this process gives rise to theological systems which contradict or even exclude each other. According to the variations of the Subject–Object Relationship God's redemption in Christ is either mis-represented in a mystical or idealistic way, or Christ is objecti-fied as the mediator between the opposing poles of God and world. This happens, when the basic form of subject–object split prevails. The concept of faith becomes hardened in accordance with the basic forms of existential awareness and by transferring human modes of existential awareness to God, His nature is defined as perceiving, willing, consciousness or activity. If the believer makes his experience, which depends on his own forms of existential awareness, the general norm for the reality of grace, he will no longer be able to recognize the abundance of grace. For one this abundance of grace may be experienced in the feeling of God's nearness, for another it will be seen in moral victories attained with difficulty, for yet

[1] A comparison of Pauline and Johannine texts shows this quite clearly. Cf. E. Schlink, *Der Mensch in der Verkündigung der Kirche*, pp. 40ff., 59ff., 75ff. and 100.

another it will be found in new knowledge. Likewise the forms of concrete and abstract thinking with their particular images, categories of feelings and patterns or diagrams (for example, that of unity in dialectic duality) may make an absolute claim on theological thought and expression resulting in the subordination or exclusion of other forms. If the basic forms of thought-progression assert themselves, they have far-reaching consequences for the whole range of theological knowledge and doctrine and also for its systematic arrangement and especially for the understanding of 'Heilsgeschichte' and eschatology.

Up to this point theological statements and theological apprehension have been the subject of our consideration. It is inevitable that the basic forms of human perception should influence theological perception as well as theological and dogmatic statements. Nevertheless we must distinguish between knowledge and its expression and bear in mind that there is no direct correspondence between thought and speech though they are related. Despite the fact that thought seeks to express itself in speech and finds its clarification and formulation in it, there is also wordless thought, that is thought which cannot be expressed adequately in words. Language exists before the individual begins to think or speak and despite its wealth it only offers a restricted range of expression whether one accepts or modifies one's inherited vocabulary. The form of perception is certainly reflected in speech, yet an existing linguistic structure may distort thought when it is given verbal expression. In this connexion the various possible relationships between thought and speech must not be overlooked.

3. THE COMPLEXITY OF THEOLOGICAL STATEMENTS

Before considering the question of the relationship between the two basic forms which have been treated up to now we shall try to give an account of the place these forms hold within the whole range of problems raised by theological statements. Obviously this problem-complex is much too intricate to be included in the treatment given to the problems already discussed, namely the personal structure of theological statements and the basic forms of human perception. Any attempt to reorient ourselves in the situation is impeded by the fact that we do not have a comprehensive theory of theological statements in present theology. It is true that in both Protestant and Roman Catholic theology a 'logic of theological statements' is lacking (G. Söhngen).[1] This deficiency is made even more striking by the fact that the problem of theological statements, in any form, is of primary significance for all Churches—not only for 'the church of the Word'.

The whole problem of human expression clearly cannot be the subject of one scientific discipline only. Without claiming completeness and without entering into detailed discussion about the range of competence of each of the following disciplines it should be stated that: Every statement raises problems of: (a) the theory of cognition, (b) logic, (c) linguistics and philology, (d) history, (e) psychology and anthropology, (f) sociology and (g) ontology. Every statement is subject to all these disciplines. The fact that we began with the theory of cognition and ended with ontology simply serves to indicate that all the particular disciplines are liable to be questioned about the truth of what they are saying.

This differentiation of disciplines is of relatively recent origin and is continually progressing. From the time of Aristotle and Stoic philosophy onwards throughout the history of Western thought up to modern times, the scientific treatment of the problem of verbal expression was dominated by logic. And because of this linguistics remained confined to Latin grammar. The attempt was made to make language and logic coincide and to reduce or to eliminate the linguistic anomalies which occurred in this philosophical logic of language. Later, in the Enlightenment, a great number of newly discovered languages were investigated. But Rationalism still showed its secularized scholastic heritage in its treatment of the problem of verbal expression by subjecting language to the criterion of human reason. This was achieved by a process of criticism and rationalization and by adhering to the principle that there is ultimately but *one* reasonable grammar. Under this domination of logic, statements were understood in a very unbalanced way as statements about facts, whereas the various forms of address such as the question, the command, etc., were ignored.

The special character of language was only realized after it had been freed from the domination of logic and ontology.

[1] *Philosophische Einübung in die Theologie*, 1955, p. 129.

This change in the situation was largely due to Herder and the scholarship of the Romantic period. The variety of languages was understood as the organic expression of the individual and of whole nations, and as the treasure of their historical insight. Romantic scholarship also recognized language as the combination of individual and collective achievements and as a process of growing consciousness, and saw the possibilities in having entirely different grammars. But there was still a long way to go through misleading and alienating influences of an ethnological, physiological, psychological and scientific nature, until a clear distinction was found between language as an objective and collective system and language as the act of speaking. A systematization of the chief functions of statements in *conversation* was the result of this long process of development.[1] The original and basic ideas were published by F. de Saussure,[2] who distinguished methodically between 'le langage', 'la parole' and 'la langue'. Similarly Karl Bühler,[3] advocated a threefold conception of language as 'proclamation, initiation and representation'. They were both concerned with the 'elementary phenomena' in the structure of language. 'If we take a sentence not only as the description of a number of facts, but also as a part of living conversation' it must 'fulfil three conditions in order to be meaningful. It must have the intended effect upon the hearer, it must truly exhibit the facts, and it must express the opinion of the speaker' (B. Snell).[4] These different and very important attempts in constructing a morphology of language have a common starting-point for their investigation in the act of speaking. 'The act of speaking is always "definite". It happens at a particular time in a particular place. It demands a definite speaker (transmitter) and a definite hearer (receiver), and a definite subject matter to which it refers. All three elements— the transmitter, the receiver and the subject matter—change from one act of speaking to another. Apart from this, the act of speaking requires that both the listener and the speaker must speak the same language in order to undrestand each other. The existence of a language which is present to the consciousness of the members of a linguistic community, is the

---

[1] Cf. H. Ahrens, *Sprachwissenschaft*, 1955, p. 204ff.
[2] *Grundfragen der allgemeinen Sprachwissenschaft*, (Ger. Ed.) 1931.
[3] *Sprachtheorie*, 1934.   [4] *Der Aufbau der Sprache*, 1952, p. 15.

F

precondition to every act of speaking. In contrast to the unique act of speaking, a language or a linguistic system is a common and constant reality.' The linguistic system 'has no other justification for its existence than that it makes possible acts of speaking and it subsists only in so far as actual acts of speaking are related to it' (Fürst Trubetzkoy).[1] Here linguistics finds its own method which is clearly distinct from that of logic. As far as the differences between the 'meaning of a word' and a 'logical concept' are concerned I refer to the important distinctions of Hans Lipps:[2] 'The *attribution* of a characteristic in *judgement* must be distinguished from *expressing* something *predicatively* as a quality.' 'The context in which something is *perceived* is different from that in which it is spoken about and recognized "as something", for instance in respect of its essential nature.'[3] 'With Kant for instance "judgement" understood as an objective entity (Konstitution) is analytic or synthetic, but not as a "statement".'[4] Concepts and judgements in logic must not be identified with concepts and judgements in normal everyday language, although the concepts and judgements used by logic are operative in language. But the evaluation and definition of the meaning of words in language proceed in such a way that they can only partly be apprehended by logic, or by the doctrine of the modality of judgements.

Thought-psychology, like linguistics, had to free itself from logic. For the question in psychology concerning the thought process is different from the inquiry into the problem of the logical correctness of a thought within the logical system. Thus psychological investigation of the thought-process yields no consistent progression within the well-known forms of logical syllogisms, even if the conclusions reached by the thought-process comply with these principles of logic. In fact, conclusions frequently break into one's consciousness by means of intuitive leaps which by-pass logical connexions. The evident logical correctness of these results is immediately perceived even though it is only subsequently proved by logical argument. Again the problem of statements is different in psychology from

---

[1] *Grundzüge der Phonologie*, 1939. Quoted acc. to Ahrens, ibid. 488.

[2] *Untersuchungen zu einer hermeneutischen Logik*, 1938; *Die Verbindlichkeit der Sprache, Arbeiten zur Sprachphilosophie u. Logik*, 1944.

[3] Ibid. p. 15.   [4] Ibid. p. 20.

what it is in linguistics. Even though statements are usually acts of the intellect, mental activity (which is later verbally expressed) does not necessarily and exclusively occur in the form of word-meanings or according to the rules of sentence construction. Mental images of words are of great importance even for unexpressed thought. Moreover verbal expression seems indispensable for the fixation of considered concepts and for the clarification of thought as a whole. Yet the problems of thought psychology must be distinguished from those of linguistics. The relationship between thinking and the subjective act of speaking, or between thought in general and objective language is very complex, and varies from person to person. In this connexion, it is important to note that neither thought psychology nor linguistic psychology is solely concerned with the mental processes. Thus in addition to the psychology of consciousness, we must take into account depth psychology and depth-physiology, and with it, the psychosomatic wholeness of man which conditions man's thought and speech.

After linguistics and the psychology of thinking had freed themselves from the bondage of logic in the second half of the last century, an attempt was made in the opposite direction, namely to construct an empirical logical system from laws of language and thought as discovered by psychology. The transformation of logic from a normative science into an empirical science dealing with the canons of thought, represents the reaction of positivistic psychology against the dominating ideas in previous Western history of science. Against this it was the decisive achievement of E. Husserl[1] and his disciple A. Pfänder[2] to demonstrate clearly the unique inexchangeable character of the logical, psychological and linguistic fields. This distinction leads also to the purification of traditional logic from the impediments with which it was formerly burdened by the classical languages and provides the possibility of a more coherent systematic approach to logic.[3]

The differentiation within Arts between the spheres of

---

[1] *Logische Untersuchungen* I[2], 1913.

[2] 'Logik', *Jahrbuch für Philosophie und phaenomenologische Forschung*, Bd. IV, 1921, p. 139ff.

[3] Cf. B. v. Freytag-Löringhof, *Logik*, 1955, and I. M. Bochenski, *Formale Logik*, 1956, p. 311ff.

linguistic, philological, historical, ethnological and sociological research, some of which are very closely connected or even overlap, caused far less dramatic and fundamental discussion about the problem of statements than the struggle between the normative sciences (Logic, Theory of Cognition, Ontology and Aesthetics) and the Arts. Since every statement is subject to every possible method of investigation, it must be admitted that there is, at present, no comprehensive theology of language. There is not even a philosophy of language, which would sum up and methodically display the results and problems of the particular disciplines, which are in constant process of differentiation among themselves and grow further apart from each other. At present philosophical anthropology and even more the philosophy of language presents itself as a variety of attempts, which have their origins in the different perspectives of the Arts and Sciences and in the differences between the various disciplines.

Under which of these aspects has the problem of statements been discussed in theology and especially in systematic theology? We shall seek to answer this question by making a brief survey at this point.

a) Although the term 'Theory of Cognition' has only gained general acceptance during the last century the problem itself is much older. Thus it may be said that the *theoretical and cognitive aspect* of theological statements has always been thoroughly discussed in theology. The whole history of dogmatic thought has been accompanied by discussions about Revelation and Reason, Faith and Understanding, Faith and Experience, Human Word and Holy Spirit, etc. The relations between them have been variously defined. It was sometimes taught that faith and knowledge are opposed, while at other times it was maintained that faith makes knowledge possible. In this discussion about the theory of cognition the *specific character* of theological statements over against other statements has been most clearly recognized.

b) In this connexion the *logical aspect* of theological expression has been discussed by dogmatics, especially by the Medieval Schoolmen and the theologians of the Scholastic Period in Protestantism. In particular, theological *concepts* were discussed within the field of semasiological problems such as the relationship between mental image, word and object. The ever-changing history of the concept of analogy shows that the problem caused by the unique character of theological statements has been most clearly seen at this point. It is the problem caused by attributing this world's concepts and words to God. In the treatment of this problem more attention was paid to nouns and adjectives than to verbs or the systematic presentation of theological *conclusions*. The conviction was that it was easier to apply elementary logical syllogisms directly to theological statements than to apply existing concepts to them. The direct applicability of existing concepts was called in question (as can be seen in the treatment of the problem of analogy). In more recent Protestant Theology, the systematic discussion of logical questions has been noticeably under-emphasized—even in cases where no attempt was made to avoid these problems by maintaining that all theological thought is fundamentally irrational. For instance, the concept of 'paradox' in theology has never received its exact logical definition—whether by Kierkegaard or Heim, Tillich or Barth.

c) Since theology has always had to treat texts in foreign languages it has always been confronted with the linguistic aspect of theological statements. However, the systematic-theological discussion of this aspect was held back for centuries by the fact that theology like philosophy did not properly distinguish between the logical and the linguistic problem of theological statements. Thus the specifically linguistic problems of theological statements remained hidden beneath the discussion of logical and cognitive aspects. Thomas Aquinas, for instance, understood by 'God's names' simply the terms by which God is designated.[1] Even in his discussion of his favourite name, 'He who is',[2] Thomas ignores the historical self-revelation of the name Jahveh, and the fact that it is God's will that men should call Him by this name. He also forgets God's promise to those who pray to Him in this revealed name. On the other hand Thomas consistently applied the term 'donum' to the Holy Spirit,[3] even though the Holy Spirit is never worshipped as a 'gift' either in biblical texts or in the Church liturgy,

---

[1] *Summa theologica* I, qu. 13.
[2] Ibid. art. 11, *corpus* and *ad primum* till *ad tertium*.
[3] Ibid. qu. 38, art. 2.

though He is asked for as gift. Just as the different functions of words in a statement (for example, concept, address, etc.) were concealed by the logical discussion of concepts, the different functions of sentences (as an assurance, a confession, a plea, etc.) remained concealed within the logical discussion of judgements and syllogisms. After linguistics had freed itself from these bonds in more recent times, the discussion of theological statements was normally conceived of as a part of general linguistics in the same way as theology understood itself as one of the Arts. On the whole, the special character of theological statements was not sufficiently recognized. And when, about 1920, the special character of the I–Thou relationship and its significance for theological statements was discovered by F. Ebner, K. Heim, Martin Buber and others, this important basic form of personal encounter was soon wrongly absolutized and placed in opposition to ontological statements. But on the whole it is striking how small a part has been played by linguistic problems in the teaching of the principles of dogma in comparison to the problems of theory of cognition.

d) There was always a historical side to theological statements, but because history was forced into philosophical or theological categories and because dogmas were understood as eternal truths this historical aspect became obscured. Thus it is not surprising that the recent development of historical research has brought an end to the previous subsumption of historical problems by dogmatic theology. Because of this polemic renunciation, the historicity of theological statements (e.g. their presuppositions, the cause of their existence, the object to which they were directed, and their terminology) was now discussed within the framework of historical research in general. Because of the use of normal historical methods, such as the principle of analogy,[1] the special character of theological statements as response to the divine revelation was not taken seriously enough. On the other hand, the dogmatic teaching at this time (in so far as it did not give up its task altogether or refuse to explain the doctrine of the unchanging Church), failed to give sufficient consideration to the historicity of dogmatic statements. In its desire for statements of eternal validity,

[1] Cf. E. Troeltsch, *Historische und dogmatische Methode in der Theologie*, Ges. Schr. Bd. II, 1931, p. 792ff.

Dogmatics has often lightly passed over the problems of identity and validity which arise in the variety of historical statements which were made in changing historical situations.

e) The psychological and *anthropological aspects* were even more neglected—not only in systematic theology, but also in the historical disciplines of theology. Of course the relation between religious experience and theological statements had been the subject of constant discussion and the theological statement was sometimes understood as the direct expression of our experience. At about the middle of the last century we can observe the rise of scientific psychological research, which after its initial preoccupation with sense psychology, moved on to thought psychology and the psychology of the emotions which subsequently developed into typological and psychosomatic research. But systematic theology has ignored the importance of this development for the problem of theological statements or only paid attention to it in so far as it impinged upon the psychology of mental processes.[1] The problem of statements is, however, as a psychological problem, much more complicated, since it is rooted in the psychosomatic wholeness of man, that is in the highly complex constitution of human perception and speech which are determined by his basic forms of Subject–Object Relationship and existential awareness, etc. Because of theology's excessive concentration on self-*understanding*, man's psychosomatic wholeness has been overlooked. And because of her undue concern to preserve an unchanging image of man throughout changing historical situations, the constitutional diversity of different men was almost completely ignored. And the significance of this constitutional diversity for the problem of theological statements and their interpretation was largely overlooked.

f) We are still in need of a systematic exposition of the *sociological aspect* which is implied in the search for the 'Sitz im Leben' of biblical texts and in the results of research into the history of literary types and tradition. This exposition should seek for a comprehensive definition of the different sociological functions which dogmatic statements have within the different Churches.

g) All these aspects are significant when one attempts to

[1] Cf. K. Girgensohn, *Der seelische Aufbau des religiösen Erlebens*[2], 1930.

clarify the questions imposed on us by the dangerous vacillation of Christianity between ontological and actualistic and existentialist statements. In any case this short critical survey indicates that today there is no comprehensive philosophy of language nor any extensive theological treatment of the problem of statements, which methodically combines and criticizes the many results and problems of the various disciplines. And wherever theological statements have been discussed under one aspect such as the linguistic, psychological or sociological aspect within theology, it is remarkable how often it was taken for granted that this could be done on the basis of general presuppositions common to all the non-theological disciplines just mentioned. The theological statement was treated within the context of general phenomena such as those of language and speech, of feeling, thinking, willing and social relationships. Undoubtedly theological statements are made within all these phenomena, but their origin is different from that of all other statements since they are the response to God's revelation. However, this origin in revelation transforms thought and language, decision and social relationships—in short, it transforms every aspect under which each statement must be considered. The special character of theological statements consists not only in its unique origin in revelation, but also in the special structure of their response to this revelation. Thus the theological statement raises special problems not only with respect to ontology and the theory of cognition, but also within the framework of logic and science. The procedure for examining biblical texts by means of the historical critical method has made increasingly clear the far-reaching transformations which non-biblical terms have undergone when they were employed in the language of revelation. The same is true of the employment of philosophical terms in the course of the history of dogma. But all the scientific aspects under which theological statements would have to be discussed are essentially concerned with the same problem. And, in this sense, it is true that the historical and philological judgements concerning theological concepts have not yet been fully and methodically examined. In other words they have not been exploited in other areas of the problem of theological statements.

Still less do we find a comprehensive attempt to treat the

problem of statements in general (not only theological ones) in the light of revelation. The first attempts made towards giving human statements in general a systematic and theological treatment were made by Luther in his pronouncements on grammar and logic, and later by Hamann and again by F. Ebner. The latter two saw the origin of their philosophy of language in the fact that man is addressed by the Word of God. Thus Hamann constructed a philologia crucis from the theologia crucis.[1]

But these attempts have not been taken farther in the present-day treatment of the problem of statements. Normally the general problem of statements is not approached from a Christian point of view; on the contrary, the Gospel is treated as part of the universal problem of statements in much the same way as the present encyclopedic classification of the Arts and Sciences is not usually carried out on the basis of revealed knowledge, but instead under the headings of Arts or Sciences with theology falling into the former group.

This critical survey is intended to place the two basic structures which have been dealt with in sections I and II into their context within the whole range of problems raised by theological statements. It should now be clear that both the whole range of problems involved in dogmatic statements and the special problem of their formal structure is much too complex to be comprehended fully, either by the personal basic form of theological statements or by the basic forms of human perception. Many further structural problems which are caused by differences of language, experience, inherited world views, social and ethical conditions, etc., would have to be included. Thorlief Boman, for instance, in his comparison of Greek and Hebrew thought has observed different structures of thought and has indicated differing verbal functions. He has also pointed out different structures in their descriptive methods, their use of numbers and in their spatial and temporal concepts. He then combined them with different basic modes of existence which are dominated by hearing or seeing.[2] The structures of

[1] Cf. W.. Leibrecht, *Philologia crucis*, *Joh. Georg Hamanns Gedanken über die Sprache Gottes* (*Kerygma und Dogma*, 1, 1955, p. 226ff.).

[2] *Das hebräische Denken im Vergleich mit dem griechischen*, 1952. E.T. *Hebrew Thought Compared with Greek*, S.C.M., 1960.

religious, philosophical and cosmological views as well as those of time and space are the result of a variety of historical, psychological and linguistic interactions as well as other factors. In comparison with them the two basic forms which have previously been discussed are *fundamental*. Although these basic forms are hardly ever considered in discussions concerning problems of theological statements, they are of primary importance, because somehow they comprehend uniquely all the linguistic, historical and other problems. The basic forms of human perception provide the actual and natural presupposition for the decision which is implied in every statement. And the basic form of theological statements represents the valid form of expression for all language about God which is used in obedient service.

4. Dogmatic Statements in the Interaction of Theological and Anthropological Basic Forms

If we abbreviate the term 'personal basic forms of theological statements' into 'theological basic forms' and the term 'basic forms of human perception' into 'anthropological basic forms', we must ask how both these forms are related to each other and how they interact.

There is a fundamental difference between the structural problems of doctrine, which result from the basic forms of theological statements on the one hand, and from the basic forms of human experience of reality on the other. The latter forms exist before man is confronted with the Gospel, while the former are evoked and challenged by this encounter. Again the latter exists in the actual constitution of different men since no individual existence is determined by all these basic anthropological forms at the same time. The basic theological forms on the other hand are essentially united in the response of every single man. Despite the variety of Spiritual gifts it remains true that every believer owes God the response of confession, prayer and witness, and thus he too participates in doxology and teaching. But the theological and the anthropological basic forms represent initial attempts at constructing systems behind which man barricades and secures himself from the abundance of the divine redemptive act. The basic anthropological forms do this automatically. They must always first be overcome by the power of the Gospel, which enables man to perceive the divine act of salvation. The basic theological forms, however, presuppose the Gospel and faith. Here a hardening of the system is caused by over-emphasizing or isolating one particular basic form of response and by giving it pre-eminence or even domination over all the others. Thus the believer's response is exposed to different dangers by the theological and anthropological basic forms. On the one hand there is the danger of theological one-sidedness, and on the other the danger of an undue emphasis of the human forms arises. We can now present the survey of the mutual interaction of both basic forms on each other.

a) If one particular basic form of theological statement is isolated from the others or is allowed to assimilate or dominate them it is possible for the corresponding basic anthropological forms to assert themselves over against revelation and to receive expression in theological statements. Every basic theological form, if it is isolated and brought into predominance, assumes a rigid pattern which can ultimately be employed without faith. Both the objectivism of theological thought derived from an unbalanced use of the structure of doxology, and the subjectivism which is partially based on the structure of God's assurance contradict one another, as do philosophical systems in which the corresponding basic forms of human perception have found their self-justification. For each of the basic anthropological forms is capable of being developed into a distinct religious, ideological and philosophical pattern or even system. The differences between the basic anthropological forms increase the one-sidedness, which is caused by structural shifts of doctrine.

b) On the other hand, if the response of faith is given in its fullness and in combination with all basic theological forms, anthropological differences and even the different basic forms of perception would enrich each other. Whenever God is addressed in the second person and proclaimed in the third and whenever He is worshipped and His deeds are proclaimed, man's systems break down. Similarly wherever man (who is addressed as Thou) prays, witnesses and sanctifies himself in doxology as 'I' or 'we' his systems are disrupted. All the rigid systems of objectivism and subjectivism, of actualism and ontology, as well as the absoluteness of the I–Thou relationship and their corresponding systems are broken up. The Gospel promotes and confirms its destruction of man's self-assertion in the co-existence of the basic forms of the response of faith. If men exhibit in their lives the complete response of faith demanded by theology, they discover one another without ceasing to exist as unique individuals. Thus they are enabled to live in fellowship, which is based on knowledge and confession, prayer and witness, worship and teaching. If all responses of faith are made, the pentecostal break-through takes place—a break-through which overcomes our limitations of language, historical ties and thought-forms. It further results in redemption from the captivity and bondage brought about by man's sin.

c) Thus the basic theological forms are of greater significance for the problem of dogmatic statements than the basic anthropological forms.

5. The Unity of Dogmatic Statements

We began by stating the fact that Christians belonging to different Churches find it relatively easy to pray and witness together while it appears impossible to formulate common dogmatic statements about the same subject. In our investigation we have refrained from discussing similar experiences, such as to point out that joint exegesis of the Bible is much easier at ecumenical conferences than the formulation of common principles of exegesis. We have instead restricted ourselves to the question of what happens when expressions of prayer and witness are transformed into dogmatic statements. The investigation of the mutual relations between the basic forms of theological statements led to the conclusion that every basic form has its inherent function. Accordingly transpositions of statements from one basic form into another have a considerable effect on their meaning. Both the form and the meaning are subject to changes, which are increased by the basic human forms of perception. We also came to the conclusion that the investigation into the basic forms is not merely a matter of phenomenology. Nor is it simply a matter of describing the various ways in which faith responds. It is the recognition by theology of ways in which faith must respond to

God's demand. This also applies—though in a different way—to the basic forms of human perception. Again we are not merely concerned with describing them, but with acknowledging the will of God, who expects a complete response of faith from every man as he is. Thus we came to the conclusion that the problem of the structure of dogmatic statements has important implications for the meaning of the statements.

In view of the extreme difficulties which the divided Churches face in their struggle for unity as a result of their different and contradictory statements, it seems obvious that we should first of all try to reach agreement in questions of joint moral action (life and work) performed by Christians. One is tempted to eliminate dogmatic considerations or declare them to be superfluous for unity in Christ. From this point of view dogma is the chief barrier to unity, while unity in prayer, witness and responsible action seems easy to achieve. We must not overlook that trends of this kind time and again threaten to gain predominance in the Ecumenical Movement in spite of the serious efforts which are being expended on questions of doctrine, worship and order (faith and order). This trend is visible both in the United States and Canada and among the Younger Churches. Nevertheless this conception is based on a fundamental error. The root of dogma is confession. And where the Church is united this unity is essentially expressed in common confession. A Church's response which consists of prayer and witness alone is incomplete. Consequently it is quite unjustified to minimize the importance of dogmatic statements within the Ecumenical Movement. Moreover, an undogmatic and anti-dogmatic Church union of this kind would not only fail to win the approval of those Churches which are dogmatically bound, it would also be frustrated, because, on closer inspection, even those Christian communities which are hostile to dogma in fact live according to quasi-dogmatic principles, which operate divisively, although they are not formulated dogmas. Similarly those who reject tradition in principle in fact live within the tradition of their own Christian community and speak and act out of their allegiance to it.

If we do not wish to trifle with dogmatic differences we must take them seriously and strive for the dogmatic unity which is essential for Church unity, by using new methods in approaching the problems. But what does unity of dogmatic expression mean? It is usually taken for granted that this unity consists in the acceptance of the same dogmatic formulation by all believers. Nevertheless the demand for uniformity in dogmatic statements and for the acceptance of the same credal formulas within the whole Church is rather late in origin. During the first centuries a variety of parallel local creeds were in use and unity was maintained by their mutual recognition by the local Churches (not by the expulsion or the replacement of other creeds by one's own). Even after the compulsory acceptance of the same dogmatic formula in all Churches of the Roman Empire, the truth was not completely forgotten that unity of dogma does not necessarily consist in dogmatic uniformity. Thus in the Middle Ages the Roman Church, in her attempt to achieve reunion with the Eastern Church, simply demanded the acknowledgement of the 'filioque' without its reception into the Eastern text of the Nicene Creed. Similarly, in our time, the Churches of the Augsburg Confession who are united in the Lutheran World Federation demanded from the Church of Batak in Sumatra the recognition of the Lutheran Confessional Documents (but without requiring complete acceptance of them) as the condition for accepting them into her Church fellowship. We should not now need to explain the merits of dogmatic uniformity nor its dangers which are mainly to be seen in the fact that a uniformity in dogmatics lessens the responsibility of local Churches when they make their own confessions in their own particular historical situation. Thus the acceptance of a common dogma weakens the existential character of the Church's decisions and replaces it with a formal act of obedience. But we are here concerned with the basic assertion that the unity of dogmatic statements need not consist in the acceptance of one and the same formula, since it can also consist in the mutual recognition of different dogmatic formulas. Even the unity of the New Testament canon includes different kinds of witness to Jesus Christ, and the one Gospel is still passed on in the form of four 'Gospels'.

If we take for granted this understanding of unity as a fellowship based on mutual recognition, the problems of identifying and expressing dogmatic unity become much more complicated than when unity is understood as uniformity. Identical formulas are easy to deal with. But unity which is based on mutual recognition is much more something which needs to be striven for, to be sought and found. It is relatively easy to decide whether dogmatic statements are uniform or not. But unity which consists in mutual recognition raises the question— in which of the different dogmatic statements may the unity of dogma be perceived and acknowledged? This question can only be answered by means of a comprehensive ecumenical dogmatics. Here we must confine ourselves to making a few points of method.

a) In order to perceive the unity of differing dogmatic statements an exact philological examination is required. In particular there is demanded the examination of the concepts which are employed both in connexion with their previous non-theological use and with regard to the influence of the biblical message in determining their meaning and use. The unity of dogmatic statements may be concealed by differences of terminology, as may be seen in the history of the development of trinitarian dogma in the Early Church where the term ὑπόστασις roused the suspicion of tritheism in its Latin translation 'substantia', while on the other hand 'persona' took on a modalistic ring when it was translated as πρόσωπον.

b) Furthermore an exact historical investigation is indispensable. We must devote special attention to the historical presuppositions and specific errors and other threats in the face of which dogmatic statements derived from Scripture were made. The unity of dogmatic statements may be concealed by differing or even apparently contradictory statements, which have been formulated against different opponents. For instance, there is a hidden unity in the Orthodox stress on human freedom amidst the danger of a gnostic and naturalistic conception of man and the Western statements about the 'servum arbitrium' which are directed against the dangerous distortion of the Christian understanding of man by voluntaristic ethnical activism.

c) But we must not confine ourselves to these two methodical aspects of philological and historical exegesis, which are now a matter of normal procedure. It is also necessary to consider the anthropological presuppositions which existed in different areas which have influenced the dogmatic statements. Thus we find that for some people, seeing plays a dominant role while for others hearing is determinative. This difference affects dogmatic statements and may have serious consequences for Christology, anthropology, the doctrine of worship as in determining the relationship between the Word and Sacrament. Here again the unity of dogmatic statements may be hidden by differing dogmatic expressions, which bear witness to the mighty acts of God in different basic structures of human perception and being.

d) Apart from this one would have to consider the place which the various dogmatic statements occupy within the basic forms of theological statements by virtue of their specific structure. Undoubtedly the Creeds are the root of dogma, because all the responses of faith are concentrated in them. But in the course of history, dogmatic statements have strayed from their origin in various ways and have suffered significant structural changes through adaption to other basic forms. We need not condemn all these structural changes, but we must clearly bear in mind that these changes influence the meaning of statements which gives rise to dogmatic problems. Thus the unity of dogmatic statements may be hidden under differing dogmatic formulations when they are made in the context of different basic forms of theological statement. Thus, for instance, the statement 'simul peccator justus' can be found throughout almost the whole of Christendom as a statement of existential confession of sin and faith. As such it may even be found within the Roman Church. But the same statement must appear as a denial of recreating grace, (and) especially. of baptismal regeneration—if it is misunderstood as an ontological and metaphysical definition of the Christian.

e) Finally it is essential to scrutinize the factual recognition which the various dogmatic statements have received and still receive within various Church spheres and confessional Churches. The unity of the Church may be hidden by differing dogmatic statements, whose authority is variously understood by the Churches concerned. They may be the present norm of every pronouncement the Church makes; they may be representative landmarks of her history, or they may be symbols with little theological meaning whose primary function is sociological Because Church unity depends on the authority accorded to dogmatic statements, this unity may exist in the actual witness and teaching of the divided Churches in spite of differences in their dogmatic formulations. The reverse may also be true— disunity may reign despite dogmatic agreement.

These indications demonstrate that in order to solve the question of the unity of dogmatic statements, a more comprehensive scientific treatment of the problem is required than has been given in ecumenical discussions up to now. First of all we are here confronted with all the problems of biblical hermeneutics since dogmatic statements must be interpreted and be judged in the light of the apostolic message—while still paying attention to each of the aspects which have been considered. For the apostolic message is the permanent basis of every Church pronouncement; it is the permanent norm for determining the content of her message and the pattern for her outgoing witness to the world. But the special problems of dogmatic hermeneutics must be added to those of biblical hermeneutics. In both cases it is not enough to make allowances for the self-understanding with which we approach the statements under consideration; still less is it legitimate to make a generalization from a specific self-understanding and apply it as a critical norm to a text which must be interpreted. Of course all understanding takes place within the hermeneutic circle between the spoken word and the hearer. Consequently our efforts to understand unity must proceed without losing sight of the differences in human self-understanding. In addition to these differences we must take into account the differences between men as whole beings with their basic forms of perception and expression. The problems of biblical and dogmatic hermeneutics are still underestimated.

Nevertheless our search for unity in differing dogmatic statements is not only more difficult, but also more promising than it is commonly assumed. We must start investigating the dogmatic statements of divided Churches by applying philological, historical and morphological methods, which involves a consideration of the whole range of these Churches' statements of faith. And if this is properly done we shall certainly find a wider range of agreement than might be expected from the isolated consideration of dogmatic statements in isolation. But we shall be surprised to find the same conceptions in completely

G

different parts of Church life and in basic forms of theological statements, which are completely different from those ideas which are familiar to us in our own Churches and which we look for in other Churches as well. We shall see that some of the dogmatic statements were originally and essentially not statements of teaching, but statements of prayer and witness, which have been transformed into doctrinal statements. In the light of this they must receive a new interpretation. At the same time we shall discover which dogmatic statements correspond to doctrine as it was originally used and understood. Thus the variety of expression which God has disclosed to believers by his revelation in Christ begins to become transparent through the differing dogmatic statements of the divided Churches. Our eyes will be opened to perceive the unity and the fullness of the Church and dogma will begin to shine again in its original form as confession, which is the focus of all other statements.

PART II

DOGMATIC FOUNDATIONS

I. THE CHRISTOLOGY OF CHALCEDON IN ECUMENICAL DISCUSSION[1]

WHEN Pope Leo IX excommunicated Michael Caerularius the Patriarch of Constantinople in 1054 the cleavage between Eastern and Western Christendom developed into a permanent schism. In all further attempts to regain unity, the common recognition of the Christological decision of Chalcedon remained undisputed. The same is true of the schism between the Church of Rome and the Reformation Churches which took place in the 16th century within Western Christendom. When Luther and his followers set up new forms of Protestant Churches after their excommunication by the Pope, the Chalcedonian Christology was never questioned. Despite the well-known Christological differences between Luther, Calvin, Zwingli and Brenz, their desire to retain the Chalcedonian Christology in common with Rome and Byzantium must not be overlooked. This desire found clear expression in the Confessional Documents of the Reformation. The term 'ecumenical symbol' is therefore merited not only by the three Creeds of the Early Church (the Apostolic, the Nicene and the Athanasian) but also by that of Chalcedon; in fact the latter deserves to be called 'ecumenical' more than the Apostolic and Athanasian Creeds, which were not recognized by the Eastern Church.

It is all the more significant that it was not possible for the World Council of Churches to take over officially the Christological statements of Chalcedon together with the Nicene or Nicene–Constantinopolitan Creed as the common basis for the Churches assembled. The reason for this is that certain younger-member Churches of the WCC who were not familiar with the decisions of the Early Church concerning dogma, wished to disregard Church traditions and seek the direct guidance of the

[1] Paper for the Committee on 'Christ and the Church' set up by the ecumenical commission on Faith and Order, Oxford 1956. Trsl. G. Overlach and D. B. Simmonds.

Scriptures and the Holy Spirit. But even in such Churches as the Lutheran and Reformed who explicitly retained the decisions of the Early Church, these symbols have been the subject of dispute. Since the Age of the Englightenment objections have been raised against the interpretation of the Chalcedonian Creed after 451 and especially against the doctrine of the 'anhypostasis' of the human nature of Jesus. Criticism was also voiced against the doctrine of the two wills of Jesus and a concept of the 'communicatio idiomatum' which implied that the human nature of Jesus Christ possessed divine qualities. It was feared that this further development of the Chalcedonian Definition would involve the loss of Jesus as man. Furthermore, neo-Protestantism protested against the Chalcedonian Definition itself, especially its understanding of 'nature' which seemed to cast doubts on the historical Jesus. This suspicion was increased when attempts were made to explain Jesus' acts in history on the basis of the doctrine of the two natures. For instance, His miracles were attributed to His divine nature whereas His hunger, thirst, suffering and death were ascribed to His human nature. This seemed to destroy the unity of the historical Christ. Among other points of controversy which we shall not now enter into, the discussions about the Chalcedonian Creed were especially concerned with the relation between ontological (Harnack: 'physical') and historical statements in Christology. In the 19th and 20th centuries there has been a tendency to eliminate ontological statements and to rest content with historical ones. Carried to its logical conclusion this procedure would result in the complete abandonment of the Chalcedonian definition.

It is of decisive importance for future ecumenical work that the Churches should not fall into two groups—one of which adheres to the Chalcedonian Creed while the other finds no use for it. The Churches should work together towards a new interpretation and a new application of the Early Church's Christology suited to the altered spirit of our age. This is necessary because large and important Churches regard the Chalcedonian Creed as an indispensable condition for Church union and because every rejection of the Chalcedonian Creed, on closer inspection, implies a denial of essential biblical statements or at least a restriction of the response of faith to the biblical witness.

In what follows we shall present a few points of view which are important for a new interpretation and application of the Early Church's Christology, and in particular for clarifying the relation between historical and ontological statements in Christology.

1. A possible objection to the Chalcedonian doctrine of the two natures is that it presents the historical Christ Jesus in ontological, metaphysical and 'physical' categories. But we must not forget that among all the different responses of faith to the Gospel, doxology has a special place because of its close affinity to ontological statements. Doxology, which is present in both the Old and New Testaments, has always been part of worship alongside petitionary prayer, preaching and teaching. All these responses (including doxology) are uniquely concentrated in confession. Doxology is based on God's redeeming action in history. It does not rest content with praising His saving act but also praises God Himself as He who is the same for ever and ever. God is not identical with His act of salvation performed for the individual, the Church and the world. But He has wrought salvation in His eternal freedom and desires to be praised for Himself and not only for His deeds. Doxology, like the prayer of petition, is not directed to men but to God. In contradistinction to ordinary prayer, however, God is not addressed as 'Thou' but acknowledged as 'He' who is the same from eternity to eternity. In doxology He is not asked to do anything, but is praised in His being, His eternal glory, holiness, might, power and wisdom. Thus we are constantly finding statements about His being and nature in the New Testament doxologies (cf. Rom. IX. 5; Rev. IV. 8, VII. 12).

The dogmatic statements of the Early Church are moulded by the structure of doxology. For they are determined by the structure of 'homologia' (confession) in worship in which the element of doxology cannot be overlooked. Homologia is not primarily directed to the world but to God. It is offered up to God as the Church's sacrifice of praise. Thus the dogmatic decisions of the councils of Nicea and Chalcedon are direct statements of belief, and although the Christological decision of Chalcedon is not formulated as a creed for use in worship nor applied as such, it is nevertheless very closely connected with the 'homologia' in worship. Its purpose is to serve this 'homologia' which may be seen by the hymnal and doxological elements remaining in its language.

2. If we have understood the nature of doxology we need not be surprised that the Early Church employed concepts derived from Greek metaphysics in her formulation, development and interpretation of it, since doxological statements about God's being, nature and qualities provided a real starting-point for this development. Furthermore, doxology had to be formulated and interpreted in the historical setting of Hellenism—in its language and terminology. But this need not imply the domination of alien influences or of syncretism. In fact it can be clearly shown that the concepts which were borrowed from Greek philosophy were broken up, corrected and transformed and that the loftiest ideas of pagan thought were admirably employed in Christian witness. Thus Paul's missionary journeys to Greece have left their imprint on the history of Early Church dogma.

3. The development of Christology in the Early Church which took place during the struggle with Adoptionism and Arianism led to the formulation of dogmatic statements about the divinity of Jesus Christ as distinct from all created things. The Christological statements of the Nicene Creed, 'God of God, Light of Light, very God of very God, begotten not made' have a distinctly doxological and hymnal character. And it is in this connexion that the ontological formulation 'being of one substance with the Father' and the term 'homo-ousios' should be understood. The same applies to the formulations of Nicaea–Constantinople.

4. The Christological dogma of Chalcedon adopted these statements from the Nicene Creed. It also employed the term 'physis' (natura) as an equivalent to 'ousia' (substantia). The former concept must also be understood within the framework of the ontological structure of doxology. In addition to the dogmatic decision of Nicaea and Constantinople, dogmatic statements about the humanity of Christ were added as a result of the controversy with Nestorianism and the Monophysites. These statements employ the same concepts as are applied in praising the divinity of Christ—for example, 'perfect', 'true', 'consubstantial' and 'nature'. Thus the humanity of Jesus

Christ is included in our praise and adoration. This is quite appropriate because the purpose of the Chalcedonian Creed is to teach us how the Church should make her 'homologia' to Christ. For the Lord to whom it is offered is the risen Christ, who in His resurrection did not cease to be very man and hence our brother. As the risen Lord He remains very God and very man for all eternity.

5. Doxological statements are based on God's act of salvation in history. Thus doxology presupposes a historical event though it makes no direct reference to it. The great deeds of God are the subject of prayers of thanksgiving. On the other hand the prayer of adoration praises God Himself in His Lordship over history and in His unchangeable divinity. Hence doxological statements are ultimate in a special way since they are based on God's act of salvation in history. Without this basis they would be impossible though they do not necessarily mention it. Therefore it is not surprising that the history of Jesus Christ, His message and His miracles up to His death on the Cross, and then His resurrection, ascension and parousia are not mentioned in the Chalcedonian Creed. The only thing that is mentioned is the Incarnation, which is the origin of the God-*man* who is confessed by the Church.

6. Although the Christological statements of Chalcedon make no reference to the history of Jesus Christ (apart from His birth), they are not unrelated to the historical tradition of Jesus' preaching and miracles and of His way through suffering to glory, but provide an adequate response to this tradition. The Chalcedonian definition is the proper response to the mystery of substitution which God has effected for our salvation by the work and suffering of Jesus Christ. The Son of God became a son of man that we the sons of men might become the sons of God. The Righteous One took upon Himself our sin in order that we sinners might be justified. He, who is the divine Life, died on the Cross, that we who are dead might live. The Chalcedonian Definition is the doxological response to God's work of salvation which was consummated in the historical life of Jesus Christ the Son of God who intervened on our behalf and took our place. If Jesus Christ were not praised as very God and very man, He would not be acknowledged as our substitute and our redemption would not be

accomplished. The Chalcedonian Creed was based on the doctrine of redemption advocated by Irenaeus in the face of the current speculations about the Logos and defended by Athanasius against Arius. This doctrine of redemption cannot be rejected on the grounds of being 'physical', since it has adopted the basic New Testament and especially the Pauline concept of substitution (though partly using different terms). It was continued in the Reformation doctrine of the blissful exchange of the Righteous One with the sinner. Thus the Chalcedonian Definition corresponds to the history of Jesus Christ who has been our substitute from His birth through His baptism, temptation and Messianic self-concealment up to His abandonment by God in His death on the Cross. It is not concerned with the two natures of Christ as such, but with the entirety of Jesus' divine and human nature, without which His substitution for us would be illusory.

7. As the Chalcedonian Definition is a dogma—without being in itself a 'homologia' for use in worship—but intended to teach how the true 'homologia' should be made in worship and to safeguard it, this creed must not be misunderstood as a theoretical statement. Its purpose is to guide our worship of the mystery of the person of Jesus Christ who is the Lord of the Church. This understanding of its function in the life of the Church has not always been retained in the history of the interpretation of the Chalcedonian Christology. Even though the 'anhypostasis' of the human nature of Christ and His two wills may be logically deduced from the Chalcedonian Creed, these concepts are not necessarily implied in the act of worshipping the Redeemer; they are rather the result of theoretical reflection on the statements of this creed and of a progressive analysis and clarification of this interpretation. Thus in the subsequent development, dogmatic statements about the Person of Jesus Christ by scholasticism ceased to be doxological (despite their emphasis on the unfathomable mystery of His person), and became theoretical and explanatory. The inevitable result of this process was the attempt to explain the life of Jesus Christ in history by making use of the Chalcedonian Christology in distinguishing between the actions of His human and divine natures. It was also inevitable that one should try to explain the Real Presence of the Body of Christ in the Lord's Supper by

the doctrine of the 'communicatio idiomatum'. But such an attempt involved reading too much into the Chalcedonian Definition. And Luther may justly be criticized for going beyond the intention of this creed (despite his formal adherence to it) in his teaching about the 'communicatio idiomatum'.

8. Since doxological statements are ultimate statements in which God's eternal deity is worshipped and praised because of His act of salvation in history, these ultimate statements must not be used as logical premises from which it is possible to make logical deductions about God's action in history. Although doxology is based on the message of God's acts in history and is a response to those acts, its function is to praise God in His eternal nature and freedom. Because God has accomplished His acts of creation and redemption in the freedom of His love and not out of necessity, and because He will perfect the New Creation in this freedom, these acts cannot be deduced from doxological statements about His nature (although such statements are proper responses to His acts). The acts of God in creation, redemption and re-creation cannot be deduced from the praise of the Holy and Eternal Trinity; neither can the details of Jesus' life be derived from the praise of the God-man. Nor is it possible to derive the important difference between the earthly Son of God in His humility and the transfigured heavenly body of the exalted Christ from the praise of Jesus Christ as very God and very man. At this point the statements of Chalcedon reach the limits inherent in doxology. For we cannot deduce or give a theoretical explanation of the historical events of Christ's humiliation and exaltation from the confession 'very God and very man'. Hence the Christological statements of Chalcedon are no substitute for the historical record of Jesus' life; but they represent the Church's later response to it, just as (in public worship) doxology is the congregation's response to the reading of Holy Scripture and the message of the humiliation of God's Son and exaltation of the man Jesus.

9. The Chalcedonian definition confesses Jesus Christ as true God and true man by employing basic concepts of Greek philosophy such as 'nature' and 'person'. This involved a complete transformation of the meaning which had hitherto

been attached to these concepts. At the same time we must not overlook the far-reaching changes which the concepts of 'nature' and 'person' have subsequently undergone.

a) The concept of 'person' in the Early Church must not be confused with the contemporary understanding of 'person' and personality in psychology and philosophy. If we understand 'person' as the individual centre of consciousness (i.e. as one's self-awareness) and 'personality' as the individual constitution of one's character derived from disposition and experience, this does not correspond to the concept of 'person' in the Early Church. Instead it corresponds to their concept of 'nature'. According to Chalcedonian terminology, the 'person' is not a subject for psychological observation.

b) At the same time, the concept of 'nature' in the Early Church must not be confused with what is now understood by 'nature' as opposed to 'spirit'. The concept of 'nature' in the Chalcedonian Definition includes both the human and divine spirit. Thus 'nature' is the perfect description of Jesus Christ's complete identity (in nature) with God and man.

c) Yet we must not overlook that 'nature' does not have the same meaning in the statements about His human nature and those concerning His divine nature. This can be seen when the Chalcedonian Definition is developed into statements about the attributes of His two natures. The omnipotence, eternity, omnipresence, infinity and immutability, etc., of His divine nature are not logically opposed to the weakness, limitation by time and space, finitude and mutability of His human nature. The complete superiority of the divine nature over His human nature excludes any complementary dependence of the statements about the divine nature on those about the human nature. Almighty God is so powerful that He remains Lord even when He divests himself of His power. It is precisely in weakness that He reveals the glory of His power. The eternal and ever-present God is so completely Lord of all time and space that He remains Lord even when He takes upon Himself the limitations of time and space which apply to all created things. He never ceases to be the Eternal and Omnipresent Lord, but in His finitude he manifests Himself as the Infinite whose eternity and omnipresence transcends all human thought. God's immutability consists in the freedom of

His love in which He stoops down to the sinner, becomes flesh and suffers the cursed death of the sinner.

10. Historical and ontological statements in Christology are not alternative but complement one another. The way in which they do this may be explained by taking account of the different basic structures of theological statements. The response of faith to the Kerygma is made in statements with different structures. The history of Jesus is the subject of didactic tradition and witness. Jesus Christ, true God and true man, is the subject of doxology which is the response to the history of Jesus Christ as taught and believed. The origin of Christological dogma is specially to be seen in doxological statements which were based on the teaching of the New Testament. As these statements were progressively understood as the doctrine of the person of Jesus Christ, it became necessary to work out a doctrine of His work, and finally a doctrine of His two statuses (i.e. humiliation and exaltation). In this process the statements about the Person of Jesus Christ (which are structurally ultimate statements), were made the premises for the doctrines of His work and His twofold status, and the criterion for the history of Jesus. In the 19th and 20th centuries protests were made against this in the quest for the historical Jesus and in existentialist Kerygma-theology respectively. But both these criticisms overlooked the contribution of the Chalcedonian Creed to the life of the Church—namely as a co-ordinate of the doxological 'homologia'. This contribution had been generally ignored in the Scholastic doctrine of the two natures of Christ. The statements of Chalcedon must be reinterpreted and re-applied. They should not be understood as inconsistent with the history of Jesus but as instructions as to how the historical Christ, who is present in His Church as the risen Lord, should be praised.

II. CHRIST AND THE CHURCH

TWELVE THESES FOR AN ECUMENICAL DISCUSSION BETWEEN THEOLOGIANS OF THE EVANGELICAL AND THE ROMAN CHURCHES[1]

IN HIS inquiries into the New Testament conception of the Church, Karl Ludwig Schmidt propounded the thesis: Ecclesiology is Christology—a thesis which is certainly not new, but which is by no means self-evident in the context of Protestant theology. At the outset I should like to say that I do not want my thesis to be understood in the sense of this equation, for the following reasons:

1. The terms in which the New Testament speaks of the Church are very manifold, and they are by no means merely Christological. Beside Christological designations of the Church —such as σῶμα τοῦ Χριστοῦ, νύμφη, γυνή—there are also pneumatological designations such as 'temple of the Holy Ghost', and theological such as ἐκκλησία τοῦ θεοῦ, λαὸς τοῦ θεοῦ. Thus ecclesiology taken as a whole must be expounded and developed in a trinitarian way; and in this we should not forget that in the primitive Confessions the articles concerning the Church are directly connected with the articles on the Holy Ghost. This suggests that, within a trinitarian context, one should expound the doctrine of the Church as the *opus proprium* of the Holy Ghost.

2. Corresponding to this variety in ecclesiological conceptions is the variety of the answers which have customarily been given to the question concerning the origin of the Church. Is it founded by the outpouring of the Holy Ghost at the event of Pentecost? Is it founded by the death and resurrection of Christ,

---

[1] These theses were propounded and discussed at a joint conference of Protestant and Roman Catholic ecumenical study groups on March 25th, 1953 at the Evangelical Academy, Tutzing. The translation is made by Miss Mary Lusk, B.D., Edinburgh. 'Evangelical' here and elsewhere in this book represents German *evangelisch*. It refers to the Lutheran and Calvinist churches and their doctrines, not to a particular church party.

and by the sending out of the apostles as the appointed eye-witnesses of His resurrection? Is it founded in the election of the Covenant people of the Old Testament? Or in the creation of the first men, or in the eternal decree of creation even before the act of creation (the truth in the sub-apostolic affirmations of the pre-existence of the Church)? We cannot discuss these questions further here, but each one of them is in a real sense to be answered in the affirmative. The question of the origin of the Church demands a trinitarian answer too. In celebrating Pentecost especially as her birthday, the Church considers herself to be the *opus proprium* of the Holy Ghost.

3. But even with reference to the specifically Christological designations of the Church, the equation Ecclesiology = Christology is not a useful one, because it expresses only one of the very manifold connexions between Christ and the Church, and this one it isolates dangerously. The equating of ecclesiology and Christology is suggested by the New Testament statements of the Church as σῶμα Χριστοῦ, in which one should certainly not overlook the irreversible relation between the Head and the Body: only Christ is both the Head and the Body, while the Church is only His body. Besides, there are the descriptions of the Church as the Bride of Christ, which in themselves, though pointing towards unity, express rather a distinction between Christ and the Church. Then one has to take into consideration all the places where Christ confronts the Church as Lord, and even as Judge. Ecclesiology has also to consider such warnings of the exalted Christ as that to the Church at Sardis: 'Repent! If therefore thou shalt not watch, I will come on thee as a thief. . . .' (Rev. III. 3). These expressions exclude a thorough-going equating of ecclesiology and Christology, in just the same way as it is impossible to equate the doctrine of the creature with the doctrine of God the Creator.

So under the heading of 'Christ and the Church' we shall deal here not with ecclesiology as a whole—not with ecclesiology in the whole of its trinitarian context, but simply with the special aspect of its Christological reference. In what follows the development of this subject is outlined in twelve theses, of which the first ten begin with the words: 'The Church is . . .'. Most of these theses will be only briefly expounded. But the statements concerning the attributes and the marks of the

Church must be developed at greater length, since these are of special significance for our theological conversation. Then in conclusion we must ask the question: What is meant here by '*is*'? and what is meant by saying the Church '*has*' attributes?

1. *The Church is the People of God called by Christ out of the World*

Jesus Christ died on the Cross for the whole world, and in His resurrection is exalted as Lord over the world. The self-assertion and self-will of the world are placed under His judgement. In Him also there is opened up a possibility of deliverance from this judgement for everyone who believes in Him. We are called out from the world by the Gospel of the death and resurrection of Jesus. This call is not merely news about Jesus, and not merely the announcement of the deliverance of those who believe in Him; but the Gospel is also the Word by which the risen Christ is Himself present and acts. It is by the Gospel that Jesus Christ accomplishes the deliverance of believers; and by the Gospel He reveals Himself in power as the exalted Lord. In baptism we have not merely received the mark of Jesus' death and resurrection: but we have become the property of Christ, we have been delivered up to His death, crucified, dead and buried with Him, so that we live with Him (Rom. vi. 3ff.).

So we are gathered out of the world by Christ and united in Christ. We are added to the New Testament people of God—both Jews and Gentiles—in which the worldly distinctions between races, classes and sexes are eschatologically annulled. In the people of God all those who are differentiated in the world are 'one in Christ Jesus' (Gal. iii. 28).

As members of the New Testament people of God we are subject to the Kingship of Christ. We belong no longer to ourselves, but to Christ our Lord. Day by day we receive from Him anew forgiveness, life and fellowship. And we are subject to His command.

2. *The Church is the Prophetic-Priestly-Kingly People sent out into the World by Christ*

Christ has called us out of the world, so that He may send us as His messengers into the world. He has given us a new point of origin outside the world, so that we may go forward into the world from this point of origin. Since we have been liberated by

Christ we must proclaim to the world its end, and to the captives freedom in Christ. Both movements—out of the world and into the world—belong essentially together in the conception of the Church.

The Church is sent into the world by the Lord who, as the Crucified and Risen One, rules the world and intercedes for it in His threefold office of Prophet, Priest and King. By virtue of His commission the Church receives a share in this office corresponding to His. The Church is the prophetic people by whom the mighty acts of God are shown forth before the whole world (Acts 2); she is 'the royal priesthood' (I Peter II. 9ff.). Under the Old Covenant *individual* men were called to be prophets or priests or kings, and these individuals stood over against one another and the people as a whole; but now the Church *as a whole* is called to be a people of prophets, priests and kings. All that we may say concerning the different gifts of the Spirit in the New Testament (and even the peculiar nature of a gift of prophecy) and concerning offices in the Church—all this is within the context of the reality of the prophetic, priestly and kingly office of Christ, which embraces the whole Church and gives her her commission, and which makes every member a prophetic witness and a royal priest. Jesus' threefold office is represented before the world in the ministry of the Church as she is sent out into the world.

Sent into the world, the Church is the proclamation and the instrument of the Lordship of Christ breaking-in into the world. It is only when we include in our conception of the Church this sending out of the Church into the world that we really grasp the relation between the Church and the Kingdom of Christ. The Church is the Kingdom of Christ, because her members are subject to Christ as Lord of the world, and because she calls the world to recognize this Lord. She is the effect and the instrument of the Lordship of the Kyrios.

3. *The Church is the Worshipping Assembly, in which Christ is Present and Active*

This twofold movement—out of the world and into the world—has its centre in the worshipping assembly in which the saving acts of God are proclaimed and glorified, and the Lord's Supper celebrated. Christ has called us into this assembly

H

by His Gospel; He has joined us to it in baptism; and from it He sends us out to our ministry in the world. The worshipping assembly is so very much the centre of the life of the Church that it has become the central designation of the Church in the concept ἐκκλησία. The designation of the Church as the Body of Christ, which is connected with the Lord's Supper, as well as the designations 'Temple' and 'House of God', all point to this centre. And the worshipping assembly is at the centre of the Reformation conception of the Church (*Confessio Augustana* VII).

The life of the Church is concentrated with peculiar intensity in the worshipping assembly. In the event of worship we have to distinguish several dimensions, of which we shall call attention to the first three now and to two others in the two following theses: (1) the active presence of the crucified and risen Lord in the Word and Sacrament; (2) our becoming the Lord's property, in hearing His Word, in receiving His body and blood, in confession, in petition, acclamation and doxology; (3) our mutual service of one another—of believers and non-believers—in witness and intercession.

It is through the presence of Christ that, in New Testament language, every local worshipping congregation is in the full sense ἐκκλησία, σῶμα τοῦ Χριστοῦ, ναὸς τοῦ θεοῦ. This is so, not with regard to the total number of believers, for these are scattered throughout the world and belong to geographically separated congregations, but with regard to Christ, who is wholly present in every local congregation of believers. So the Church comprising all the believers in the world should not be conceived as the sum of local churches; rather she is a κοινωνία in the sense of a common participation in the one Christ, who is present whole and undivided in every local congregation.

4. *The Church is the Bride waiting for Christ, and already in the Worshipping Assembly she Participates in the coming Marriage Supper*

We are going towards the coming Lord, whose appearing in glory we await. So the Church is like the Bride who awaits the coming of her Bridegroom to the marriage.

In the worshipping assembly it is not just that we *pray* 'Maran atha'; but the Lord whom we invoke actually *comes* into our midst. In the Lord's Supper it is not only the crucified and risen Christ who makes Himself present to us, but the Christ who is to come again. In Him we already partake now of the great Supper in the Kingdom of God—the eternal Marriage Supper of the Lamb. The Church is not only the Bride, but the Wife of Christ. It is true that in this life we are still moving towards the goal: yet it is also true that we have already reached the goal. Although we do not yet see the promised glory, we have a share in it already by faith in the Lord, who gives Himself to us in the Lord's Supper.

So the worshipping assembly is also the present followship of believers on earth with the perfected believers of all ages, whom Christ will one day gather in glory. The invisible unity of the Church militant with the Church triumphant is realized in the presentce of the Christ who is to come.

This is the fourth dimension of the event of worship.

5. *The Church is the Body of Christ, which in the Worshipping Assembly will be built up into the New Universe*

As we receive the body of Christ in the Lord's Supper, we who are baptized and believe in Christ are built up as the body of Christ. Christ is the Head of His Body. As Head He rules the Church, His Body; He confronts her as Lord. But it is also true to say that Christ is not just the Head, but the Head and the Body. The Church does not just live under Him as her Lord; she lives in Christ, she is a part of Christ, she is the Body of Him who is Himself both the Head and the Body. The unity of the Church and Christ is not the unity of identity; for it is Christ only, and never the Church, who is the Head of the Body. But it is the unity of the Body of Christ.

The Body of Christ is growing—growing up '*into him* in all things, which is the head, even Christ' (Eph. iv. 15); and growing *from the Head*, 'from which all the body by joints and bands having nourishment ministered, and knit together, increaseth with the increase of God' (Col. ii. 19). This growth takes place in knowledge of faith, in the fruits of good works, as well as in the sufferings of the martyrs, who 'fill up that which is lacking of the afflictions of Christ . . . for his body's sake, which is the church' (Col. i. 24). But the increase of the body consists above all in the adding to it of more members as the fruit of the Gospel preached in the world. The Body of Christ grows in the increase of the faithful and in the size of their company, inwardly and outwardly, upwards and in the dimensions of space and time, in her struggle with the trials of the world. So Christ who is the 'firstborn from the dead' is 'the head of the body', 'the beginning' (Col. 1. 18) and the goal of the growth. But Christ Himself is also the 'perfect man' (Eph. iv. 13), in whom the Body and all the members are fitted together under the Head.

As the Body of Christ, the Church has an even greater significance: she reaches forth beyond mankind—and, in fact, pervades the whole universe. She is 'the fulness of Him that filleth all in all' (Eph. 1. 23). The power of Christ which fills the universe is present in the Church; the Church is the fullness of Christ, which is extended by Him into the universe; the Church is, indeed, 'the universe in its eschatological form' (E. Käsemann). It is in the Church that the creation reaches its goal—not as the world, but as the Kingdom of Christ. So in the Church there is brought about the harmony of voices of all creatures who praise God as their Lord. In the worship of the congregation we join in the praise of the angels who offer the *Sanctus* to God. No doubt the praise of the Church in this world will not be without entreaties and supplications and sighings; and yet the new creation is already realized in Christ and in the people who praise Him.

This is the fifth dimension of the event of worship.

6. *The Church is the Fellowship of the Gifts of Grace, in the diversity of which the one grace of Christ makes itself Effectively Present*

All the Scriptures of the New Testament bear witness to the fact that the Holy Ghost is given to every member of the new people of God. Paul in particular bears witness to the fact that the outpouring of the Spirit works a diversity of spiritual gifts (but cf. also e.g. I Peter iv. 10f.). To each believer, a particular *charisma* is imparted: 'one and the self-same Spirit, dividing to every man severally as he will' (I Cor. xii. 11). Paul taught the diversity of spiritual gifts as so fundamental a doctrine, that his statements should not by any means be considered to be limited to the churches in Corinth (I Cor. xii-xiv) and Rome (Rom. xii. 6ff.), nor even to the Pauline Churches or to the Early Church. Rather, the diversity of spiritual gifts is essential to the Church in all times and places. As the Body of Christ the Church is an organism of manifold gifts, in which particular spiritual gifts are divided to each believer by the Spirit as He will.

Every spiritual gift is a διακονία, given for the edifying of the Church. No one receives spiritual gifts for himself alone; and so among all *charismata* love is the 'more excellent way' (I Cor. xII. 31), the transcendent, the 'more costly way' (Luther).

In the diversity of the divine gifts the fullness of the one Christ is made present in the Church, and, through the Church, in the world. The diversity of *charismata* may appear in different forms in different churches (cf. I Cor. xII. and Rom. xII.) and at different times. But it is always the manifestation of the one χάρις of Jesus Christ. As the Head of the body He is the bearer and the originator of all *charismata*, and all are related to Him in the ministry. So the community of spiritual gifts consists in their common participation in the one χάρις of Jesus Christ.

7. The Church is the Congregation led by Christ Himself through the Office of Pastor

From the calling of everyone to membership in the prophetic-priestly people of God and so to ministry, we have to distinguish the calling which commissions and authorizes individual members to a particular ministry. From the diversity of the spontaneous *charismata* and ministries of all the faithful we have to distinguish the ministry which is exercised by virtue of a definite commission and authorization in the Church (as was the original basic ministry of the apostles). It is true that everyone who exercises a charismatic ministry is to an extent related to such a definite 'Word' of the Church, since he is subjected to the testing and judgement of the congregation. This is the significance, for example, of the Amen by which the Pauline congregation recognized free testimony among them as a testimony of the Spirit. This is also, in a different way, the significance of the Pauline admonition that they should submit themselves unto the ministry of Stephanas, for the sake of the work which he was actually doing for the congregation (I Cor. xvi. 15). But the 'Words' on which the charismatics and their ministries are *subsequently* dependent are different from the calling which *precedes* a ministry, which sends out particular men to a particular ministry and authorizes them for it in prayer.

In this case we speak of ecclesiastical office: this means that charismatic ministry which among all the diversities of the charismatic ministries of the Church rests on a special calling, commissioning and sending. Nevertheless all offices in the Church are distinguished from the historic apostolate, because it alone possesses the unique and incomparable authority of those who were directly called by the Lord to be eyewitnesses of His resurrection. This authority is the basic norm for the Church of all ages. All other offices in the Church have authority only in obedient submission to the apostolic authority. Those ecclesiastical ministries which are based on a special precedent calling are in particular the functions of founding and leading the Church. They are embraced in the concept of the pastoral office; and in addition to the different forms of the pastorate there are further offices of the diaconate in the narrower sense.

If the apostolic message is proclaimed by the pastor, the same promise which Jesus once made to His apostles holds good for the pastor too: 'He that heareth you, heareth me' (Luke x. 16). When the pastor cries: 'Be ye reconciled to God', he like the apostle is an 'ambassador for Christ', an instrument by which God Himself intreats the Church and the world (II Cor. v. 20). The consoling, admonishing and judging voice of the pastor is not merely a human voice, but the voice of Christ using human words as its organ of speech. The same commission and the same promise which were given to the apostles are given to pastors of all ages: 'Whose soever sins ye remit, they are remitted unto them; and whose soever sins ye retain, they are retained' (John xx. 22f.; cf. Matt. xvi. 19 and xviii. 18). In everything that the pastor does in obedience to his commission, he confronts the congregation as the representative of Christ, the one Good Shepherd. As the pastor leads the congregation in worship, Christ Himself through this ministry leads the Church; thus He consoles, admonishes, strengthens and directs her.

Because Christ is actively present in the gifts and ministries of the whole membership, the leadership of the congregation cannot in any way be a lordship of the pastor over the congregation. Not only the office of pastor but also the free charismatic testimony stands over against the congregation. For in that, too, Christ encounters the congregation. Christ acts upon the congregation through the office of pastor; and He acts upon both the congregation and the pastor through the diverse charismatic ministries. Thus the pastoral office stands in the midst of the reciprocal ministries which all members exercise toward one another. The pastor stands in the midst of the diverse operations of the one grace of Christ through diverse ministries one to another. So it is not only that the charismatic testimonies of the congregation are to be proved by the pastorate; but the opposite is also true—the congregation has the duty and the authority to prove, to criticize and to judge the ministry of the pastor, as it does every free ministry.

8. *The Church is 'one, holy, catholic and apostolic' (Nicaea)*

These four attributes of the Church are in a peculiar way interwoven. The first three are of the same Christological structure, while the fourth occupies a special position.

1. The *unity* of the Church. We see not only a number of spatially separated assemblies, but already in the New Testament epistles we read of various tensions, oppositions and groupings within the local congregations—for example, differences of opinion at Corinth which extended even to the celebration of the Lord's Supper; and also of tensions and differences between the apostles (Gal II. 11ff.). These tensions and even the forming of cliques did not hinder Paul from testifying to the unity of these very churches and their members, nor from speaking to those who were disunited among themselves about their unity, nor from exhorting them to unity by appeal to that unity.

The unity of the Church is not primarily the unity of her members, but the unity of Christ who acts upon them all, in all places and at all times. It is one and the same Christ who by Word and Sacrament has called them all and incorporated them into Himself; one and the same Christ who is actively present in the diversity of spiritual gifts. All members of the Church have been chosen by the one God, called by the one Christ and renewed and endowed by the one Holy Ghost. Hence, the unity of those who believe in Christ, are baptized into Christ and receive the body of Christ in the Lord's Supper is an object of faith, transcending all their visible tensions, oppositions, cliques and local differences. Faith regards it as the reality created by God in Christ through the Holy Ghost.

Because those who believe in Christ, who are baptized into Him and receive His body are one, they should strive for oneness; because they are one, they ought to be one. On the ground of the unity given in Christ, the apostle exhorts them to give expression to this unity in an ordered, common celebration of the Lord's Supper and in a mutual ordering of the *charismata* in love; and, beyond the local congregation, in a mutual recognition of ministries and in mutual intercession and assistance. So the exhortations of the apostle to the Church at Corinth which refer to this subject are of the structure common to New Testament *paraklesis*. The imperative is given on the ground of the indicative of the saving act which has taken place and which is recognized by faith. The unity of the Church is not the task and achievement of men; rather, it is on the ground of the unity which Christ has achieved that the faithful ought to be one.

2. The *holiness* of the Church. This holiness is not to be seen by looking at all those who belong to the Church. Nor is it to be seen by looking at the picture which the New Testament epistles give us of the early Churches. There we read of many and various sins; and even when the incestuous and some of the grossest sinners were excluded from the Church, there was still enough to be admonished—presumptuousness, covetousness, legalism, lack of faith, licentiousness and uncharitableness of every sort. Added to that were the hidden sins, then just as now. In fact, the Church was from the beginning a 'bed and sick-room of those who are ill and in need of healing' (Luther, *Röemerbriefvorlesung*, Fi. II, III).

The holiness of the Church is not primarily the holiness of her members, but the holiness of Christ, which is imputed to this gathering, and the holiness of the Spirit, who sanctifies these men in Christ and dwells in them. Only in this way can we understand the indifference with which the writers of the New Testament epistles address as saints those same members of the Church whose sins they so clearly expose. The holiness of the Church is not the sum of the holiness of her members, but the holiness of Christ, who gives Himself to the Church and dwells in her midst—in the power of the Holy Ghost, who makes sinners holy. If we look at the members of the Church, they are all sinners, and the Church is a fellowship of sinners and not of saints. But if we believe in the Christ who is present and active in her through the Spirit, we know that by the gospel and by the sacraments this multitude of sinners is justified and will be daily justified anew. In this sense the Church is both a sick-house and a palace for the cured—to the natural eye a sick-house, and to the eye of faith a palace for the cured.

Because the Church is holy through God's sanctifying work, her members ought to put away sin and strive after holiness. The exhortation to holiness presupposes the saving action of sanctification. Because the members are sanctified, they ought to lay hold on holiness. Because they are holy, they ought to live as holy. Yet we should notice that this New Testament imperative is directed not only to individual members of the Church, but also to whole Churches. So we can say even of the Church as a whole: Because she is sanctified, she ought to be holy.

3. The *catholicity* of the Church. If by catholicity we understand that the Church encompasses the world geographically, we see very little of that in the New Testament writings. For what significance has even the road from Jerusalem to Rome in comparison with the whole world? Nevertheless, according to the Nicene Creed, the Church was already the catholic Church at Pentecost.

The Church is catholic because Christ, who is exalted as Lord, the Pantokrator, acts in her—He to whom is given all power in heaven and on earth. The word 'catholic' is not to be found in the New Testament writings; it is found first in Ignatius, and there in a Christological context: 'where Christ is, there is also the catholic Church' (Smyrn. VIII. 2). As the concept is further developed, the geographical extension of the Church on the earth becomes more prominent, and later a distinction is made between actual and virtual geographical extension. The Reformers, on the other hand, in accordance with the original line, liked to translate 'catholic' by 'Christian'. We may connect with this an understanding of catholicity, which one comes across repeatedly in the ecclesiology of the Eastern Church, according to which the catholicity of the Church consists in the comprehensive diversity of charismatic

gifts, of theologies and of believers. The catholicity of the
Church is the catholicity of Jesus Christ, Lord of lords, Lord of
the universe. As this Lord, He is present and active in the
Church; He incorporates believers into His Body, which is the
πλήρωμα of Him who fills the universe; He gives them, in the
diversity of spiritual gifts, a share in the all-embracing riches of
His grace; and He sends them into the world to proclaim to it
the end of its self-will and to proclaim Him as Lord of the world.
It is because Christ the *Pantokrator* is in her midst, because He
empowers and sends her, that the Church is catholic. She is
catholic on the strength of the catholicity of her Lord, which is
imputed to her.

Because in Christ the Church is catholic, He ought to be
catholic. She does not have to achieve her catholicity primarily through her own extension, but she has to believe in her
Lord who encompasses the universe and to be obedient to Him.
Because in faith she is catholic, she should give scope to the
abundance of His gifts of grace in the manifoldness of the
knowledge of faith, of witness, of ministries in the widest sense,
through which the Lord in His riches is present in her midst.
Because she is catholic, she ought to advance into all regions of
the world, to proclaim to all men Him who is already their
Lord, whether they know it or not, whether they confess or
deny Him. Since we do not have by our own effort to make
Christ the *Pantokrator*, nor even to make the Church catholic,
our ministry, in spite of all troubles and trials, is in the end an
easy and joyful one.

4. *Apostolicity* occupies a special position among the four
attributes of the Church. Certainly it is true of each one of these
attributes that it is only realized in conjunction with the other
three. They are inseparably interwoven in like manner as are
the attributes of God: and their enumeration is incomplete, as is
that of the attributes in the doctrine of God. Yet, within this
belonging to one another and this unity of the four attributes,
apostolicity has a special place in so far as the Christ—one, holy
and exalted over the universe—really encounters the Church
only in the apostolic witness. Without the apostolic witness He
would simply be hidden, and only on the basis of this witness is
He really known. So the significance of apostolicity is that it is
the attribute on which the other attributes of the Church rest in

a special way; because Christ neither rules the Church, nor is He present in her, without the ministry of the apostles.

If by the apostles we understand the called and enlightened eyewitnesses of the resurrection of Jesus Christ, they are the foundation of the Church, and that not only in the historical sense that once the Church was founded through their ministry and so on them. As the chosen eyewitnesses of the victory of Christ, they have beyond that a lasting, an incomparable, an unrepeatable, a normative position as authorities *vis-à-vis* the Church of all subsequent ages. One cannot approach Christ if one by-passes the apostolic witness to Christ. Consequently it is only in faith in the apostolic Gospel that the Church is one, holy and catholic in Christ. If she is the apostolic Church obedient to the apostolic message, then she is also the one holy catholic Church.

Because this is so, the Church of all ages must heed the exhortation to abide by the apostolic Gospel, and, where she has departed from it or gone beyond it, to return to the apostolic message. This is the meaning of the challenge: *ecclesia semper reformanda est*.

9. *The Church is Indestructible*

The structure of the attributes of the Church becomes even plainer here. For of the relevant New Testament passages none speaks, strictly, of any attribute of the Church, of any capacity of *her own* to abide on earth, or of her incapacity to be destroyed; they speak, rather, of *the promise of God in Christ*.

The world resists the message of the Church. The message of the end of the world and the summons to submission to Christ the Lord cause disturbance in the world. The world wants its own kind of eternity; it wants to continue to be the world. So it struggles against the Church on a double front: in open attack, oppression and persecution on one side, and, on the other, in adapting itself to the Church, in bringing the Church into subservience and in secularizing her—of which the second is the more dangerous. In one way or another this struggle takes place under ever new camouflage and on continually changing historical fronts.

The promise is given to the Church that she will abide, in the midst of all trials and struggles. 'The gates of hell shall not prevail against it' (Matt. xvi. 18). The woman (the Church) remains on the earth, even when her seed (the individual members) are killed (Rev. xii. 6, 13ff.). Even though she is almost choked by the tares that the enemy has sowed secretly, yet she will remain until the time of harvest (Matt. xiii. 24ff.).

This promise does not mean that the Church will always remain in the same place, with the same increase in her membership, with the same order, in the same clarity of knowledge and of love, with the same diversity of spiritual gifts. But never will the earth be without those to whom is given the promise that they will 'inherit the earth' (Matt. v. 5). Never will the earth be without her for whose sake and for the completion of whose number God preserves the world in spite of sin and death. The one holy catholic apostolic Church will always remain.

Because the Church is given this promise, she is subject to the imperative to combat the powers of the world. Christ does not only promise, 'neither shall any man pluck them out of my hand' (John x. 28); He also commands, 'abide in me'. The combat in which the Church is ordered to engage is an extremely strange one, and it is waged on both sides with quite different weapons. The Church fights as she is gathered for the Word and Sacrament, as she thanks God even for her trials and intercedes for her enemies, as she confesses Christ before the world and takes upon herself suffering for the sake of her confession. She fights as she continues in her λειτουργεῖν in the widest sense, and as she continues to be that which she originally is—as she abides in Christ. She fights for the victor's crown by abiding in Him who is already Victor over the world.

In order to abide in Christ, the Church has in the course of her history fixed the canon of the New Testament and defined dogmas and orders. These decisions all have their common origin in the service of the worshipping assembly, and they have, historically, been pronounced as the Church combated threats to this assembly.

In the canon, the Church has gathered the documents of the apostolic message. It is the norm of the Church's speaking and acting—and that not because the Church made it, but because the apostolic message is the normative foundation of the Church for all time. The Church has recognized in the canon the norm of the apostolic witness to Christ.

In dogma, the Church has acknowledged Christ. Dogma is authoritative for the Church's speaking and acting, not because it was formulated by the Church, but because in it confession is made of the Christ to whom the apostles bore witness—the Christ who is the same yesterday, today and for ever, and who has ever to be confessed anew by the Church on her historically changing fronts.

In her order, the Church has appointed the manner in which the ministry of preaching and of the administration of the sacraments is to be exercised. Even order has its binding validity not because it was instituted by the Church but because of the commission of the Lord to preach the Gospel and because of His institution of the sacraments. In her particular historical situation the Church has to acknowledge by her orders the ordinance of Christ.

Notice the increasing width of the field of possibilities within which the Church has come to these three decisions. In the fixation of the canon, she was bound (notwithstanding the whole problematic of the antilegomena) to the historical documents which had been handed down, and to their text. In dogma, the Church has ever to use her own words to bear her witness, making her choice between various ideas and in controversy with continually changing heresies and *Weltanschauungen*. Ecclesiastical order in its details is to an even greater extent conditioned by the external presuppositions of the contemporary situation in which the Church is obedient to the commission of her Lord. From this result the problem of the historical variability of these ecclesiastical decisions and the differing manner of their authority and validity for the Church.

10. *The Church is Visible in this World*

The Church is hidden from the eyes of the world, like the earthly Christ and the operation of the Holy Ghost. Admittedly everyone can see the worshipping congregations and hear their witness, and discern the temporal duration and the spatial extension of Christendom. But without faith the Church cannot be discerned as the people of God. In the eyes of the world she is concealed in the abundance of religious-historical and religious-sociological analogies. She appears as only one religion among many. Neither her unity nor her holiness nor her catholicity may be discerned without faith in her Lord.

But the Church is also hidden from the eyes of believers. Certainly it is clear that those who have separated themselves from the worshipping fellowship do not belong to the people of God. But the company of the children of God is further hidden among the many who may take part in worship but who nevertheless do not lead a new life—whether it be that they deny Christ before the world, or that they persist in adultery, covetousness, ambition, etc., or self-righteously boast before God and men of their irreproachable conduct and of their confession. Often enough the number of hypocrites seems greater than that of true believers. One must not, however, stop at such judgement of others; and on no account may one anticipate the separation between the living and the dead in the Church, which is reserved to Christ as the Judge who is to come. Rather, it is precisely the believer who discerns again and again in himself the sinner, the hypocrite, the denier! Who could boast of his obedience before God? Who must not cry daily, 'Forgive me my debts?' The one holy Church is concealed not only beneath the disunity and the unholiness of others, but also beneath my own sins.

In the midst of the assemblies of this world one may only discern the Church in the same way as the sinner discerns in himself one who is justified and holy—namely, by faith in the Gospel. The Church is not the Gospel, but the congregation of sinners in which the Gospel is preached. But the Gospel is God's Word, powerful and active, by which He produces faith and justifies and sanctifies believing sinners. In spite of every contradiction brought against it by men, the Gospel will never fail to produce its effect, namely to awaken faith and to save. Where it is preached, one may reckon with certainty that God is gathering His people, however questionable may appear the gathering in which this takes place. Where baptism is administered there is an incorporation into the Body of Christ, and where the Lord's Supper is received the Body of Christ is built up, even when unbelief is judged in this event and believers are concealed among hypocrites. So the preaching of the Gospel and the administration of baptism and the Lord's Supper are the marks by which the Church can be discerned with complete certainty in this world.

Certainly, where the Gospel is preached, there arise, as a result of faith, new obedience, prayer and witness, as well as trials and suffering. Gifts of the Spirit break forth, by which men minister to one another and in which the love of Christ is manifested in the midst of the world. In a wider sense all these effects may be designated as marks of the Church. But they remain in the twilight of all human action. Often prayer is concealed under groanings which cannot be uttered; and often beneath a witness to the world is concealed the boasting of the confessor. The Church is also made visible in a wider sense by her order, her liturgy and her diaconate. But in the midst of all such visible signs the Gospel and the sacraments remain the *notae ecclesiae par excellence.* They are related to all these others as the message of Jesus is related to His signs. Without faith in the message Jesus' miracles were not discerned as signs of the kingdom of God. Other miracle-workers also worked miracles. Only on the basis of the *notae ecclesiae* do all the rest become marks of the Church, and only thus is the Church discernible in the religious-historical and religious-sociological structure of Christendom. The Gospel, baptism and the Lord's Supper are the only marks by which the reality of the Church in the world can be *infallibly* discerned. The question concerning the one holy catholic Church is decided according to the apostolicity of her message.

Now the Gospel is an 'outward' word, which everyone can hear; and baptism and the Lord's Supper are as water, bread and wine 'outward' signs, which everyone can see and consider. The world knows them only as human words and earthly occurrences. But faith discerns in them God's Word and Action. God's own Word encounters men as an outward, audible human word; and Christ, the Crucified and Risen One Himself, is imparted to the believer in an outward, visible, earthly occurrence. So the Church is *visible* in this world to faith. Although hidden beneath the sins of her members, she is revealed in the Gospel which justifies believing sinners. If, with Augustine, Luther and Calvin, one distinguishes between the visible and the invisible Church, that is, between the company of all who are baptized and that of the real believers, one must add this: that in the visible Church of sinners, in which the gospel is preached, the invisible Church is *visible*. In conformity with the usage of the New Testament epistles, we may now even in this Church, by the judgement of faith, love and hope, regard and address *all* those gathered as the saints of God, because the Gospel is at work here as God's active, justifying, sanctifying word. So the Church is *visible to faith*, although she is hidden precisely in her worldly visibility; and she is invisible to unbelief, even although it sees her—as Jesus was visible to faith as the Christ, although in His self-humiliation He pointed away from Himself to the coming Son of Man; and as the Christ remained invisible to unbelief, even although it saw and heard Jesus.

So the Church has her place in the creed: 'I believe in the Holy Ghost, one holy catholic and apostolic Church'. It has often been remarked that there is a difference made here: 'I believe *in* the Holy Ghost', but 'I believe *the* Church'. The Holy Ghost is the Lord, but the Church is His creation. The Church does not have her place in the creed in the same way as God, the Father and the Son and the Holy Ghost. I believe in God as my 'Thou', who has created and redeemed and sanctified me, and who daily acts upon me and all men anew as Creator, Redeemer and Re-Creator. But the article on the Church is an article on men upon whom God is acting. I cannot believe in the Church, any more than I can believe in myself as a Christian. But I believe in God—Father, Son and Holy Ghost—who in His faithfulness has created and preserves the Church. Inasmuch as I believe in the triune God, I also believe the Church. God's re-creating work through the Gospel creates the Church and makes her discernible.

So the attributes of the Church and the *notae ecclesiae* are not identical. The attributes are the effects of the *notae*. For the marks of the Church—Word and Sacrament—are the means by which Christ acts upon the Church and gives Himself to her. By Word and Sacrament He gives the Church her unity, holiness, catholicity and apostolicity as well as her indestructible duration.

11. *The Threat of Judgement applies to the Church*

Christ will come in glory. He will overthrow all opposition.

He will redeem the poor, those who hunger after righteousness, those who are waiting for Him. Yet He comes not only as Judge of the world, but also as Judge of the Church. It was in this sense that the early Church understood the parables of the wheat and the tares and of the net with the good and the bad fish (Matt. XIII. 37ff. and 47ff.). In this sense, time and again in the New Testament, we find the call to repentance addressed to the churches—not merely to individual members, but to whole churches (cf. especially the letters to the churches in the Apocalypse). Yes, the call to repentance is addressed to the whole of Christendom.

This call to repentance extends not only to false doctrine and vice, to unbelief and disobedience of every kind. Beyond that it applies also to the special dangers which only emerge through the kind of decisions by which the Church in her conflict with the world seeks to abide in her Lord. It is not the Church that preserves the Word of God, but God through His Word preserves the Church. The Church does not preserve herself against all assaults; but God preserves her, and therefore she abides. If she has in this faith fixed the canon and determined dogma and order, that does not exclude the possibility that her preservation by Christ may be perverted into a self-preservation of the Church, and that the Church may misuse the canon, dogma and order as a means of self-preservation. Consequently, we know even in the Church the danger of the scribes, who in their appeal to Scripture miss the call of the living Christ. We know the danger of that kind of orthodoxy which by its sticking to dogma overlooks the riches of the Scriptures and misses the witness which the Church has to bear in new historical situations and in face of quite different menaces and heresies. We also know the danger of an ecclesiastical legalism which obstructs the abundance of the gifts of the Spirit and the historical leading of the Church by her living Lord. There is a self-confidence in the Church which makes her deaf to the call of the living Christ and to the brethren scattered throughout the world, and which makes her blind to the constantly changing camouflages under cover of which the world seeks to devour the Church. The canon, dogma and ecclesiastical order have to *serve* her abiding in Christ. But Christ remains the living *Lord* of the canon, of dogma and of Church law.

I

12. *The Promise of Glorification by Christ at His coming applies to the Church*

Out of the Judgement Christ will save, perfect and glorify the Church. His Parousia will be the end of the believing, waiting, hastening, struggling and suffering Church; of the Church which is also sinful which allies herself with the world, and seeks her own security. It will be the end of the Church as *corpus mixtum*, in which the true believers are concealed among the hypocrites. At His coming Christ will show forth the Church in her purity. Though the Church militant and the Church triumphant are now divided, then there will be an end of this distinction. There will be an end of the veiling of Christ in the human word of the message and under the water, bread and wine of the sacraments. Then we shall see Him, and there will be revealed the reality of the dying and rising again with Christ and the communion of the Body of Christ. At His coming Christ will encounter the Church not only as her Perfecter but also as her Judge. But He encounters her above all as her Perfecter—as the Bridegroom who goes to meet His bride so that He may celebrate with her the eternal Marriage Supper.

The first thesis began with the words, 'The Church is. . . .' Now, in conclusion, we ask the meaning of this word 'is'.

The Church is, because Jesus Christ, the Crucified and Risen One, acts upon her ever anew. Looking back over the theses we may now say: The Church is, because Christ calls His people out from the world (I), Christ sends them into the world (II), Christ makes Himself present in the worshipping assembly (III), Christ prepares the Marriage Supper (IV), Christ builds up His body (V), Christ unfolds His grace in the abundance of the gifts of the Spirit (VI), Christ leads the Church through the office of pastor (VII). The expositions of the other theses too were determined by the work of Christ. But Christ does not merely work here and there, much less in a spasmodic, arbitrary fashion; He works continually, in the faithfulness of God. That which He has begun He will also complete. The Church is, because Christ constantly is acting upon her. She was not before this action; and she is not for an instant without this action. Christ's action upon the Church is also the life of Christ within the Church. For in baptism He takes the sinner into His death and resurrection, and in the Lord's Supper He gives Himself bodily as food to sinners. He is present in His Church as the Living One. It is in Christ's living presence that the Church has her being.

Christ acts upon the Church through the Gospel (through preaching as *sacramentum audibile* and through the sacraments as *verbum visibile*). The Word of the Gospel encounters the Church as a double form of address: as a consolation and a claim, as a gift and a demand, as Christ's act of grace upon the Church and as Christ's command to the Church to live in accordance with the grace received.

In the consolation of the Gospel Christ gives to believers His righteousness. His holiness, His life. In the Gospel He shows Himself as the Lord who gives to believers all that is His. In faith in the Gospel the Church is one, holy, catholic, indestructible.

In the claim of the Gospel exhortation Christ commands us to live by His power. Because we have been justified, we ought to strive after righteousness. Because we have been sanctified, we ought to pursue holiness. Because we have been transplanted into His life, we ought to live. Because Christ lives in the Church we are thus exhorted: Be ye one, be ye holy, be ye catholic, abide in Him—be that which in Christ ye are.

From this follows the answer to the further question: In what sense does the Church 'have' the attributes of unity, holiness, etc.? These attributes come to the Church in Christ's operative consolation and claim; or, more precisely, in an ever new consolation and an ever new claim—in His giving and in His commanding, which are new every day. The Church 'has' these attributes in a daily new acceptance and a daily new striving. In other words: She has her attributes only in the double movement—that of being called by Christ out of the world and that of being sent by Christ into the world.

The Church is one in being gathered by the one Christ, and in striving for unity on the strength of being united with Him. The Church is holy in the acceptance of the holiness of Christ, and in sanctifying herself on the strength of having been sanctified. The Church is catholic as the possession of Christ, the *Pantokrator*, and as His instrument for proclaiming His lordship to the world. The Church is one, as she repents of disunity and believes in the one Christ. She is holy, as she repents of her sins and believes in the holy Christ. As the Church discerns her errors by submitting herself to the judgement of the apostolic message, she is apostolic. As she surrenders herself to die with Christ, she lives and abides. But should a Church desire to hold fast as her own possession both her being and her attributes, cut loose from Christ's daily renewed consolation and claim, then such an understanding of unity would lead to schism, such an understanding of holiness would lead to a denial of repentance, such an understanding of catholicity would lead to a claim to world domination, and such an understanding of apostolicity would lead to a breaking away from the historic apostolate and so to self-assertion over against Jesus Christ. The attributes of the Church should be acknowledged with fear and trembling as the ever new gracious acts of God's faithfulness in Christ. In this faithfulness the Church has her being.

Statements concerning the being and the attributes of the Church, therefore, share the same form as statements concerning the being of the believer in Christ and concerning the attributes of the believer: his righteousness, his holiness, etc. Certainly this analogy is limited in an important respect: my being in Christ, my being as justified and sanctified stands or falls with my ever new acceptance in faith of the righteousness and holiness of Christ, which He bestows on us in Word and Sacrament. But the Church does not stand or fall with my faith. She was, before the individual came to believe; and she will remain, even when the individual ceases to believe. So statements concerning the Church can never be resolved into existential statements. But on the other hand, it should never be forgotten that the Church is the fellowship of believers, and that only in faith can we make true statements about the Church. To that extent, statements about the Church can never be severed from the existence of believers; and we should beware of hypostatizing the Church.

III. THE MARKS OF THE CHURCH ACCORDING TO THE AUGSBURG CONFESSION[1]

IN ARTICLE VII of the *Confessio Augustana* the Church is defined as the congregation of believers; and this congregation of believers is further defined by means of what happens within it: The Church 'is the congregation of believers, where the Gospel is purely preached and the holy Sacraments offered in accordance with the Gospel'.

It is to be observed, first, that what is here mentioned is not the Word of God in general, or the law, but the Gospel. The Gospel is the glad tidings of the justification of the sinner by God for the sake of Jesus Christ out of sheer grace. Justification is not received on account of man's good works but only on the work achieved by Christ on the cross. Law is not indeed thereby excluded. But the Gospel can only be purely preached when law and Gospel are rightly distinguished. The Gospel is God's proper Word, while the law is God's 'alien' Word. Thus Gospel is mentioned in connexion with preaching; the Gospel is the oral affirmation of *Christus pro nobis*, the oral call to forgiveness. In the German and Latin texts 'preaching' and 'teaching' correspond. What is meant is not the dumb possession of a doctrine but the act of oral communication of the doctrine; and again, not a communication divorced from challenge and comfort but a communication which is preaching.

In the same way, the important thing is not to know about the Sacraments but the actual administering of the Sacraments. This must occur 'in accordance with the Gospel'. This means first that every celebration must employ the words of institution. A celebration of the Communion without the words of institution would not be a celebration. Nor must this principle be restricted to the liturgical order and administration of the Sacraments; the principle of 'in accordance with the Gospel'

[1] Originally appeared in R. N. Flew (ed.), *The Nature of the Church*, S.C.M., 1952, p. 58ff.

reaches out to the doctrine of the Sacraments. Again, the Church is not essentially constituted by the silent possession of a sacramental doctrine in accordance with the Gospel but rather by the 'administering of the Sacraments', that is by the event of their being offered and received in the context of the appropriate sacramental sermon.

If Gospel and Sacraments thus belong to the idea of the Church, so do the sole 'means of grace' belong to the essence of the Church, through which God gives the Holy Spirit (Article V) and by which the Holy Spirit operates.

In Article VII the 'congregation of believers' and the event of the preaching of the Gospel and the administering of the Sacraments are connected by the disputed words 'in which', *in qua*. A corresponding 'in' occurs in a like connexion in Luther's Small Catechism: 'The Holy Spirit has called me through the Gospel and enlightened me with His gifts, . . . just as He calls, assembles and enlightens the whole of Christendom on earth...; and within this Christendom He abundantly forgives both me and all believers our sins' (II, Section 6; cf. *Greater Catechism*, II, Section 54f.). The Holy Spirit addresses Christians through the Gospel, and preaches the Gospel among them. These phrases suffice to show that in the context of the confessional documents this 'in' must be interpreted in several relations.

a) Gospel and Sacraments are *in* the congregation of believers the means by which the Holy Spirit arouses faith, effects the assembling of believers.

b) Gospel and Sacraments are *in* the congregation of believers the service imposed upon it and discharged by it. The Church is 'the mother who conceives and bears individual Christians through the Word of God' (*Greater Catechism*, II, 42).

From this it appears that in the definition of Article VII of the Augsburg Confession of Faith the expression 'congregation of all believers' and the predicate of the relative clause belong quite inseparably to one another. The relative clause adds nothing new to the expression 'congregation of believers' but defines it. Hence it is possible to define the Church as 'the congregation of believers and saints', without any mention of Gospel or Sacraments (Article VIII). This does not mean anything different from what is said in Article VII. For the congregation of believers cannot exist at all without Gospel and Sacraments.

Without preaching and Sacraments it would dissolve into nothing and would never have arisen.

In this definition of the Church in Article VII of the Augsburg Confession there is lacking any mention of the Ministry. This occurs in Articles V, XIV and XXVIII. These articles show that there can be no thought in Article VII of a ministry divorced from the proclamation and celebration of the Sacraments. For no one may preach *nisi rite vocatus* (Article XIV), i.e. without a call to the office founded by Christ. While in Article VII the office is implicitly and not explicitly contained, attention is focused on God's deed in the Gospel, and it becomes clear that the office is no independently existing institution but is at the service of the Gospel alone.

Further, it is striking that not even the Confessions of Faith are mentioned in the definition of Article VII, though they deal with the question of the meaning of *pure* and *recte* (i.e. 'pure' and 'in accordance with the Gospel'). But the Confessions are a response to the preaching of the Gospel, the fruit of the Holy Spirit, and not His means like Word and Sacrament.

Finally it should be observed that in the definition of the Church there is no mention of the Bible. This is all the more striking in that the Reformation emphasized the basic principle of *sola scriptura* very strongly, and recognized Holy Scripture as the sole norm of all ecclesiastical doctrine. That Holy Scripture is not named in Article VII of the Augsburg Confession cannot therefore mean that the purity of Gospel preaching and the validity of sacramental celebration consisted in anything else than conformity to Scripture alone. But something comes here to expression which is very characteristic of the Augsburg Confession, which contains no article on Holy Scripture, and which hence also appears in the Formula of Concord. It is this, that in its 'Summary Ideas' (the *Epitome*) there is no list of canonical Scriptures. Scripture is the sole norm of all Church doctrine on the basis of the Gospel to which the Scripture bears prophetic and apostolic witness, i.e. on the basis of that central figure to whom both Old and New Testament bear witness, namely Jesus Christ.

Thus the Church is constituted by the event (*Ereignis*), of the preaching of the Gospel and the administering of the Sacraments, and so by Christ Himself acting through and present in

Gospel and Sacraments. The Church does not exist where men possess Bible, Confession and Ministry and yet keep silent, but rather where on the basis of Scripture, and in agreement with our Fathers and brethren, the Gospel is preached and the Sacraments celebrated, where the voice of Christ is heard and Christ offers Himself.

Thus the idea of the Church is separated from a false ontology and also from dissolution into a succession of individual acts without any continuity. The continuity of the Church consists in the identity of the Gospel preached ever anew, and it thereby becomes visible. In that this Gospel is essentially identical with the apostolic Gospel, preaching takes place in apostolic succession. Since public preaching takes place through the Church's ministry (*nemo debeat in ecclesia publice docere aut sacramenta administrare nisi rite vocatus*, Article XIV), one can speak of an apostolic succession of office. But this succession rests not on a succession of ordinations (calling to office can take place both through an individual bearing office and by the congregation), but rather on an identity of the Gospel and Sacraments which Jesus Christ instituted and which He commissioned the Apostles to continue. If the chain of ordination in the Lutheran Church from the ancient Church to the present day remains unbroken, this is to be regarded as an outward sign of the continuity of the Church. The true apostolic succession of office is neither based upon laying on of hands, nor guaranteed by it. The Church through all time and change preaches because it believes the Gospel; doing this it is apostolic and will persist 'always' until the end of the world (Article VII). This continuity receives expression in the acceptance by the Lutheran Church of the confessions of the ancient Church, of the Church Fathers, as *testes veritatis*, and of the structure of the liturgy of the ancient Church.

2. In Article VII of the Augsburg Confession the Church is declared to be *una sancta*, 'one, holy and Christian'. As holy and Christian it is essentially one (cf. the 'holy, catholic and apostolic' of the Nicene Creed). As holy it is one, since the one Holy Spirit operates in it. As Catholic it is one, since the one Christ, the Lord of heaven and earth, rules it ('Catholic' is translated 'Christian' in the Formula of Concord). As apostolic it is one, since its unshakeable foundation is the office of the Apostles.

These statements about the unity of the Church require in agreement with Eph. IV. 5 delimitation at various points.

It is taught in Article VII 'that one, holy Christian Church must always be and remain'. This is not at all to be understood as if the unity of the Church were a future goal or an imposed task. Unity belongs rather to the essence of the Church. Either the Church is one, or it is not the Church.

But neither is the *Una Sancta* a transcendent possibility on the other side of time. It is a reality here on this earth. 'We do not dream of a Platonic state ('a Church of the imagination which is nowhere to be found'), but we declare that this Church exists ('is really here on earth'), (Apologia, VII, 20).

The oneness of the Church on this earth consists, however, not only (so to speak) in vertical relations, namely in ever re-newed acts of the one Christ and the one Holy Spirit through Gospel and Sacrament. The oneness of the Church is always at the same time a fellowship of men with one another, upon whom God operates in Word and Sacrament. This is indicated by the definition of the Church as the 'congregation of all believers'. While the Gospel is always being proclaimed in the local community of believers, Article VII looks beyond the greatness or the smallness of the local gathering, out to the whole of Christendom on earth. The Augsburg Confession indeed speaks not only of the Church, but also of the Churches (*ecclesiae apud nos docent*, I, 1; II, 1; III. 1; and elsewhere). Like Christen-dom on earth, so the Christian fellowship at a particular place is in the most proper sense the Church of Jesus Christ. The definition of Article VII does not contradict this, but rather erects a barrier against an idea of the Church on such inde-pendent lines as would isolate the individual congregation. The word 'harmonious' in the following sentence of Article VII points in the same direction. It is not only by reception of the one grace in individual isolated cases, but in the consensus of hearing and proclaiming the Gospel and the receiving and dis-pensing of the Sacraments that the *Una Sancta* consists. This consensus in Lutheran confessional documents is always under-stood in a double sense, as agreement with contemporary living brothers and with the fathers who have gone before. Hence the unity of the Church means essentially the fellowship of the Holy Communion of all believers on earth.

On the other hand, it is no part of the unity of the Church 'that similar ceremonies, instituted by men, should everywhere take place'. 'Rites', 'traditions' and 'ceremonies' should not in this connexion be too narrowly construed. Into this class of things fall not only particular festivals and seasons, but fundamentally everything that pertains to or is taken over by the ordering of the Church of believers in the freedom of faith, whether it be the order of divine service, or ministerial orders. The idea of the Church in the Augsburg Confession contains no definition of national Church, free Church and the like, or of the form of church leadership. Nor are there any definitions of episcopal or synodical church government, or concerning the concrete discharge of the ministerial office, in a local congregation through the supplementing of the preaching office by deacons, presbyters, etc. Thus the Lutheran Churches in Germany, most of which since the cessation of the National Church in 1918 have gone over to an episcopal order, stand in complete agreement with those other Lutheran Churches (e.g. in the United States), which are synodically ordered, or which (as in Sweden) have retained the episcopal office without interruption since the Middle Ages, and hence an unbroken succession of ordination. The constitutive factor for the unity of the Church is not the form, but rather the function of the ministry alone, namely the preaching of the Gospel and the proper celebration of the Sacraments.

This doctrine of the unity of the Church means for the Lutheran Church as it confronts other confessions a great and constant uneasiness. This would not be the case either if the Augsburg Confession taught a merely eschatological unity on the other side of time, or if the Lutheran Church were sure that outside its frontiers the Gospel was nowhere preached. But at this point the Augsburg Confession is extremely cautious. The congregations that made the confession at Augsburg, in that they were at one in agreeing on the purity of the preaching of the Gospel and of an administration of the Sacraments in accordance with Scripture, did indeed understand themselves as the *Una Sancta*; but they always took account of brothers in other, even heretical, Churches, with which the Church of the pure preaching of the Gospel was in conflict. Even if in the Roman Church, bishops, teachers and monks taught justification through human works, and thus obscured Christ's work, 'there yet always remains among a few pious persons a recognition of Christ' (Apologia, IV, 392). Even if, in the doctrinally false Roman Church of the late Middle Ages and pre-Reformation days, preaching and Communion were distorted, even at this time there was always a Church on earth. And if the Gospel were witnessed to in a heretical Church even only in its liturgical prayers (*ibid.* 385) or became effective only in the right administration of Baptism, even here because of the overwhelming grace of God one has to take account of believers in dispersion. This realization was seriously regarded as an obligation to unite with these brothers. That the Augsburg Confession trod thus softly is not to be negatively judged only, but is also to be taken as the expression of a concern for unity as cautious as it was persevering.

The Augsburg Confession's conception of the Church, when taken seriously, always and necessarily gives rise to the strongest impulses towards unifying believers. For the *Una Sancta* is recognized as a reality upon earth. Divisions between believers are distortions of the one, holy, catholic and apostolic Church, dishonouring to Christ, gravely blameworthy, and permitting no congregation to rest at ease.

3. The reunion of divided Churches has to begin with their reciprocal discovery of the Church. How is the Church to be recognized?

Here distinction should be made between the problem of the recognition of the members of the Church and the task of recognizing the Church, even though of course it never exists without members.

Article VIII affirms that 'in this life, many false Christians and hypocrites and even open sinners remain among the pious'. 'The Church is hidden under the large number of the evil' (Apologia, VII, 19); these constitute 'the Cross with which the Kingdom of Christ is overshadowed' (18). At the same time the confessional documents debar the Church from separating itself from all nominal Christians. This would be to anticipate the Last Judgement, which the Lord of the Church Himself will conduct. The confessional documents do indeed teach the exclusion from the Church by excommunication of gross sinners, heretics and those that despise the Sacraments, and this excommunication is an eschatological judgement of

God just as much as absolution. But the majority of those nominal Christians the Church neither can nor ought to exclude. The *ecclesia proprie dicta* remains hidden till the last day within the *ecclesia large dicta*.

Nevertheless the Church is recognizable in all distinctness, not only the Church as an external religious fellowship but as the 'assembly of believers'—not of course in its believing members who are hidden among the nominal Christians, but once again in the Gospel and the Sacraments which are infallible signs. These are fundamental for the Church not only in a cognitive but also in a causative respect. Where the Gospel is purely preached and the Sacraments administered in accordance with the Gospel, there we have in the most proper sense the reality of the *ecclesia proprie dicta*, of the fellowship of true believers, even if we cannot distinguish them individually from the *ecclesia large dicta*, the merely external community. For the Gospel is the power of God and is never without effective capacity to arouse and renew faith. In this sense the true Church, though concealed in the multiplicity of hypocrites, is visible for faith on earth.

These *notae ecclesiae* are taught as exclusive in the strict sense of the term.

Good works on the part of the believers, of love to God and their neighbour are, for example, not marks of the Church. These works are not rejected. They occur in the Church 'as thanksgivings to God' and are the weapons of Jesus Christ against the devil (Apologia, IV, 189ff.). But hypocrites also can exhibit works, and the good works of believers are the very ones concealed from themselves.

Moreover, a particular form of order is not a mark of the Church, whether it be the order of divine service, or of the ministry, or of the relations between Church and State. The significance of order is in no way belittled. But no particular form of order is constitutive of the Church.

Finally, neither is Church discipline a mark of the Church, even if the power of excommunication is committed to the Church by its Lord Himself (cf. Formula of Concord: Epitome XII, 26). Characteristic of the Church is exclusively the preaching of the Gospel, not the Word that condemns but the Word that saves.

More striking is the fact that, in distinction from many statements of the confessional 'Revival Movement' (*Erweckung*) theology of last century, not even say confessional documents are named as marks of the Church. The Apology indeed speaks in this connexion occasionally of the Confession (VII, 3). The statement appealing to Nicolaus of Lyra that declares the Church to be wherever 'a right confession and declaration of faith and truth' is made (22) agrees with this. Since the act of confessing is always and essentially a public declaration or word, it may not be far-fetched to set it beside Word and Sacrament as a mark of the Church. Confession is bound in the closest way to Word and Sacrament as to content since it pronounces what proclamation of the Word is pure, and what administration of the Sacraments is right. Is it thus fairly obvious that the confessional documents, even if not a third *nota ecclesiae*, should be regarded as *nota ecclesiae* derivatively, since they teach and declare the two true marks of the Church, Gospel and Sacraments. Yet one must exercise reserve at this point. For in the passages of the *Apologia* named the thought is evidently less of particular confessional documents than of the act of confessing. Just as the norm of the Church is the biblical Gospel, and as the Church is defined through the preaching of the Gospel and the administering of the Sacraments, so the Confessional documents are not as such, that is as documents, constitutive marks of the Church. They are marks within the event (*Ereignis*) of preaching and administering the Sacraments, which take place in accordance with the confessional documents, namely in accordance with the Gospel. A Church does not get its title to recognition where the right confessional documents are constitutionally valid, but the preaching is not in accordance with them. On the other hand, a Church merits recognition where no particular confessional documents are valid, but where preaching and the administering of the Sacraments is in accordance with the Gospel. Confessional documents are important for the Church's proclamation. A Church acts irresponsibly in abandoning its confessional documents. Yet the confessional documents, on the view of the Augsburg Confession, are marks of the Church only in the event of proclamation in accordance with the confession. Without thereby intending to dissolve the confessional documents as such into constantly novel personal acts of confession, what has been said implies this for the marks of the Church: the confession is a mark of the Church *within* the limits of the two sole marks, preaching of the Gospel and the administering of the Sacraments. Since the confessional documents are by their very nature intended to serve the maintenance of Gospel preaching and the proper administering of the Sacraments in the Church, they are *in* this their proper function a *nota ecclesiae*. Thus the confessional documents are, a mark of the Church just in so far as this mark coincides with the two first *notae ecclesiae*, and only in them can be recognized as a *nota ecclesiae*.

4. This doctrine of the Augsburg Confession concerning the Church implies an inescapable and lasting obligation for the Lutheran Church within the ecumenical endeavours of our time.

Neither the common threat of secularization and of anti-Christian powers to everything Christian, nor the general disorder which draws all Christians sympathetically together, neither church struggles, nor war-time needs, can be as such the basis for the reunion of the Churches. Neither common scientific researches and liturgical movements, nor common social and political demands or obligations, can as such effect and bring about the unity of the Church. Even the mutual assistance which Churches render each other in time of need does not amount to the recovery of Church unity. The Lutheran Church holds open the door to co-operation with other Churches in all such cases and amid the shocks of our time is aware of its place within the community of seeking and helping. Yet it can recognize the unity of the Church only where *consensus de doctrina evangelii* exists. The Lutheran Church is at this point bound by its confession.

What is meant by 'bound by its confession'? The Augsburg Confession is obligatory for the speaking and acting of the Church as a fellowship of brothers and fathers agreed in the exposition of Holy Scripture. The factor of fellowship of agreement is strongly emphasized (e.g. Article I: *ecclesiae magno consensu apud nos docent*, and the numerous citations from the Fathers, and also the relation to dogma of the ancient Church), but consensus has no importance of its own. The confessional documents are not obligatory simply as a consensus, but only as a consensus concerning the right understanding of Holy Scripture. It is not the consensus that is judge over Church doctrine and activity, but Holy Scripture. To be bound by a confession is to be bound with the Church to Holy Scripture as the sole norm. This obligation is not taught formally by the Augsburg Confession. There is no special article devoted to the normative significance of Scripture. It is taught in the attestation of the central point of Holy Scripture, namely the Gospel. Confessional documents are thus obligatory for the speech and action of the Church, since they jointly witness to the Gospel on the basis of Holy Scripture. But the obligatory power of the confession does not manifest itself in the claim to conformity with Scripture, but in an actual agreement with Scripture which has to be always freshly confirmed in the course of exegetical work.

Confessional obligation includes another possibility for the Church when facing fresh situations of heresy. In certain circumstances it may indeed be the duty of the Church to develop its Confession, supplement it, secure it against misunderstandings, and even to issue, in this exposition of Holy Scripture, new confessional documents. Confessional obligation fundamentally even includes the possibility that statements of the confessional documents, hitherto current, may be corrected in the light of biblical exegesis, and on the basis of a better understanding of Holy Scripture. Such correction, indeed, is not capable of being undertaken by an individual member of the Church, or by one theological school, but only by the Church as a whole. Meantime confessional obligation precludes Churches proclaiming unity where *consensus de doctrina evangelii* is lacking, or where the confessional documents of the other Church reject the doctrine of the Augsburg Confession on Gospel and Sacraments.

5. This obligation of the Church to the Augsburg Confession means also on the other side the widest liberty for reunion with other Churches.

a) The Augsburg Confession is a constant and radical challenge to the Lutheran Church. For the Church according to its doctrine does not exist wherever the Augsburg Confession is 'held' or is by the church authorities 'unimpeachably' guaranteed in law, but only where the Gospel is purely preached and the Sacraments administered in accordance with the Gospel. The Church does not exist merely because someone calls himself a Lutheran. The reality of the Church is determined through the event in which Christ speaks and gives Himself in Word and Sacrament. The Augsburg Confession is always putting the question to the Lutheran Church, whether in its speech and action it is really a Church. All ecclesiastical self-glorification, all resting on the laurels of the Reformation of the Fathers, all security based on confessional property, all comfortable self-sufficiency within the framework of its historically developed form—all these are destroyed by the Augsburg Confession. For by it the Church is asked what is happening *hic et nunc* within itself. This challenge frees the Church for Christ who is constantly at work upon it in novel ways, but who is and was and will be always one and the same.

b) The Augsburg Confession opens up, in a profound way, concern for the brothers who are in Christ, and therewith for the one holy Church beyond the limits of the Lutheran Church. Those who differ from one another in the conception of the limits of the Biblical Canon (e.g. in the value placed on the O.T. Apocrypha) can still recognize one another as members of the one Body of Christ. For the norm of all church speaking is the Bible, not in any formal or quantitative sense, but in substance, as the prophetic and apostolic witness to the Gospel. Differences in the confessional documents current in the local Churches do not constitute limitations to the one Church—if only they agree in substance on the doctrine of the Gospel and of the Sacraments. Fundamentally, the unity of the Church can be a reality even without confessional documents—if only the pure Gospel be preached and the Sacraments celebrated in accordance with it. Even the variety in orders of divine service and of the ministry is not hostile to the unity of the Church. The Augsburg Confession does not merely allow but requires that we break through all these differences and boundaries, and penetrate into the length and breadth of Christendom, and seek and find our brothers there.

c) Allegiance to the Augsburg Confession is an ever new liberation of the Lutheran Church, since it is a matter of allegiance to the Gospel. Allegiance to the Gospel, however, is not an enslavement of doctrine and life—slavery would be the effect of the law—but a liberation for the public praise of the great deeds of God. The Augsburg Confession sets no legal limits to the service of the Church, but opens up to the Church the great joy of service to all the world which Jesus Christ through His death and resurrection has made His own possession. The Augsburg Confession imposes no law of pure doctrine to correspond to the justification by works of a so-called orthodoxy, but calls us to Gospel proclamation. Thus the Augsburg Confession frees the Church from the danger of becoming doctrinaire, and from anxious fear of the world, and from a merely defensive and conservative attitude. The Augsburg Confession constantly reminds the Lutheran Church of the overwhelming richness of the gifts which Christ through Word and Sacraments bestows upon it, so that it may serve the brethren in all confessions and join in their praise and adoration.

K

IV. WORSHIP FROM THE VIEWPOINT OF EVANGELICAL THEOLOGY[1]

W E all arrive at one present situation from the historical event of Jesus Christ's death for the world, and we are all approaching the coming final historical event when Jesus Christ, as judge and saviour, will reveal His glory to the world for which He died. The whole of humanity is encompassed by these two events whether it knows it or not—whether it wants to admit it or not.

But we are not only encompassed by Jesus Christ as an event of a past which is becoming ever more distant and an event of an indefinitely distant or near future, but we are all under the command of Jesus Christ as the present Lord. The crucified man is the present Lord. In His resurrection God has already given him all power and glory, which He will reveal in His parousia. At the same time, however, as the risen Lord He does not cease to be the man who bears the scars of His death on the cross on His transfigured body. As the man who sacrificed His life on the cross the risen man is the eternal high priest who intercedes for His brethren by reason of His unique historical self-sacrifice before God. Here too it can said: the whole of humanity is under the command of this Lord—whether it acknowledges him as Lord or not.

In the midst of the world, however, the Church is the community of those who have yielded themselves to this Lord in faith, who extol Him as Lord and proclaim Him to the world as the one salvation.

The Church exists in this world in a dual life movement: it exists as God's people called from the world, who have received a new beginning by baptism in Jesus Christ and have been

[1] Lecture delivered on August 1st, 1960, at the Roman Catholic International Scientific Congress which took place on the occasion of the Eucharistic World Congress in Munich and discussed the theme 'Worship and the Modern Man'. Trsl. by I. H. Neilson.

saved from the bonds and subjection to judgement of this world. It also exists as the race of prophets, priests and kings sent into the world to proclaim salvation to the world and to intercede for it. It is thus the proclamation and the mouthpiece of the sovereign power of God which is overtaking the world.

This dual life movement of the Church has its centre in the congregation assembled for divine worship. What happens in this assembly?

In attempting to answer this question I must first say that in the realm of evangelical theology there is discernible again and again a distinct inhibition about terming Christian worship a cult. One speaks of the pagan cult, and also of the Old Testament cult, but only rarely of the Christian cult.

For Jesus Christ presented to God the sin-offering for the sins of the world once and for all on the cross. Indeed God Himself did this in giving His son to the cross. Christ's death is thus the end of the cult of sacrifice by which man tries to appease God. But the risen Christ does not present Himself a second time to God as a sacrifice; the man sacrificed once and for all on the cross is the eternal high priest, who unremittingly intercedes before God for His own.

Because of this act of salvation on the cross Christian divine worship is in the last analysis not the service of man to God but the service of God to man. God lets the congregation participate in what Christ accomplished for it. Christ the Lord presents Himself in public worship to the congregation He has gained by His blood on the cross.

Thus Christian divine worship is different from the Old Testament cult as the Gospel is from the law. By the law God demanded the obedience of man and made the attainment of life dependent on obedience to His demand. But in the Gospel God gives life with the exhortation to change to a new life by reason of this new creation.

Just as Jesus Christ is the end of the law He is also the end of the cult. That Christ is the end of the law does not of course mean that He was the end of divine rule. But God's commandment encounters believers in the Gospel no longer as the law but as the Paraclete, as comforting, fatherly exhortation. Accordingly the New Testament letter-writers—not only Paul— avoid calling the imperative mood of the Gospel the law. That

Christ is the end of the cult means just as little that He was the end of divine worship. Something so completely new takes place now in him that the old names no longer suffice.

What happens in the assembly of the Christian congregation for divine worship? Luther answered this question in his famous sermon at the consecration of the Schlosskirche at Torgau in 1544, 'that nothing else should happen there but that our dear Lord (Jesus Christ) speak with us Himself through his holy word and we in our turn speak with Him in prayer and praise' (M. Luther's *Works*, Weimar, Vol. 69, 588, 1.15ff.). Thus divine worship is God's act to the congregation and the answer of the congregation to God's act. We can also say: divine worship is God's service to the congregation and the service of the congregation before God. This dual answer of reformation theology to our question recurs in the history of the evangelical theology of divine worship, as also in the more recent most significant presentation of the 'Doctrine of Divine Worship of the Congregation gathered in the Name of Jesus' by Peter Brunner (*Leiturgia, Handbuch des evangelischen Gottesdienstes*, Vol. 1, 1954, 82–361). In what follows I will endeavour briefly to comment on both these statements on the act of divine worship in order later to develop them ecclesiologically and cosmologically.

1. *The Service of God to the Congregation*

In divine worship there takes place the remembrance of God's great deeds and of the promises which God has given. This remembrance relates to all God's deeds: to the creation and preservation of the world, to the choice and direction of Israel and the Church, but above all to His act of salvation in the death and resurrection of Christ. It relates likewise to all the promises of God, but above all to the promise of the parousia of Jesus Christ.

This remembrance takes place according to the holy scriptures: as scriptural reading, doctrine and proclamation. In this remembrance expression is given to the claim and the consolation, the command and the gift which are resolved upon in the deeds and promises of God for the assembled congregation. But above all it takes place in the claim of the Gospel: Christ has given Himself in death for you! He is risen for you!

God Himself is present as saviour in this remembrance of God's act of salvation. He gives salvation by the proclamation of His act of salvation. The New Testament expression 'Gospel of Christ' says not only that the Gospel proclaims Christ but that it comes from Him, and again not only that it came from Him historically but that He works through the Gospel as the present Lord—that He shares His death and life through the Gospel. The Gospel is God's active word, God's strength. Thus it is not only the message of God's act of reconciliation on the cross but through the Gospel God makes us the ones who are reconciled. It is also not only the doctrine that God justifies the sinner for Christ's sake, but through the Gospel God speaks justice to the sinner. And this judgement, as God's merciful judgement, is at the same time His new creative word, which is both declared and effective. In conferring upon us through the Gospel the righteousness which He revealed in Christ on the cross He takes us from the judgement of anger and even now gives us the life which is to become visible in the resurrection from the dead. Through the Gospel He gives us a share not only in Christ the crucified but also in the risen Lord who will come to judge the world.

In remembrance of Jesus Christ bread and wine are then taken, blessed and offered to the congregation to eat and drink. In remembrance of the last supper of Jesus the same words are spoken here which have been handed down as Jesus' words of giving: 'This is my body for you', 'this is the new covenant in my blood'. In this deed too Christ's death is made known. At the same time we think of the future communion promised by Jesus which He will celebrate in the kingdom of God with his own.

Jesus Christ is also present and active in this communion of remembrance. He Himself, the risen Lord, invites the congregation to the communion. He Himself gives it what His words of giving say: His body and the new covenant in His blood. He Himself, the Lord, is here both the giver and the gift, for forgiveness of sins and union with Him. In distinguishing in His giving, His body and His blood the Lord gives Himself to the congregation as the man who gave His life for it on the cross. As the eternal high priest He shares in this communion the sin-offering which He presented to God on the cross. In giving

Himself he takes the congregation into the new covenant which God enacted in His blood. Even the remembrance of the coming communion in the kingdom of God promised by Jesus does not remain merely a remembrance or expectation. In presenting Himself to the congregation as the man who was sacrificed the Lord at the same time lets them participate in His victory and in His coming in glory. The entreaty 'maran atha' is also the confession 'the Lord cometh!' In the Lord's Supper He comes to earth and shares even now the coming wedding feast of the lamb with the congregation.

Thus God serves the congregation in word and sacrament. In both He gives a share now in Christ's victory on the cross and His parousia and includes us in His act of salvation. In both He justifies, sanctifies, brings life to and unites the congregation with Christ. The proclamation is neither only the leading to the life-giving communion, nor is the Lord's Supper only the confirmation of the life-giving word. But in both together God gives us life. Is it one and the same word become flesh which is given to us in word and sacrament? The determination of the relationship of word and sacrament is in the last analysis such an exceedingly difficult theological problem only because the gift of divine grace is immeasurable.

2. *The Service of the Congregation before God*

How does the congregation serve God who descends so far to it in Jesus Christ?

The service of the congregation consists above all else in that it allows God to serve it and receives His inexhaustible gift in a manner befitting the majesty of the divine giver. How does it receive the Lord 'truly, worthily and rightly'? In no other way than in the total surrender of man, of the heart and every limb to Him who gave Himself for us men and goes on giving Himself to us. This surrender takes place in our turning away from ourselves, in repentance of our past sins, in the renunciation of self-chosen plans and ways and at the same time in the surrender to Him, in clinging to His word and taking one's stand at the communion of the new covenant. For both these—the conversion and the bestowal—we can also say: the service of the congregation before God is above all faith. For faith is not without repentance and is the laying hold upon mercy. At the same time, however, faith in salvation is certain not because of our repentance and our grasping but only because of God's apprehending act of mercy to us. This reception in the faith cannot remain silent. God has made man in His likeness so that He may give him the answer conforming to His address.

Thus the congregation serves God with the *confession of sins*. It acknowledges itself unworthy to receive the Lord in its midst.

It serves him further with the hymn of praise of His mercy. It thanks Him for all His great deeds and promises, above all for the act of salvation on the cross, for His erstwhile deeds and for the act which He Himself now accomplishes in God's service, for His act of salvation for us and the whole world.

The community serves God further with *prayers* in the name of Jesus for the Church and the world. To pray to God in the name of Jesus—that is, to bring to God in prayer the sacrifice that Jesus brought to Him on Golgotha for the sins of all men.

In its service it does not stop, however, with thanks for the historical act of salvation and with the entreaty for further deeds which God has promised but because of these deeds it glorifies God in Jesus Christ as the one who *is* from everlasting to everlasting. In the doxology it praises the everlasting sameness of the divine being and substance, in which the truth of the promise is established.

But all these answers are concentrated in the *confession of faith*. Confession of sins, praise, adoration and public testimony are concentrated in the creed in a particular way—as in baptism so also in worship. In the diversity of these answers and in the spontaneity of their expression the Church professes to live a new life from day to day by God's grace alone.

In this surrender of self in faith and confession the congregation comes through Jesus Christ to God as an offering. The service of the congregation before God is the thank and praise offering, which extols the sacrifice that Christ made to God on the cross for the sins of the world and which He shares by word and sacrament. This is a total sacrifice. It cannot be confined to the heart and mouth of man. It demands also the sacrifice of the body and of all that is of man. Thus earthly gifts, which were brought to God for the service of the church by its members, are termed offerings.

I pause here first and ask: How are the service of God to the congregation and the service of the congregation before God related now in Christian divine worship? Can they be differentiated at all?

The service of God to the congregation takes place by the service of men. God speaks and acts towards the congregation by human speech and action. Not only the answer of the hymn of praise and of prayer but also the encouragement of the proclamation and the prayer of thanks for bread and wine take place in the spontaneity of the believing church and its members. Once again the service of the congregation before God with all the spontaneity of the believing Church is at the same time God's act. This service is not only the answer to God's act but has effect by God's act. It is the praise offering which God Himself prepares through the Holy Ghost. Thus the service of God to the congregation and the service of the congregation before God not only belong together but penetrate each other in a pneumatic event.

Thus the sequence of God's service and service of the congregation cannot mean the sequence of words and actions in the composition of divine worship. Nor does this distinction mean that the service of God and the service of the congregation could be distributed in an exclusive manner to the different parts of divine worship. But certainly this distinction and this sequence of God's service and service of the congregation characterizes an irreversible inner order of the Christian divine service, an inner order which at the same time corresponds to the historical order of salvation on which Christian divine worship is founded and in which it exists.

Before the divine worship of the Church there took place God's act of salvation in Christ: the sending of the son in the flesh, the giving of Jesus on the cross and the proclamation of the victory of Jesus on the cross in his resurrection from the grave. Before the divine worship of the Church there is the charge of Jesus Christ to think of Him and to proclaim Him to the world. Before the divine worship of the Church there is the promise that He will always remain with His own and do His deeds through them. Before the divine worship of the Church the Apostles stand as the summoned witnesses of the resurrection of Jesus Christ and as the citizens and servants of His charge and His promise. And before the divine worship of the Church there took place the descent of the Holy Ghost, but not only as a unique deed, as Christ's death and resurrection, but as a first act of salvation followed by more and more new descents of the Holy Ghost on more and more new people.

This historical order of salvation on which divine worship is founded is at the same time the inner order in which Christian divine worship must take place. All human action through which God wants to serve the congregation here is ultimately determined by God's historical act of salvation and the charge connected with it and the promise of the Lord. The spiritual spontaneity of the witnesses and pastors, through whom God acts towards the congregation, has only to serve the realization of the historical mission which Christ gave to the Church and which is handed down to us by the Apostles. It is the essential nature of the Holy Ghost that he 'shall not speak of himself' (John xvi. 13) but brings 'remembrance' of all that Jesus Christ said (John xiv. 26). All realization, development and concrete expression of the Lord's words confirms the conclusiveness of what Jesus Christ said and did once and for all time. Thus the human speech and action through which God serves the congregation is completely enclosed by God's action and included in the one great movement of the descent of God into the depths of humanity, included in the one great movement of His self-humiliation from His becoming a man to the administering of Christ's body and blood to the congregation at the Lord's Supper. This one penetrating movement of divine descent cannot at any point be pierced or reduced by man, either in the action of the man who conducts divine service or in the thinking of theological reflection. For the movement of divine compassion alludes to the consolation 'given for you'. It reaches fulfilment in the acceptance of His gifts by the congregation.

Thus man, through whom God serves his congregation, is only the agent of God's devotion to men. He does not need to reconcile God with men. Indeed God reconciled the world with Himself in Christ (II Cor. v. 18). Man has only to proclaim this act of reconciliation and to warn: 'be ye reconciled to God!'—and herewith he may be sure that God warns through him (v. 20). Man does not need to bring God any sin-offering. God brought this sin-offering on the cross. Man has only to proclaim God's covenant in Christ's blood, he has only to take bread and wine, to bless and administer. And in this he can be sure that Christ Himself in this communion administers His body and His blood to the community and thus lets it participate in His sacrificial death on the cross.

Evangelical theology is strongly and ascetically against all obvious religious, historical and syllogistic possibilities of a symbolic or even a realistically intentioned interpretation of the human act of blessing and bestowing by which God serves the congregation. However, the New Testament scriptures are, as is known, exceedingly reticent in their pronouncements on just this subject. In divine worship we are not sacrificing Christ, nor does Christ sacrifice Himself again by our act. Christian divine worship is no sin-offering brought to God by men but the once for all time accomplished sin-offering of Christ bestowed on men by God, which the congregation accepts with faith and praise. The act of the Church in divine worship is not *sacrificium propitiatorium* but *sacrificium eucharistikon* because of the *sacrificium propitiatorium* of Christ on the cross, in which God lets us share in word and sacrament (cf. Article XXIV of the *Confessio Augustana* and its apology, particularly par. 16ff.).

3. *The Ecclesiological Development of the Service of God to the Assembled Congregation*

In serving the people assembled here in Christian divine worship God unites them with Himself and among themselves. In receiving Christ's body they are a body, His body. But God unites those assembled in one place not only with one another but with all believers on earth. For it is the one Lord who gives Himself here and in all places to His own. Accordingly the same word 'ekklesia' in the New Testament denotes both the local congregation and all God's people on earth. In the local assembly of worshippers is manifested the communion of all the faithful.

This communion is not only communion with the brethren who live contemporaneously with us but at the same time communion with the fathers who have gone before us in the faith. For at all times there is the one Lord by whose mercy the faithful live, the same Lord who once acted for them and who acts for us today. All of them, even the devout men of the old covenant lived by Christ's sacrifice. The Old Testament cult of sacrifice already foreshadowed this coming truth. Thus we serve God in communion with the Apostles and the Old Testament prophets and with the known and unknown members of God's people of the Old and New Testaments. The Church of all places and times is manifested in Christian divine worship. And indeed this communion consists not only in an historical remembrance of those who have gone before us and whose service is our foundation; it consists not only in that we preserve its doctrine in divine worship and praise God with its prayers. In divine worship we have communion with them as with those live, even though they were dying. In partaking now in the Lord's Supper in the coming wedding feast of the lamb we have, over and above the interval of time and also the intervening state, communion with all whom the Lord will one day in his parousia gather from all lands and times to eternal joy. In the worship of the one Lord God's people wandering on earth and God's people who have reached the goal are one.

4. *The Cosmological Development of the Service of God to the Assembled Congregation*

By His service God also opens up for us the cosmic dimension of the hymn of praise which He prepared for Himself in the non-human creature, the hymn of praise which has not been silenced by the fall of man. In Christian divine worship God is present as the Lord whom the throngs of angels praise without ceasing. In singing the gloria in excelsis and the sanctus the congregation joins this heavenly liturgy.

At the same time God opens up for it the hymn of praise for which he created the non-human visible creature. In spite of all misrepresentation and all the sighing of the earthly creature faith recognizes that it serves the glory of God. Thus from the congregation with the psalter comes the call to heaven and earth: 'Praise ye the Lord *from the heavens* . . ., praise ye him, sun and moon, praise him all ye stars of light . . .!' and: 'Praise the Lord *from the earth*, ye dragons, and all deeps, fire, and hail; snow . . ., mountains, trees, beasts . . .!' (Ps. 148). Every creature must praise the Lord in his own way.

In Christian divine worship the unanimous hymn of praise, for which God created the world, begins thus. Heaven and earth are to praise the Lord and at their centre man as God's image.

The hymn of praise of the congregation on earth is still expressed only among prayers, supplications, sighing and lamenting. We still share only in faith in the worship of what is perfected and of the heavenly throngs of angels. The divine worship of the congregation is still encompassed by the sighs of the non-human creature. And yet the Church is now the mouthpiece of the hymn of praise, which the whole new creation will one day offer to God.

Thus the whole story of the life and sufferings of Christ is in a peculiar way concentrated in the event of divine worship, namely the deeds which God has done and will do for humanity and the world as creator, redeemer and new creator, and the appropriate answer of man in the midst of all creatures to these deeds. The act of God and the act of man are unified in divine worship, in that God comes down and serves in Christ and the congregation pays the crucified Christ honour as Lord and God.

I shall conclude by returning once more to the introduction to my statements:

As the concentration of God's saving activity the congregation assembled for divine worship is the life-giving centre of the life-movements of the Church in the world. For again and again the Lord gathers here from the world those people scattered throughout the world, cleanses them from their sins, strengthens them in their temptations, unites them afresh with Him. Again and again the Lord also sends His own into the world. In serving them He commands their service in the world, and in strengthening them He gives them full power for this service, the service of saving those who have become subject to judgement if they do not believe. Thus the sacrifice of surrender cannot be confined to the congregation assembled for divine worship. If it is true surrender the praise-offering of the congregation reaches from here into the world and the whole life of the members of the congregation becomes the praise-offering which extols Christ. 'And whatsoever ye do in word or deed, do all in the name of the Lord Jesus, giving thanks to God and the father by him' (Col. XIII. 17). Thus the divine worship of Christians is the daily offering of the whole man in obedience to action and suffering. The faith which receives God's gift cannot, according to reformed doctrine, remain without good works, even though the believer does not receive grace on account of the works. But faith in Christ makes us slaves of this Lord, and as His slaves we are freed for the joy of His service.

In this dual life-movement, out of the world and into the world, the Church of God is built up and is the growing body of Christ, growing in talents and growing in members. It grows from Christ the head, who shares His sacrificed body with the congregation assembled for divine worship.

Both the gathering from the world and the mission into the world would of course be misconstrued if we were to think here only of the locally assembled congregation. As the one Church of all places and times manifests itself in local divine worship by the self-offering of the one Lord, divine worship by its nature releases the urge to make visible the congregation of all believers in Christ beyond the local limits in mutual comforting and admonishing, in helping and giving and in the mutual share in talents and sorrows with which Christ distinguishes his own. This urge cannot halt at the frontiers of the schisms which separate the various parts of Christendom. It is much more the yearning and loving search of the community with all who are characterized by the name of Christ, with them all together to proclaim to the world the Lord whose possession it already is, even if it does not yet realize it.

V. LAW AND GOSPEL AS A CONTROVERSIAL THEOLOGICAL PROBLEM[1]

U NDOUBTEDLY we are here concerned with one of the most difficult themes of controversial theological discussion, and for a variety of reasons: not only because in the various parts of Christendom the same thing is by no means always and everywhere understood by each of the two concepts 'law' and 'gospel'; again, not only because the 'and' linking the two concepts contains many possibilities of correlation (as between connexion and contrast, or unity and incompatibility), which are by no means viewed and stressed in the same way everywhere. Furthermore, the difficulty of this theme consists in the fact that in its treatment special problems affecting the ability to make dogmatic declarations and of susceptibility to fixed formulation spring up which we do not encounter in this way in the Christological and trinitarian dogmatic decisions of the Early Church. This is all the more valid the more consciously one treats not only the sequence of Law and Gospel in *Heilsgeschichte* but also their co-existence, in which both God's messages are encountered together by each individual afresh again and again. This, however, has happened over and above the New Testament terminology in all Churches in that they speak of a lasting validity of the law for Christians even if in very different fashion. Thus the ever new and overwhelming encounter of God with men in the word puts difficulties of particular kind in the way of dogmatic declaration. The problem of expressibility of this event as dogmas requires special elucidation.

In what follows the theme will first of all be developed systematically in six sections. A beginning will be made here not with

[1] The basic thoughts of this paper were expressed at the joint conference of an evangelical and Roman Catholic ecumenical work-group on April 6th, 1960, in Heidelberg. Cf. in this connexion the lecture given by Gottlieb Söhngen at the same conference and published under the title 'Law and Gospel' in the *Vierteljahrsschrift für Kontroverstheologie 'Catholica'* (Jahrgang 14, 1960, pp. 81–105). Trsl. by I. H. Neilson.

Luther and the Lutheran creeds but with the New Testament and above all with a few elementary conceptual distinctions in Pauline theology. The beginning is thus made with biblical presuppositions which are common to all Churches. The seventh section then has as its subject the ecumenical significance of the distinction between Law and Gospel. Our theme here will not primarily be a presentation and discussion of the well-known controversial points in reformation and tridentine statements but an attempt to elucidate the methodical presuppositions and points of view among which the controversial theological discussion of these distinctions had to proceed in the midst of the scholarly statements of the problems in our time. Perhaps in this way some new approaches for the discussion will be achieved.

1. *The Problem of the Distinction between Law and Gospel*

In God's message to the sinner are to be distinguished:[1]

a) The word of the Old Testament Law and the word of the New Testament Gospel. After the broken old covenant God concluded the new covenant. After Moses came Jesus Christ. Νόμος is according to Paul the essence of the commandments revealed by God to Moses and through Moses to the Old Testament people of the covenant. Εὐαγγέλιον is the message of Jesus Christ, pre-eminently the word from the cross which is always, however, at the same time the word of the risen crucified Lord. The difference between God's Old Testament and New Testament word consists not only in the sequence of divine speech in time but also in what God said and is saying in both these messages, indeed in what He did and is doing through them. The well-known and most important antitheses in which Paul contrasts Law and Gospel read: By the Law God requires the works of man, by the Gospel God calls to faith. The Law proclaims the principle: the man who does the required works shall live (Gal. III. 12), but by the Gospel the believer will have life without the works of the Law. By the Law God makes sin evident (Rom. VII. 7), alive (VII. 9) and abundant (V. 20), by the Gospel on the other hand God justifies the sinner. The Law

[1] In the five distinctions made in this first section I link up with my paper 'Gesetz und Paraklese' (in '*Antwort*', *Festschr. z. 70. Geburtstag Karl Barths 1956*) and refer to the more exact New Testament proofs given there (p. 324ff.).

brings death (Rom. VII. 10), but the Gospel brings life. The Law is powerless, cannot give life (Gal. III. 21; Rom. VIII. 2), but the Gospel is 'the power of God unto salvation to every one that believeth' (Rom. I. 16). The Law is the outward letter on stone tables, but through the Gospel the spirit of the living God works in the hearts (II Cor. III. 2ff.). The antitheses in the Letter to the Hebrews are perhaps more acute. The Law of the old covenant is termed here as 'weak and unprofitable, for the law made nothing perfect'. But Christ 'disannulled' the Law and 'brought in a better hope, by the which we draw nigh unto God' (Heb. VII. 18f.). In the neighbourhood of the Pauline antitheses comes also the sharp Johannine comparison of Moses and Christ, Law and grace (John 1. 17). Thus it is true to say that the Law commands, but the Gospel bestows. The Law uncovers sin, the Gospel covers it up. The Law judges, the Gospel justifies. The Law kills, the Gospel makes alive. And indeed all this is valid not only of the Old Testament ceremonial and judicial law but also of the moral law.

b) On the other hand a dual message is to be distinguished in God's Old Testament Law itself: God's consolation and demand, God's electing call and exacting call, namely the Old Testament promise and the Old Testament demand of the Law. With *nomos* Paul denotes not only the Old Testament demand of the Law, in particular therefore the Pentateuch, but in a wider sense all Old Testament scriptures, even the prophetic books. Within this broader concept of *nomos* he distinguishes again Law and promise and uses in this, in addition to the broad concept of *nomos*, a specific concept. More correctly the sequence reads 'promise and law', for the Law 'entered' after the promise (Rom. v. 20). This difference between νόμος and ἐπαγγελία is no less great than that between νόμος and εὐαγγέλιον. In the old covenant God already promised as a gift of faith: righteousness (Rom. IV.; Gal. IV. 21), life (Gal. III. 21f.), the Holy Spirit (Gal. III. 14), the son (Gal. IV. 22ff.), etc. The faithful already had a share in these promised gifts in the old covenant, though all these promises referred to fulfilment in Jesus Christ. But they share in the promise independently of the Law and independently of the works of the Law. If the promise were tied to the Law and dependent on the fulfilment of the Law it would be void. 'The promise, that he should be the heir of the world, was not to Abraham, or to his seed, through the law, but through the righteousness of faith' (Rom. IV. 13). The antithesis in Gal. III. 18 reads no less strongly: 'For if the inheritance be of the law, it is no more of promise: but God gave it to Abraham by promise'.

c) In the New Testament Gospel we must also distinguish between consolation and demand, between God's gift and God's commandment, namely between Gospel and admonition. The Gospel comes to the congregation as the consolation of righteousness and as the challenge to serve righteousness (Rom. VI. 19), as the consolation of salvation and as the command to 'work out your own salvation with fear and trembling' (Phil. II. 12), as the power which creates new life, and as the commandment to change to a new life. The apostolic proclamation makes itself heard as the indicative, as the remembrance of the eschatological 'perfect tense' of the act of salvation experienced by the believer, and as the imperative. Moreover the imperative is based on the indicative, namely on the act of salvation which God accomplished for the believer by the Gospel, in particular in baptism. This foundation of the imperative in the act of salvation experienced by the believer is over and above Paul characteristic for the admonitions of the New Testament letters. For the sake of this foundation the suitable sequence in which the dual address is to be distinguished within the Gospel reads: consolation—demand, Gospel—commandment. Otherwise than in the contrasting relationship of Law and Gospel as of Law and promise, consolation and demand are here peculiarly merged. For here God does not demand from the believer anything that He had not previously bestowed upon him by the Gospel. He demands of the believer only that he live as the man he has become by the Gospel: as the man made righteous, free, alive, as a member of the body of Christ. For the unique character of this New Testament command Paul uses the words παρακαλεῖν and παράκλησις, which can be rendered only imperfectly as 'exhorting' and 'admonition'. For in the paraclesis exhortation and comforting fuse in a particular way. Yet this command of the Gospel is the disclosure of the consolation of God's act of salvation in Jesus Christ.

These three fundamental distinctions contain two others: Although God's word comes to men in a double message both in

L

the old and the new covenant, namely as consolation and demand, we must distinguish between the Old and the New Testament consolation and also between the Old and the New Testament demand:

d) We must distinguish the Old Testament promise from the consolation of the New Testament Gospel. For the Gospel proclaims the promised man in the old covenant as the man who came in Jesus Christ. It proclaims the beginning of the promised time of salvation in him and the completely new thing that God has done and is constantly doing through the Holy Ghost to His people in the midst of this decayed world, the new thing which is now hidden but will one day be revealed and accomplished in the parousia of Jesus Christ. The difference between the Old Testament promise and the Gospel is thus not merely a temporal difference of sequence in the divine consolation before and after Jesus' coming or of sequence in a human perception, first expectant and then discerning, or even first obscure and then clear, before and after Jesus' coming. The difference is characterized rather in the fact that God accomplished in Jesus' death and resurrection the act of salvation by the descent of the Holy Ghost, which changes everything.

e) We must distinguish the Old Testament demand of the Law from the commandment of the New Covenant, i.e. *paraklesis*, and with the same precision as we distinguish the Old Testament promise from the consolation of the New Testament Gospel. For *paraklesis* does not command the change to righteousness so that man will become righteous by these works, but because he is made righteous by the Gospel *paraklesis* ordains righteousness. Here it does not hold good as in the Law that he who doeth these works will live; but because new life is given to you, change to a new life. Paul nowhere calls *paraklesis* a Law, although he occasionally admits commandments of the Law in it (Rom. xiii. 9). He nowhere terms obedience to *paraklesis* the work of the Law, although love is the fulfilling of the Law (Rom. xiii. 10). Law and *paraklesis* are different just as Law and Gospel are. The Law is powerless, but *paraklesis* shares in the sin-destroying and renewing power of God which works through the Gospel. The reluctance to call evangelical exhortation law is also characteristic of other New

Testament letters. Thus the Household Codes are nowhere called the Law and the same is true of the admonitions to love which are expressed anew again and again in the first letter of John according to the love of God which appeared in Christ: the subject here is the ἐντολή which is both old and new (2, 7ff.), but not νόμος. Only at the fringe of the New Testament canon does this begin to become something else. But even the letter of James shows a reticence in that he does not characterize his imperative with the same word νόμος (absolutely) as was customary with the Old Testament Law. The early Church did, of course, soon go over to calling the New Testament imperative and even the Gospel the *nova lex* or, even without the addition of distinctive attributes, to calling it quite simply the Law (absolutely). In this respect it cannot refer to Paul, nor to his occasional statements about the 'νόμος τοῦ Χριστοῦ' (Gal. VI. 2) and the 'νόμος τοῦ πνεύματος τῆς ζωῆς' (Rom. VIII. 2). For the *nomos* concept is taken up polemically here in order to express most sharply the opposite of the *nomos*: the Law of the spirit is not the counterpart of the demanding Law but the living working of the spirit in the believer. The Law of Christ is not the counterpart of the demand of love of the Law but the present truth of the love of Christ to which room is to be given in faith. But if the concept of Law is to be used to characterize New Testament *paraklesis* over and above such occasional paradoxical points and in systematic breadth, then it will decisively depend upon its not being used absolutely and upon the novelty of this Law being very clearly worked out in distinction to the Old Testament Law.[1] The same is true if *paraklesis* is called the *tertius usus legis*, as did most emphatically happen through Calvin. Here too it will decisively depend on whether this *tertius usus* is very clearly differentiated from the other truly legal methods of proclamation and operation of the Law (*usus politicus* and *elenchticus*). If these differences are adhered to the concepts *nova lex* and *tertius usus legis* need not necessarily conceal the individuality of *paraklesis*. Looking back at Church history one must of course declare that a particular force of gravity is inherent in the concept of Law which has actually operated again and

[1] Cf. the statements of G. Söhngen (*Gesetz und Evangelium, ihre analoge Einheit*, 1957, p. 51ff.) about the doctrine of the *nova lex* in the *Summa theologica* by Thomas Aquinas (II, 1, qu. 106).

again in a legal undervaluation of the New Testament imperative. Thus Luther did not call *paraklesis* as such *nova lex* or
tertius usus legis, but understood it appropriately as *usus practicus
evangelii*.[1]

The theological problem of the distinction between Law
and Gospel within the one word of God comes out clearly only in
the coalescence of the three basic differences of Old Testament
Law and New Testament Gospel, of Old Testament promise
and Old Testament demand of the Law and of New Testament
Gospel and New Testament exhortation, and the two further
differences contained therein between Old Testament promise
and New Testament Gospel and between the Old Testament
and the New Testament commandment. And in fact these five
differences overlap literally and effectively in the cross of Jesus
Christ. Jesus Christ, the Word become flesh, died for the Law in
order that the Gospel would be proclaimed as the message of the
end of the Law. His death was the transformation of the Old
Testament demand of the Law into the comforting exhortation
of the Gospel. Christ is simply the end of the Law, of the Old
Testament promise as well as the Old Testament demand of the
Law. For He fulfilled both. He also fulfilled the Law whose
demand God has written into the hearts of all men (Rom. II. 15)
and by which God makes all men responsible at His judgement
seat. As the fulfiller of the Law Christ is the Gospel. In His death
God put into operation the new covenant with sinners.

Like the whole question of the correct distinction between
Law and Gospel the question of the sequence—'law and
gospel' or 'gospel and law'?—is a question of many dimensions.
The sequence Gospel and Law is necessarily valid for the Gospel
is the presupposition for the true understanding of the definition
of the Law. Historically the sequence 'law and gospel' is valid,
for after Moses God sent His son, after the old covenant He put
the new one into operation. Within the tenets of the Old Testament Law and the New Testament Gospel the reverse sequence
is on the other hand valid, namely 'promise and law', and
'gospel and exhortation'. For God's command is based both in
the old and the new covenant on His act of salvation which He
accomplished out of spontaneous love for Israel and the Church

[1] Cf. W. Joest, *Gesetz und Freiheit*, 1951, 1956, esp. p. 82ff.; P. Althaus,
Gebot und Gesetz, 1952, and Lauri Haikola, *Usus legis*, 1958.

and by which as this very redeemer He at the same time promised to lead His own also in the future. But both these sequences 'promise and law' and 'gospel and exhortation' remain encompassed by the historical succession of the old and the new covenant which cannot be cancelled out. For this reason the formula which unites the many dimensions of the problem of the sequence of Law and Gospel reads from time immemorial 'law and gospel'—not 'gospel and law'. For the rest the historical sequence 'law and gospel' recurs in the ever new hastening of the believer from the word of judgement to God's word of grace, from the appreciation of the divine 'no' to the hymn of praise of the divine 'yes' in Jesus Christ.

Now, of course, we have to distinguish Law from Gospel not only in the historical consideration of the historical succession of the old and the new covenants, and certainly not from a theoretical point of view away from the old and new covenant—such a point of view which looks on in contemplation does not exist— but in faith in the Gospel, as members of the New Testament people of the covenant, as those who by baptism have been given into Jesus' death and in the midst of the temptations of this world are going towards the coming judge of the worlds. Then, however, we appreciate not only the difference between Old Testament Law and New Testament Gospel but appreciate at the same time the Gospel in the Old Testament Law and the Law in the New Testament Gospel. Consequently our theme becomes an exceedingly existential problem which concerns again and again afresh the life and death of Christians.

2. *The Gospel in the Old Testament Law*

As members of the Church we can no longer read the Old Testament scriptures as the Jews did. For in faith in Jesus Christ we recognize that the Old Testament Law is fulfilled. Because the Old Testament *promise* is fulfilled in Jesus Christ we no longer see it as the promise but as the Gospel, as the joyful message of the salvation which has come. Because the Old Testament demand of the Law is fulfilled by Jesus and we have died with regard to the Law in faith in Jesus Christ, we no longer understand the Old Testament demand of God as a Law which kills but as comforting evangelical exhortation.

The fact that the veil of the Old Testament is done away in

faith in Jesus Christ (II Cor. III. 12ff.) means first of all the recognition that service to the old covenant condemned, judged, killed, that it was service to the letter not to the spirit and it was only of little (indeed—in comparison with service to the new covenant—of no) splendour (v. 6ff.). The unveiling of the Old Testament thus means the questioning and refutation of the understanding spread abroad in Israel and particularly ex-pressed in the psalter, as if the covenant of Moses had already given the sinner righteousness and life and complete sufficiency. It is clear now too that the historical change of the Old Testa-ment demand from the free commanding word of God to God's Law fixed in letters, which finally encompassed life having no way out, was no chance happening. Paul at all events explains the function of the Law to make sin 'abound' as the divine task allotted to it from the beginning. Through Christ life under the Old Testament Law is unveiled as preparation, waiting, ques-tioning, failing, as the not-yet intended by God, which is now passed and done away. Thus in Christ the covenant of Moses is unveiled as the 'old' covenant.

This unveiling, however, brings the perception that the Old Testament testifies to Jesus Christ. Not only do individual passages testify to the coming Lord, but the Old Testament as a whole gives an outline of the coming Saviour. Not only the Old Testament promises, which expressly point to a coming Lord who will bring righteousness and peace, but also the peculiar contradictions which exist between divine authority and the human reality of the Old Testament prophets, priests and kings, and beyond that the existence of the Old Testament people of the covenant and its devout men are considered now as proofs of the coming redemption. We then hear of the proofs of the Old Testament expectation in their connexion with the Old Testa-ment contradictions and questions as testimony to the final answer which God in Jesus Christ gave to sinners. In faith in Christ we may live by the fulfilled Old Testament promise as by the Gospel and we may understand the rule of God in the old covenant as divine fatherly direction.

In this double revelation the Old Testament scriptures are the Bible of the congregation of Jesus Christ. In the light of the glory of the Gospel it becomes clear that the glory of the Law can hardly be termed glory (II Cor. III, 10). It is, however, by this unveiling of the Law that the exuberant glory of the Gospel comes to light. The Old Testament Law attests simultaneously the splendour and non-splendour of the inexhaustible wealth of the Gospel to him who believes in Christ.

3. The Law in the New Testament Gospel

The Gospel proclaims God's act of salvation in Jesus Christ: God placed Jesus on the cross under the judgement which is the sinner's lot, and revealed Him in the raising from the dead as the man who knew no sin, and who, suffering and dying, took the sins of the world upon Himself. Thus the Gospel is by its nature at the same time the proclamation of the judgement deserved by the sinner. It proclaims this judgement as the judgement borne by Jesus and thus as the acquittal and salvation for everyone who believes in Jesus Christ. But the Gospel does not cease to demand the acknowledgement of the judgement deserved by us. The call to faith is always at the same time a call to repentance. But thus the saving Gospel can become God's word of judgement. The Gospel brings life to him who believes in the coming of God's son and it brings death to him who refuses obedience to faith. 'He that believeth on him is not condemned: but he that believeth not is condemned already, because he hath not believed in the name of the only begotten Son of God' (John III. 18). Thus Paul, the preacher of the Gospel, sees himself as 'a sweet savour of Christ, in them that are saved, and in them that perish: to the one we are the savour of death unto death; and to the other the savour of life unto life' (II Cor. II. 15). Just because God, the justifier and life-giver, acts through the Gospel, no one can hear the Gospel and remain the same person that he was. Either he surrenders to this divine saving act or he incurs the judgement of divine anger. Indeed, through the Gospel God does the work of the Law with extreme pointedness and final radicalism. For Jesus Christ is the last message of God, after He previously spoke through Moses and the prophets—the last message, followed by no other one. As this last and final message Jesus Christ is to be proclaimed and believed. Yet he suffered in a final manner God's judgement on men. There is no acquittal for the sinner in all eternity other than in the faith in this Lord judged for us.

What is true of the consolation of God's act of salvation in

Jesus Christ is true also of the imperative of the Gospel, which is based on the indicative of the act of salvation. The exhortations of the New Testament letters demand of the believer not only that he believe in salvation through Christ but also that he await the coming day of judgement. The same people who receive justification through faith alone without works are now exhorted to do such works so that they can stand on that day. Paul referred again and again to the coming day of the revelation of God's righteous judgement when each will be rewarded according to his works. This judgement will be double according to the work: for some acquittal for life, for others sentence of destruction. Paul announced this judgement not only to the world but also to the congregation and expressly included himself in it (cf. e.g. II Cor. v. 10). Thus he announces the judgement to those whom he comforted by the Gospel with the judgement of justification and thus eschatological acquittal. Consequently within Paul's proclamation there are the eschatological judgement of justification which is received independently of the works by faith, and the judgement according to the works. Paul did not solve this antithesis logically and it cannot be solved logically. It can neither be removed as a Jewish residue from the Pauline message, nor can the preaching of judgement be confined to non-believers. Rather does the announcement of the judgement belong inseparably to the Gospel of Paul. In this sense he can say: 'God shall judge the secrets of men by Jesus Christ according to my gospel' (Rom. 11. 16). According to this we must distinguish within a broad concept of the Gospel not only between Gospel and paraclesis but also between the Gospel as the message of salvation and the proclamation of judgement according to works.

In expectation of the coming judgement the exhortations of the apostle with regard to the sins in the congregation can become not only confirmatory and admonitory but also threatening, judging and punishing. For they are then not only the comforting, entreating disclosure of the Gospel and the new life given by the Gospel but they also become the exhibition of sins, the threatening proclamation of divine judgement and reproving struggle for the endangered members of the congregation. This warning is most sharply expressed in the anathema upon those members of the congregation who do not live by grace.

With the anathema the apostle proclaimed not only the coming divine judgement, but by the anathema the delivery of the sinner to the vengeance of God is carried out.

Thus God acts through the New Testament Gospel in a way that is not only justifying, but also judging, not only saving but also condemning, not only lifegiving but also killing. As long as we are journeying through the world we must take seriously the dual effect of God through His word. In faith in Jesus Christ we must acknowledge our sins daily and pray: 'Forgive us our debts'. We hear the Gospel not only as the message of Him who died for us but also as the message of the Son of God brought to the cross by us. We hear the evangelical exhortation not only as the comforting imperative, by which God develops our faith, but also as a threatening warning and judging verdict by which God exposes the disobedience of believers. The believer is free of the Law only in recognizing at the same time in repentance the demand of Law, which is proclaimed by the joyful message as the demand fulfilled through Christ.

Even though this function of the Gospel to proclaim and accomplish the judgement corresponds to the function of the Law as judge, Paul nowhere called his exhortations Law, even where they became threatening, indeed judging—far less his Gospel even when it judges the unbeliever. Even where Paul sees himself as 'the savour of death unto death' (II Cor. II. 16) he knows himself to be the servant of the Gospel, not the Law. For the Law had only a temporary validity lasting until the revelation of the Gospel (Gal. III. 19). Christ is the end of the Law (Rom. x. 4). In spite of this clear concept of Heilsgeschichte which also prevails elsewhere among the New Testament letter-writers, we are entitled to call Law the function of the Gospel which proclaims and judges. Questionable as it is to call the New Testament paraclesis as such Law it is obvious with regard to the special threatening and judging function which it fulfils towards the sinful member of the congregation. In this sense Luther also taught the lasting validity of the Law for the Christian. If Paul had defined the concepts Law and Gospel from their sequence as Heilsgeschichte, Luther, like the early and Medieval Church, understood the Law, no longer only as the past but as the oppressing present. He had of course perceived, as distinct from usual Church usage, the function of the

Law for the Christian in the exposing of sins, judgement and killing, but avoided the concept of Law to designate paraclesis, the comforting, fatherly direction of God which is based on the renewing power of the Gospel.

4. *The Unity of Law and Gospel*

Thus in the Old Testament Law we encounter at the same time the Gospel and in the New Testament Gospel we encounter at the same time the Law. The difference between Law and Gospel is thus not only a difference between the Old and the New Testament but goes right through the centre of God's word in the Old Testament and right through the centre of God's word in the New Testament. It is not only a difference in the historical sequence of God's act to humanity but in the simultaneity of God's act to each man—to ourselves.

But how, in view of such simultaneity and intertwining, are Law and Gospel to be distinguished? In fact they are properly distinguished only by the person who knows about their homogeneity, indeed about their unity. For the homogeneity of Law and Gospel is founded in the unity of their origin, in the triune God who speaks and acts through both Words.

Law and Gospel are the message of the one God. This unity is by no means only that of a temporally unclear origin, but by Law and Gospel the Redeemer speaks and acts. God's demanding and bestowing, God's judging and saving message, God's old and new covenants are spontaneous deeds of one and the same divine love, deeds of His merciful descent to sinners. And indeed the same God speaks and acts through Law and Gospel who at the beginning created man in His own image and placed him under the promise and the command of being the exact image of God. The Creator, who attests Himself as the Lord to all men by the works of His creation, acts by Law and Gospel as the Redeemer towards those who have come under judgement. Law and Gospel are the revelation of one and the same righteousness of God. The same righteousness which God demands of the sinner by Law, He consoles him with in the Gospel. The same love which He offers by Law He produces by the joyful message of the act of love on the Cross as the fruit of the Holy Ghost in those who believe in Christ. The same hallowing which the Law demands is produced by the Gospel. We can continue: Law and Gospel are the revelation of one and the same divine love and righteousness, faithfulness and wisdom, compassion and holiness in Jesus Christ.

Law and Gospel are united in Jesus Christ in whom God came to us sinners. Law and Gospel attest together Jesus Christ: as the promise of the coming Lord and as the message of the Lord who has come, as the challenge of obedience and as the message of the judgement carried out on Him. By the Law which kills God drives the sinner to the same Christ in Whose life he changes Him by the Gospel. Thus Jesus Christ is the one *logos* of God which God proclaims through the Old Testament Law and the New Testament Gospel, through the prophets and the Apostles.

Law and Gospel are the work of the one Holy Ghost. Even if God bestows the spirit which renews hearts not through the Law but first through the Gospel, the Law is still also 'spiritual' (Rom. vii. 14). For God shows through the Law the same spiritual man whom He creates through the Gospel. Thus God, even though He does not create the new man through the Law, drives the sinner through the Law to the supplication of the new creating work of the Spirit. On the other hand the Holy Ghost produces in believers the fruits which the Law had previously demanded in vain, had demanded namely but had not produced. The effect of the Holy Ghost is the same love which the Law demands but had not bestowed because of its powerlessness. Where the fruits of the Holy Ghost are love, joy, peace, etc., the saying holds good that 'Against such there is no law' (Gal. v. 23), for the fruits of the spirit are in accordance with the Law's demands. But they are not effects of the Law but of the Gospel.

The homogeneity of Law and Gospel is consequently based on the unity of their origin in the triune God, in the unity of His divine will, which is manifested in both messages. The same love, in which God created man in the beginning, so that the latter might love Him again, faces the sinner in the Law as a demand and in the Gospel as a gift. The same image of God in which God created man at the beginning, faces the sinner in the Law as a command ('you shall be holy, for I am holy!') and in the Gospel as the consolation of the work of Jesus Christ who sanctified Himself for the world. Through the Gospel ensues the transformation into the likeness of God, which appeared in Jesus Christ, the transference into the sonship, which is inferred in the 'only begotten son'. In the different forms of the Law and the Gospel and ways of encountering them there is manifested one and the same divine will to love which is directed from the beginning of creation on to God's people, the community of brethren of the eternal Son of God.

The revelation and accomplishment of this one decree of love takes place in the historical sequence. The homogeneity of Law and Gospel is not to be understood as a timeless unity. It emerges rather on the path of the historical act of God. It is not a static unity but the decisive turning-point which took place in the humiliation and elevation of the Son of God and in the descent of the Holy Ghost, an historical turning-point which is accomplished afresh in those who come to believe in Jesus Christ by the event of the preaching of the Gospel. Law and Gospel consequently belong together in an irreversible co-ordination of functions. The Law is the task-master to bring us to Christ (Gal. III. 24), so that we become righteous by faith and freed from the Law. But freedom from the Law means living in the power of the Holy Spirit, whose fruits are in accordance with the Law's command. The unity of Law and Gospel consists in the event of the transition from the existence of the sinner under the Law into the life of the believer under the Gospel. The unity of Law and Gospel will therefore be properly shown only if a distinction is made between Law and Gospel.

5. *The Difference between Law and Gospel*

But how are Law and Gospel to be distinguished if in the Old Testament Law we encounter at the same time the Gospel and in the New Testament Gospel we encounter at the same time the Law? How are they to be distinguished if they are one in Jesus Christ?

Does the difference between Law and Gospel consist only in the difference between unbelief and belief, so that the same word saves the believer and judges the non-believer? As certainly as the Gospel can be distinguished from the Law only in faith, the difference between Law and Gospel is not to be found in the acts of non-belief and belief. Neither belief nor unbelief creates the difference between Law and Gospel. This rather precedes belief and unbelief as a difference in God's word. Faith and with it certainty of salvation are possible only by the difference in God's word.

Is the difference between Law and Gospel only the difference between God's dual activity, so that with one and the same word He saves some and condemns others? As certainly as God is free to kill some and bring life to others with one and the same word, so the difference between Law and Gospel is not only a difference in divine activity but is also the difference of a double message in which God proclaims two different things.

The difference between Law and Gospel consists also not only in the fact that God acts towards each individual through His one word in a dual manner, exposing and concealing, tearing down and erecting, scolding and loving. As certainly as God works for the Christian in a dual manner, just as certainly is this dual activity not a miracle hidden behind the one word, but this dual activity takes place in the dual *message* of God and is apparent in God's dual message.

Through the Law God demands everything from us; through the Gospel he bestows everything on us. Through the Law God demands that we offer ourselves to Him; through the Gospel God offers Himself to us in Christ. Through the Law he announces judgement for the sinner; through the Gospel He announces to him the judgement suffered by Christ as an acquittal. Through the Law God discloses the reality of the sinner; through the Gospel He clothes the sinner with the righteousness of Christ. These are not only different effects of the one word of God, but also different words by which God does the deeds of judgement and acquittal, of killing and life-giving, which are proclaimed by them. In spite of the unity of the speaking and acting God both words cannot be identified. In spite of the historical arrangement of the Law with the Gospel in the unity of the Divine will we are made uncertain and are astonished again and again by the dual message of God in such a way that it is impossible to derive logically the Law from the Gospel or the Gospel from the Law and to resolve their different nature.

Law and Gospel are to be distinguished as long as we are on our way through this world. For the whole human race is approaching—whether it knows about it or not, whether it recognizes or denies this—the day when Christ will come in His glory and will judge all the living and dead. Then He, Who is the one Word of God, will say two different things— to some: 'Come, ye blessed of my Father'—and to others: 'Depart from Me, ye cursed' (Matt. xxv. 34 and 41). The Church is hastening towards this coming day. Both words are to be proclaimed to every individual. But one day both words will separate so that only one of them will be addressed to each individual. This final subjection of the world under Jesus Christ, the Judge of the World, must be served by the Church in the proclamation of the different words of the Gospel and the Law. In the expectation of its Lord the Church proclaims acquittal to believers in the judgement and judgement according to the works and thus calls everyone to repentance and to faith.

Beyond this, however, the difference between 'binding and loosing' is an exceedingly concrete one: in God's mission men's sins are *either* forgiven *or* retained. As certainly as the message of God's judgement and grace is given to each man just as certainly are there decisions against God's grace by which the sinner who is not ready for repentance now finally places himself under God's 'no'. If the Church no longer dares to bind the sins to the sinner who is not ready for repentance and only intends to be able to remit sins—whether sinners desire it or not—then it fails to recognize the mission given to it and indeed fails to recognize not only the gravity of divine Law but also the glory of the Gospel, the heavenly joy over the sinner who repents.

6. *The Gospel as God's true Word*

Now it is of course absolutely decisive that things did not stand still with the affirmation of the succession and inter-mingling, the unity and differences of the Law and Gospel. Law and Gospel are not timeless values but the ever new, exceedingly concrete historical event of divine demand and bestowal, judgement and salvation, killing and life-giving. There is also a highly existential question to be considered: Is God merciful to me *or* is He angry with me? There is also a further question to be considered: Have I to award my fellow creatures God's acquittal *or* God's judgement? It is ultimately a question of either-or and not only of 'as well as'. Differentiating Law and Gospel means answering these daily new questions *in concreto*. If only the indefiniteness of an 'as well as' were to remain, only doubt would remain.

But how can man accomplish the differentiation? How can he grasp this differentiation completely in a dogmatic formula? Is this differentiation not quite concrete and thus to be accomplished again and again anew? As a matter of fact one cannot disregard for a moment that this concerns the differentiated speaking and acting of *God*: God Himself is the Lord Who distinguished Law and Gospel and goes on distinguishing them anew. The dogmatic assertion must refer to God's own actual distinction, but it cannot replace it. Dogmatic thought develops here into a hastening, imploring, grasping, humbling action. For the concrete distinction of Law and Gospel takes place by God's works in the power of the Holy Spirit. The gift of the Holy Spirit and the dual commission of remitting and retaining sins belong together according to their nature (John xx. 22ff.). Neither by a dogmatic formula nor by ethical casuistry can the concrete distinction of both God's words be anticipated. The distinction between Law and Gospel must be elicited prayerfully from God Himself. In distinguishing both words Himself He takes us towards the coming day.

There is of course one thing which dogmatics has to teach with certainty about sequence and commingling, unity and differentiation, and everything depends utterly on its doing so clearly: *God's own word* is the Gospel, not the Law. *God's own judgement* is the acquittal, not the sentence. God's *own work* is giving life, not killing. 'God sent not His Son into the world to condemn the world; but that the world through him might be saved' (John iii. 17). Jesus Christ died on the Cross not to perpetuate men's guilt but to extinguish it. So long as the age of mercy lasts, so long as humanity still awaits the arrival of the Judge of the World, the last decisive word has not been spoken, but God presses on in all His commanding, judging and killing to salvation through belief in the Gospel. The Judge of the World is Christ Who died *for us*. In this sense the Law is God's *alien* work and the Gospel his *real* work. This is true even of the word by which God binds and retains sins. Even this most extreme word of the Law serves the Gospel. For it is the most paradoxical extreme preaching of divine love, even though it forgoes any consolation of love and leaves the man who is not ready for repentance expressly to the judging act of God. For this extreme word of the Law is the last summons to those who are not ready for repentance: turn back, so long as there is time!

The distinction between Law and Gospel is thus on no account the recognition and proclamation of a timeless dialectic of two equally stressed statements which contradict each other, but the ever new proclamation hastening to the sinner, pushing into the most varied historical situations, the proclamation of the superior splendour of the Gospel to the Law. The distinction between Law and Gospel occurs then, in that the Christ who has been killed is proclaimed and praised above all, while the Law which kills is acknowledged and proclaimed. He is the revelation of the divine love of God which annuls sin, death and Law. The preacher of the Gospel cannot be prevented from distinguishing between Law and Gospel thus and not otherwise by any magnitude of sin, any abyss of perdition, any hopelessness of despair.

The distinction between Law and Gospel is consequently learnt in temptation. What is temptation?

One terms it temptation if people attack the community of Jesus Christ and persecute the believers, take them prisoner and even kill them. Such hurt which men bring to the community is by no means to be underrated and yet it is as such not real temptation. For in this hurt the Christian can know himself completely secure in the hand of his Lord.

Furthermore one terms it temptation if unseen powers of destruction surround and attack the community, produce desires and anxieties, lead it to revolt and arouse enmity against it. Even the attacks of devilish powers are not to be underrated and yet even they are not the real temptation of the community. The promise is given to it: 'The gates of hell shall not prevail against it' (Matt. XVI. 18).

Real temptation begins where we realize that neither people nor powers can attack, tempt and torment the community if God had not given them the power to do it. Real temptation arises in the community not by inimical people and powers but by God's word, namely if the community sees itself in its needs measured by God's holy commands and recognizes that it is given over to God's righteous judgement. That is the true temptation, when the same God who has given the community His promise, reveals their sins, takes away by His demand the promises behind which it conceals its vice, and leaves no doubt that He is the deadly enemy of sin. If the fall of the community becomes evident Moses and the prophets, Jesus' Sermon on the Mount, the Cross and even the comforting, exhorting Apostles become gigantic threatening figures which take one's breath away. Then only sin instead of mercy, only anger instead of love is shown by God. Then sins are harshly manifested and not one deed remains of which we could boast or which we could even excuse.

In temptation Christ cannot deny God's judgement which is passed on Him, but He must recognize it as righteous judgement, He must humble Himself under God's powerful hand: yes, we have deserved God's judgement. But at the same time He may and must in faith contrast God's promise with God's judging word. If God says to you: I am angry with you, hold out to Him: you were angry with your Son. If God says to you: I hate your sins, say to Him: you have made your Son a sin. If God says to you: I abandon you, affirm to Him: it is not true, you abandoned Jesus Christ. You yourself in your Son have taken upon you our isolation from God. His righteousness is now mine. I am secure in His steadfastness, in His steadfast suffering unto death. Christ was not only tempted by the devil and by men but by God Himself, who abandoned Him on the Cross. He named the God 'mine' who had become to Him the distant God. He still named Him His God who seemed powerlessly to contemplate the torment of His dying. In recognizing divine anger the tempted community in their faith in Christ has to praise divine love.

By bowing in repentance to the word of the judging God and clinging in faith to the word from the Cross the Christian distinguishes between Law and Gospel. This is the distinction:

M

in the knowledge of God's righteous Law to hasten to the Gospel, in recognition of God's deserved judgement to grasp the righteousness of Christ in faith. It is not as though Law and Gospel were first distinguished by this distinction. God distinguished them once and for all in His act of salvation on the Cross. Here the legal claim of the Law was taken completely in earnest and at the same time ended. We have always only to grasp this distinction.

In this daily hastening of the believing sinner from God's deserved anger to God's undeserved love, in this daily fleeing from God's 'no' to God's 'yes', in the daily request 'forgive us our debts' the sequence recurs in which God first revealed the Old Testament Law and then the New Testament Gospel. The succession of the dual divine message in world history is at the same time the direction in which the community goes towards its returning Lord and Redeemer.

The teaching of the Church cannot isolate the Gospel: the joyful message would no longer be proclaimed if the challenge and judgement of the Law were denied. The teaching of the Church also can not isolate the Law: God's challenge would not be taken seriously if God's mercy were concealed in Christ's death. Law and Gospel also can not be given equal status: this too can end only in hybris and despair. The Church must distinguish Law and Gospel by proclaiming the Gospel as God's real word—by holding open and indicating the escape road of salvation from the Law's condemnatory judgement to the Gospel's judgement of justification. Dogmatics serves the distinction of Law and Gospel by leaving a place open for the distinction which God himself accomplishes: 'For as the heaven is high above the earth, so great is his mercy toward them that fear him. As far as the east is from the west, so far hath he removed our transgressions from us' (Ps. ciii. 11f.).

7. *The Ecumenical Significance of the Distinction of Law and Gospel*

The distinction of Law and Gospel is really of the greatest significance for the whole of Christendom. For God is always encountered as the One who is challenging and giving, and on the other hand as the one who is giving and challenging. Again and again God calls to repentance and faith and new obedience. Again and again man tries to withdraw from this calling of God, whether through libertinism, or through legalism, or through despair, or through self-assurance. Moreover, this assurance in which man shelters from the living God can refer to his own works, but also to the use of the means of grace. In the midst of such very different temptations and obduracies which change in place and time the Church must proclaim both God's demand and also His mercy, in order to destroy the self-assurance of men and raise up those lying on the ground. The correct distinction of Law and Gospel is thus constantly a new task of the sermon and ministerial work. The orders of the liturgy of divine worship, catechetic instruction, confession and Church training must also serve this distinction.

It is all the more striking that this central theme 'Law and Gospel', of pressing importance at every moment of religious speaking and acting, plays only a small role in the *dogmas* of the different parts of Christendom seen as a whole. It becomes immediately clear if one compares the few dogmatic decisions on this theme with those which in one way or another have been pronounced upon by all Churches in Christological and trinitarian questions and made obligatory.

The Church of the Augsburg Confession is in an exceptional position here. Luther again and again called the distinction of Law and Gospel the decisive theme of theology. If he also called the doctrine of justification the *articulus stantis et cadentis ecclesiae* this is not a contrary position to hold. For justification is the acquittal which the man sentenced by the Law received in faith in the Gospel without the works demanded by the Law. The justification of the sinner can consequently not be taught without the distinction of Law and Gospel. This distinction on the other hand embraces all problems: judgement and justification, God's anger and God's mercy, obligation and freedom, faith and works, etc. The distinction of Law and Gospel is encountered by us, however, not only in the theology of the reformers but also in statements of Church dogma, which has been formulated and prescribed by the Reformation Churches in the creeds with claims to obligatory recognition. It is true that in the Augsburg Confession the formula 'distinction of Law and Gospel' is lacking. But appropriately to the subject this distinction is carried out in that in two separate articles 'of justification' (IV) and 'of the new obedience' (VI) are dealt with, in which there exists between both, and not fortuitously, the article 'of the preaching office' and of the Gospel and sacrament as 'means' of the Holy Spirit. The Vth article in the formula of the concordat deals expressly with 'the Law and the Gospel' and the VIth article turns 'from the third use of the Law' against antinomianism but without paraclesis as such being characterized by the concept of Law.[1]

In view of the differences between the Lutheran distinction of Law and Gospel and Karl Barth's doctrine of the unity of both[2] it may be pointed out that in the 16th century no contrast was perceived between the Lutheran and the reformed doctrine on this point, which like the Last Supper or predestination would have become the object of controversial theological arguments. Even though Calvin emphasized more strongly than Luther the unity of the old and new covenants[3] and also in his doctrine of the *tertius usus legis* went beyond Luther's concept of the Law, one must affirm that within the Christian world the old reformed doctrine of Law and Gospel is nearer the Lutheran one than the corresponding doctrinal statements of other confessions. Karl Barth's doctrine is on this point new in an important respect relative to Calvin.

The fact that in the Eastern Church a dogma about Law and Gospel is lacking is not to be wondered at as it did not go in general significantly beyond the trinitarian and Christological dogmas. It remained in its dogma at what can be expressed in the structure of the doxology. It is true that in the letters of the ecumenical patriarch Jeremias II in the years 1574–81 to the Tübingen Lutherans,[4] in which he took up a position towards the Augsburg Confession which had been sent to him, there exist statements which concern our theme and on occasion these letters are even awarded the rank of

[1] In this connexion R. Bring, *Gesetz und Evengelium und der dritte Brauch des Gesetzes in der lutherischen Theologie*, Schr. d. Luther-Agricola-Ges. 1, Helsinki, 1943.

[2] Cf. particularly *Evangelium und Gesetz*, 1, 1935.

[3] H. H. Wolf, *Die Einheit des Bundes, das Verhältnis von Altem und Neuem Testament bei Calvin*, 1958.

[4] A German edition of this correspondence appeared under the title *Wort und Mysterium*, 1958.

creeds.[1] But these texts have never acquired the same significance in the Eastern Church as the Early Church dogmas and by their content they make clear in their more parenetic treatment of the questions of justification and obedience that in the Eastern Church there exists no firm dogmatic tradition and no fixed conception for the treatment of this theme.

It is all the more surprising that the Council of Trent did not take up the theme of Law and Gospel—astonishing too because this theme had played an important role for Augustine and also, as G. Söhngen has recently shown, for Thomas; and because the reformers referred expressly to Augustine. The concept of the Gospel in the Pauline sense as the power of God, as the message of Jesus Christ, by which Jesus Christ is present and active—the Gospel as *verbum efficax*, as *sacramentum audibile*, as the saving act and word of God—is lacking. It is true that the Gospel is occasionally mentioned in the statements about the condition of justification (sess. VI, ch. 4). But as *causa instrumentalis* only baptism (ch. 7; cf. 4) is named, with a later mention of the sacrament of repentance. The justification of the sinner takes place not through the Gospel but through baptism. The significance of the Gospel is in this respect reduced to the call to baptism and thus at the same time to the call to repentance, faith, hope, love as acts of preparation for receiving baptism (ch. 6). If, however, the Pauline concept of the Gospel is lacking, the distinction of Law and Gospel makes an appearance neither *verbotenus* nor in the structuring of the Tridentine statements. For all that is said about the new obedience exists here under the one heading 'de iustificatione'. Justification and obedience are not thematically distinguished as in the Augsburg Confession but permeate each other. One cannot of course overlook that the formula Law and Gospel is to be understood as the concentration of the themes judgement and justification, faith and works, etc. But these themes were also thoroughly dealt with by the Council of Trent even though in contrast to Reformation theology. To that extent the Tridentine decree of justification and the *canones* belonging to it are to be taken seriously as an indirect contribution to the doctrine of Law and Gospel.

[1] Thus in the collection of Johannes M. Karmiris, Athens, Vol. I, 1952, Vol. II, 1953.

In the dogmatic treatment of the distinction of Law and Gospel considerable differences exist consequently within Christendom. The particular answers have not yet been mentioned here which, for example, are given to our question by Methodism and other movements of sanctification as they have come in a number of ways from different Churches. The differences exist not only between the dogmatic decisions themselves but also in whether this theme has been dealt with in a dogmatic decision.

Now in controversial theological discussion one cannot be satisfied with affirming the lack or even the presence of dogmatic statements and with comparing these statements with one another in order to establish and defend them according to the standpoint of the participants. Rather must some fundamental methodical considerations be taken into account and corresponding steps be taken in order to push forward to the affirmation of the real differences and to a true comparison of the dogmatic statements.

a) We must not disregard the fact that the dogmatic statement—in spite of the central position of the Creed in the life of the Church—is only *one* in the midst of many other statements of faith. Faith answers God for His act of salvation also in prayer, worship, testimony, doctrine, etc. The dogmatic statement is also not the only statement in which the *consensus* of faith achieves formulation. Even statements of the liturgy, of catechesis, of the traditions of the fathers, of religious tracts, etc., signify in the life of the Church more than just the statements of the individual believers who formulated them, but they are effective as statements which form and define the Church community. We must consider all this in connexion with our theme. For the dogmatic statements about Law and Gospel are not an end in themselves but they are appointed to serve other statements of faith, namely the *proclamation* of Law and Gospel. The elementary statement is the proclamation itself. The dogmatic statement about the proclamation wants to serve the proper accomplishment of the proclamation, but it cannot take the place of the proclamation itself. Since by no means all statements of faith and all functions of religious life have become the subject of dogma and this cannot be expected at all, we must always bear in mind the other statements of faith if we want to perceive the doctrine of a Church in its entirety. On account of the peculiar complexity of our theme we will moreover have to reckon with the possibility that only one side of this theme emerges in dogmatic statements, but the other emerges in the proclamation or in the liturgy or in other places in religious life. In the living encounter with other Churches so many different kinds of surprise are possible. Even where the reformation formula *simul peccator et iustus* is strange as a *dogmatic* statement it can still emerge *in practice* as an existential statement in the confession of sins of just such people as are recognized in their Church as saints. Even where the necessity of the works for salvation is emphasized most strongly *dogmatically* it can *in practice* be self-evident that *in articulo mortis*, and not only here, the saving grace is awarded without any condition. The situation of temptation is also known in every Church. Even though it has not been raised into the *dogmatic* consciousness and been made the starting-point of dogmatic statements, frightened consciences have again and again lived *in practice* from faith alone. On the other hand it can also follow that a doctrine of justification which exclusively portrays the idea of *sola gratia* and *sola fide* has become in some way a possession, that its knowledge *in practice* plays the role of a work.

b) We must then bear in mind the different historical situations in which statements of dogma achieved formulation. This is particularly important in our theme as it is a question here of the proclamation which must be delivered in face of very different possibilities of endangering Christian life. Paul already proclaimed God's consolation and demand in a different way from the Jewish lawyers and the gnostic libertines. Other situations arose in Church history. The dogmas did not grow equally on all sides from the confession of Christ and the principle of systematic integrity was not decisive in their formulation. They were rather provoked by concrete false doctrines and dangers threatening the Church and formulated at times in this concrete defence. The dogma grew rather by fits and starts than in an even, organic growth. Thus it is not unimportant from which presuppositions the dogmatic statements about Law and Gospel were made: from despair under the Law which one tries to fulfil or from fear of the hybris

which despises God's Law. Doubtless the Lutheran creeds
and the Council of Trent do not make their statements in the
same situation. The Lutheran creeds like Luther wage war
primarily against justification by works, which obscures the
Gospel, and then no less intensively against antinomianism
which isolates the Gospel from the Law and wants to claim
validity as the only Word of God for the Christian. The Council
of Trent, on the other hand, turns primarily to the danger of
a libertine scorn of the Law and the works of obedience, in
which it at the same time turns against pelagianism with which
it does not want to be and cannot be confused. The variety
of these situations was radicalized in that the Tridentine
fathers apparently did not heed the Reformation struggle
against antinomianism but treated the reformers in their
canones as antinomians. Even Jeremias II in his answer to the
Tübingen Lutherans—certainly under the influence of Roman
information—above all turned his attention to an attack on
the antinomian danger.

c) We must further bear in mind the concepts which the
dogmatic statements use—biblical as well as later ones—in
which in the historical situation of the moment the answer of
faith was to be given. With every dogmatic statement there
takes place an act of selection of individual concepts from the
many which discuss the same theme in the Bible and besides
this from the many possibilities which the concepts of the
surrounding world suggest at that moment. Out of the many,
individual ones are emphasized, developed and defined in
order to be used then as dogmatic concepts to unite that large
number. Thus in the New Testament scriptures the dual
divine message is by no means always characterized by the
concepts Law and Gospel. 'Gospel' is not the only name given
to the divine act of salvation by the Word, 'Law' is hardly
the term for the questioning of the Christian by God's command, and the formula 'Law and Gospel' is not itself to be
found in Paul. The dogmatic formation of concepts is always
an act of systematic concentration which goes beyond biblical
exegesis, even though it must also justify itself in relation to
exegesis. Thus the New Testament statements about the act
of salvation which God performs for the believer through the
Gospel are manifold: justification, sanctification, transforma-

tion into God's likeness, etc., without every one of these concepts being found in every New Testament writer. The dogmatic formulation of concepts in the Eastern Church has taken up above all sanctification and transformation into God's likeness (deification), the formulation of concepts in the West has taken up above all justification and sanctification. To this can be added that in the New Testament scriptures righteousness, sanctity, life is awarded as a gift and demanded from the believer and is promised as the reward of obedience. As the righteous the believers must seize righteousness. As the sanctified they must become holy. As those wakened to life they must struggle to achieve the crown of life. Dogmatic statements have however not extensively retained this dual use of the same concept for God's consolation and demand in their ideas. Thus in the Eastern Church, in certain respects also in the Roman Church, God's act of mercy is taught above all as sanctification, his challenge however as the command of righteousness, while in the Evangelical Church the act of mercy is called justification and often God's challenge is called not only in the selection of concepts but beyond it differences result from the fact that in the New Testament scriptures God's gift and challenge are not always attached to each other in the same way. Jesus' message and challenge is handed down differently in the Jewish–Christian circle in which the Gospel of Matthew originated (Jesus is attested here in the Sermon on the Mount, in spite of His transgression of the commandment of Moses, as the bringer of a new *torah*), differently in the Gospel of Luke. Paul taught the New Testament imperative differently from James. Thus in dogmatic statements differences result, if one starts from Paul and then takes up also the imperatives of James, or if one wanted to try to go the opposite way, which of course in view of the one-sidedness of the letter of James and his lack of explicit statements about God's act of salvation in Jesus Christ does not from the outset suggest itself.

d) The structure of the dogmatic statement[1] deserves particular attention in the distinction of Law and Gospel. For it is a question here of dogmatic statements about other statements, namely about the proclamation of God's consolation

[1] Cf. p. 16ff.

and demand and consequently of the consolation and demand of God Himself which encounters the sinner in the human word of the proclamation and the administration of the sacrament. If one inquires into the structure of the reformation and Tridentine statements about the event of justification characteristic differences result.

The structure of Luther's statements is determined by the act of listening to God's message. It is not as if this act were only the presupposition of his statements and then was made the subject of the doctrine. It is rather for Luther characteristic that in his doctrinal statements he remains very close to the structure of the actual listening. To put it crucially he makes them in the act of listening, in the act of sacramental receiving.

Naturally he does not stop here, he also makes statements about the proclamation and the proper administration of the sacraments. But here too it is characteristic that they remain very close to the act of proclamation and administration. It is not fortuitous that in reformation theology *docere* and *praedicare* are used synonymously. Luther does not make the event of the divine message, the personal encounter of God with men, namely the questioning by God's Law and the salvation by the Gospel, the subject of consideration; but makes his statements in the act of occurrence, in the event of encounter, in the personal visitation, whether it is that he hears the message of God, or that he serves this in proclaiming the Word and administering the sacraments. This structural beginning must be kept in sight when scholastic-ontological concepts are used in Reformation theology. They are now in another frame and no longer mean the same thing.

In the occurrence of the divine message I recognize myself as the lost sinner, as the man who has not fulfilled God's Law, who cannot put aside the spell of his guilt and has incurred God's deserved judgement of anger. And indeed I perceive not only individual sins by my being as a sinner. Each of the foregoing statements is totally valid in the visitation by God's Word. At the same time, however, I am called by the Gospel to receive justification, sanctification, life wholly without a reason in faith in Christ. In the act of faith I do not look at myself—everything I see in myself conflicts with what the Gospel awards me—but at Christ. I do not look at my act of faith but only at Christ in whom God is merciful to me. In the act of faith it is not my act of faith, my obedient acceptance of the Gospel, my withdrawal from sin, my turning to the mercy content of my faith, but the Gospel to which I cling, the promise of God who is merciful to me for Christ's sake and separates me from my sin. In the act of faith justification through faith alone and justification through Christ alone are consequently identical.

If the dogmatic statements remain in the structure of this occurrence the anthropological statements experience a characteristic limitation.[1] They are essentially statements about man as a sinner. But the statements about the righteous, the sanctified man, the man to whom life is given, are made as statements about the act of salvation by which God justifies, sanctifies and gives life to the sinner. As certainly as God justifies, sanctifies and transfers *man* to a new life, just as certainly is man a righteous, holy and living man only because God acts towards him in Christ, lets him share in the righteousness, sanctity, life of Jesus Christ. In the structure of personal encounter dogmatic statements about the permanence of the new life which had its beginning in baptism are not concerned with statements about an inherent quality or about a *habitus* which man now has. They remain rather engaged in the promise of the faithfulness of God who will complete the work begun. Just as reformed theology spoke expressly of the comforted conscience, of new impulses of the heart, of new desire for God's command, of the urge to new obedience, etc., so in these dogmatic statements it is not a question of a new quality of man but of the living working of the Holy Ghost who has descended into the hearts, at the same time Lord of the hearts, who as the gift remains at the same time the spontaneous divine giver. Man cannot boast of the workings of the spirit. He also cannot make them valid before God as the reason for justification. God bestows them merely out of mercy.

The dogmatic statement which is made in the structure of personal encounter consequently remains linked to the word

---

[1] On the question of the position from which the anthropological statements of the Lutheran creeds are formulated, cf. E. Schlink, 'Der Mensch als Sünder' (lecture at an evangelical-orthodox evangelical conference), *Ev. Theol.* 1952, p. 324ff.

by which God addresses man. It is not fortuitous that the reformation formula is not Law and Mercy but Law and Gospel. For the 'means' by which God acts towards men are above all under observation. Moreover the dogmatic statement stops at the distinction of Law and Gospel which is to be accomplished constantly anew in the act of recognition of sins and faith. Reformation theology is so gripped by the event of the divine message that it cannot go beyond the distinction encountered in it between God's demanding and bestowing, judging and saving action and cannot seek any theoretical settlement between Law and Gospel. All interest is rather directed to the fact that both messages remain acknowledged side by side unbalanced and unmingled. The sinner, whom the Law condemns, may believe that he will be saved by the Gospel without the works of the Law.

In the face of this the Tridentine decree of justification makes its statements in the structure of description (descriptio, ch. 4) and indeed of description of the human course of life from its beginning with original sin (ch. 1) to the last judgement and the attainment of eternal life as a reward for the good works accomplished by reason of grace (ch. 16).

This course is described by dealing successively with the preparation for the justification (ch. 5 and 6), with the justification in the event of baptism (ch. 7ff.), with the growth of justification in obedience towards the commandments (ch. 10ff.), with the renewed justification by the sacrament of repentance (ch. 14) and with the possibility of the loss of the grace of justification by mortal sin (ch. 15). Not only the construction but the structural basis of the dogmatic statements is different here from the Lutheran creeds. It is true that one must not misunderstand this displacement of structure, as if in the description of the human way the theological statements had been replaced by anthropological ones. Throughout the talk is strongly not only of the works, which the commands of God demand, but also of God's mercy. But the statements about God's speech and action do not occur in the structure of encounter with God's dual message as a listener, nor as statement of the 'I' disclosed and called by the addressing divine 'Thou'. The encounter of God and man is rather made here the object of consideration and description, and it will thus have emerged thoughtfully and assertively from the immediacy of the visitation of the encountering God. As the dogmatic statements about God's judging and justifying act are made in the framework of the human course of life they share in the objectivizing individuality of the consideration and description.

It is self-evident that in this structural beginning human action becomes more strongly the object of dogmatic statements. In the event of being addressed by God I recognize myself as the lost sinner; but I do not recognize myself as a righteous man when I look at myself, but only in faith in Christ whose righteousness the Gospel awards me. In the consideration and description of this event there occur with increasing importance statements not only about man as a sinner but also about the process of the perception of sin, and statements not only about the righteousness of Christ awarded to faith but also about the process of faith. There now arises the interest of describing this process as completely as possible in its connexion with love, hope, turning away from sin, new resolution, etc., and to protect it by such a description as exists in the Tridentine statements about the *modus praeparationis* (ch. 6) from a corruption which is seen in the Protestant idea of *sola fide*. But the Protestant statement did not serve a description but served the invitation promulgated through the Gospel to receive righteousness as a sinner without all special presuppositions. Moreover the reflecting consideration and description of the process which prepares for justification does not stop with the process itself but questions behind it the possibilities which man has of being able to prepare himself for justification. In contrast to the reformers the freedom of fallen man is taught without which that preparation appears impossible. The Protestant *servum arbitrium*, however, was not primarily a statement of theological reflection but the confession of the sinner that he cannot break through the spell of guilt and forlornness by any act of his own.

From the structural beginning of the description results further that the effects of grace in man become more strongly the subject of dogmatic statements than is the case in the act of listening and believing. If it is decisive in this act that through the Gospel the *iustitia aliena* of Jesus Christ is awarded to me a sinner, then an increasing interest arises from the fact that God's righteousness is poured into man and becomes his righteousness (Denz. 809). If in the actual encounter with God it is a question of His turning mercifully to me for Christ's sake, in the structure of description and reflection it is increasingly a question of grace as a *habitus* of man which makes good works possible for him. The statements about the personal working of the Holy Spirit are replaced by statements about the merciful new nature of man. Thus 'a certain anthropocentricity'[1] on the Tridentine decree of justification cannot be overlooked. It is not to be confused with the structurally quite different definite 'pro me' of reformation theology.

These shifts bring with them a shift in the statement of the problem in general. If in the reformation creeds it is a question of the difference, encountered in God's message and irremovable by any theological reflection, of God's demand and consolation, challenge and gift, judgement and justification, then in the structure of the Tridentine consideration and reflection there results as a basic problem the relationship of God's mercy and human obedience with regard to the goal of salvation which is to be attained and beyond that the relationship between the possibilities of human freedom and the possibilities by God's mercy. It is now not a question of the ever new discovery of the difference of Law and Gospel but of a definition of the relationship between divine and human action which is free from contradiction.

Important differences in content correspond to the different structure of the dogmatic statement. I shall explain these briefly in the following groups of concepts:

a) The judgement of the Law and the judgement of the Gospel: By the judgement of the Law God determines what man has done and judges him according to his deeds. By the judgement of the Gospel God declares the godless to be righteous, awards the sinner what does not correspond to his deeds. Moreover this judgement is not only the establishment of a principle that the godless is held to be righteous; it is also a creative active word of God: God makes the godless righteous. Accordingly the apology of the Augsburg Confession in agree-

[1] H. Küng, *Rechtfertigung, die Lehre Karl Barths und eine katholische Besinnung*, 1957, p. 20.

ment with Luther understood the declaration of justification at the same time as the renewal of the sinner. This deep-seated difference between the analytical judgement of the Law and the synthetic judgement of the Gospel has been portrayed throughout by the Reformation creeds which dispense with a theoretical adjustment. The justifying judgement of the judgement of the Law formally suited the Tridentine doctrine, however; the righteous declaration follows as an analytical judgement by reason of the mercy which has been dispensed, namely: 'according to the measure which the Holy Ghost apportions to the individual' (ch. 7). In the act of justification the effects of grace and judgement are so adjusted to each other that the effect of grace makes possible the analytical judgement of the declaration of justification.[1]

b) Man under the judgement of the Law and under the consolation of the Gospel: under the Law man recognizes that he has not only sinned but that he is a sinner and indeed as a whole man with all his thoughts, words and works. He cannot in any way exist before God and must agree with God's judgement of damnation. Through the Gospel, however, there takes place the salvation of the sinner from the divine judgement of anger, there is promulgated to the sinner his acquittal at the coming last judgement. In faith in the Gospel the sinner knows he is justified and accepted by God as a whole man. All his further life is surrounded by this eschatological acquittal, even though he prays daily anew for the forgiveness of sins. The reformation creeds retained both the totality of statements on the confession of sin and that of statements of the belief in justification. The Tridentine doctrine has also made an adjustment here by introducing quantitative concepts: man is righteous according to the 'measure' of the Spirit given to him (ch. 7), he 'grows and becomes more righteous' according to the co-operation of faith and good works (ch. 10). It corresponds to this that the reformation formula *simul peccator et iustus* undergoes today a change of interpretation in the sense of *partim peccator–partim iustus*,[2] even where it is kindly admitted by Roman Catholic theologians.

[1] Cf. Thomas, *Summa theologica*, II, 1, qu. 114, art. 8.
[2] H. U. v. Balthasar, Karl Barth, 1951, p. 378ff. and H. Küng, *loc. cit.* p. 231ff.

c) Faith and works: the justification of the sinner takes place without his works through faith[1] in the Gospel. It is demanded of the righteous man that he does works of righteousness in obedience to God's command. The reformers spoke of faith in thoroughly active expressions: faith seizes the divine promise, it holds to it, it ventures with it; faith is an intention, a turning of the self to Christ, an 'active thing'. But however emphatically they also called to decision and to the act of faith, in the event of justification faith is merely passive, pure acceptance of the act of salvation which God in Christ accomplishes in the sinner through the Gospel. All active statements are here only statements of need and desire. The difference between trusting and accepting faith in the Gospel and the new obedience of faith to God's commands is retained in all its rigour by the reformation creeds. The Tridentine doctrine, however, eliminates the difference here too. In the statements about the preparation of justification (ch. 6), but completely in the chapters of the growth of justification (10) and of the final justification in the last judgement (16) it already adds human action to faith, indeed it expressly rejects the understanding of faith as mere trust in the mercy of God who forgives the sinner for Christ's sake (can. 12–14).

d) The certainty of salvation and the fear of judgement: without being equated in theory the proclamation of the eschatological acquittal and the announcement of judgement according to works are side by side in the Pauline proclamation. On the justifying verdict of the Gospel is based the certainty of the believers that no one can accuse them and nothing can separate them from the love of God—a certainty which bridges the distance between the now and the final judgement still to be expected and at the same time includes the election preceding the call (Rom. VIII. 29ff.). The intimation of judgement according to works holds good for the same believers: even if they are conscious of no disobedience they are not justified in it (I Cor. IV. 4). They are called to earn eschatological salvation in fear and trembling (Phil. II. 12). Reformation theology has retained both, the certainty of faith and un-

---

[1] The formula 'by faith alone' is first found, as is known, not in the reformers but previously, e.g., in Basil, Chrysostom, Cyril of Alexandria and Augustine among others.

certainty on account of works, and rejected a *securitas* of the Christian. In faith in the Gospel and in the recognition of the deserved judgement the creeds teach the *certitudo salutis*. The Tridentine doctrine of justification, however, systematically settled both opposing statements in declining for the sake of the judgement according to works not only the *securitas* but also the *certitudo* and in confining the certainty of election to the questionable special case of private revelation.[1]

In the definition of the relationship of each one of the four named pairs of concepts the reformers taught the distinction and renounced a theoretical resolution of the contradictions.[2] If both statements in spite of this do not at a given time become completely incompatible it is not on account of a theoretical adjustment, nor only because in both it is a question of the same God and the same man, but because God's *true* message comes to us in the *Gospel* by which he allows us to flee to the crucified one in view of the Law. This theoretical inconclusiveness of dogmatic statements is determined by listening to this dual message of God which is at the same time exuberant in its consolation, for whose judging and saving freedom room is left open. In the Tridentine statements also it is a question of the prevenience and prevalence of grace. Grace begins to work on man through the calling, without

---

[1] The limits of the special structure of the Tridentine doctrine of justification were clearly visible in the speech of Seripandos of October 8th, 1546, on the question of the final justification of the last judgement. 'One cannot speak about it from the point of view of speculation, but practically, not as a pure systematizer, but as a pious Christian! And with all seriousness he considers each of the fathers individually with the decision of conscience on which everything depends: "Will you, if you will step up to the judgement seat of God, be judged severely according to right and righteousness based on works which you believe to have done in the mercy of God?" If man considers the position properly he must—thinks Seripando —perceive the truth of the word of Augustine: "woe also to the most pious man if God tested him without mercy!"' (Hanns Rückert, *Die Rechtfertigungslehre auf dem Tridentinischen Konzil von Trent*, Vol. II, 1957, p. 209). But 'just as the support which the Christian conscience gives to the adherents of dual righteousness appears to be strong, so it is weak, if placed under the magnifying glass of severely theological consideration' (ibid. p. 215).

[2] On the peculiarity of the theological paradox in view of the logical concepts of antinomy, aporia, absurdity, ineffability, etc., as well as the theological concept of vexation, cf. H. Schröer, *Die Denkform der Paradoxalität als theologisches Problem*, 1960.

N

merits existing in him, and only through grace can man turn to righteousness before God (ch. 5). In other parts of the decree of justification also the knowledge of grace, which is shared in spite of the demands of the Law, is not lacking. But while the Council of Trent departs in the structure of its statements from the event of divine speech and action and makes this the subject of consideration, description and declaration and strives beyond the recognition of the difference in God's speech and action for a systematically concluded definition of relationship, this happens in each of the four cited groups of concepts in the horizon of the Law, namely in diminishing adaptation of the statements about the verdict of justification, justified man, faith and the certainty of salvation to the judgement, the challenge and the announcement of the judgement of the Law. In this matter the Council of Trent not only continues that old weakening of the Pauline distinction of Law and Gospel[1] which began already with the apostolic fathers, but beyond that it is true in principle that the Law by its nature offers a logically more consistent frame for a systematically closed way of thinking than the Gospel in which God's incomprehensible generous mercy breaks into the world which exists under the Law.

We may, however, add to this comparison the reference to the fact that the old Protestant orthodoxy unfortunately did not stop at making their dogmatic statements in the act of listening to the dual message of God. Rather it went over to separating the doctrine of the appropriation of salvation (*de gratia spiritus sancti applicatrice*) from the article on Law and Gospel (*de mediis salutis*) and to developing it descriptively in the erection of an *ordo salutis*, whereby the law here too protected the systematic representation of the statements in a form different to that of the Council of Trent. From this transition to description it was an obvious step, if pietism made the statements about grace in an emphatic manner often disengaged from the means of grace statements about *experiences* of grace, which had been far removed from both the reformers[2]

---

[1] Cf. Thomas F. Torrance, *The Doctrine of Grace in the Apostolic Fathers*, 1948, and V. E. Hasler, *Gesetz und Evangelium in der alten Kirche bis Origenes*, 1953.

[2] Thus the Lutheran theology of the 19th and 20th centuries had to

and the Council of Trent. But the more the statements about God's encounter with men are made statements about human experiences the more individual differences of the religious experience of individual persons or groups or even epochs hasten to step in in place of the dogma and further schisms always result.

e) Dogmatic statements may not be compared with one another as timeless and isolated statements. We must rather bear in mind (i) their place in the midst of other statements of the Church; (ii) their historical situation; (iii) their conception and (iv) their structure. To the comparison of different dogmatic statements belongs consequently a questioning and seeking which breaks through the mere wording, namely the attempt to transpose them from the one historical situation into the other, from the one conception into the other, from the one way of thinking and structure of statement into the other, etc. This task of transposition is valid for every controversial theological theme. But it is scarcely anywhere so difficult as with the theme Law and Gospel. For here fundamental difficulties of dogmatic formulation are opened up, which were foreign to the Christological and trinitarian dogmas of the Early Church.

The root of Church dogma is the confession of Christ and consequently the doxology. In the doxology it is possible to speak 'objectively'. Its content is Jesus Christ himself, without any talk in it of historically changing men who make the confession. The doxological confession of Christ was developed by statements about the story of Jesus (birth, death, resurrection), thus by statements of historical tradition. Even here the talk can be 'objective', for these acts are accomplished once for all and they are well known without explicit statements being made about historically changing men who make this confession. Even the later Christological and trinitarian dogma contains according to its nature only statements which praise the triune God in His eternal sameness and Jesus Christ as true God and true man, as God's son, who became man once for all for the sake of our salvation. In dogmatic statements

pursue afresh the difference of Law and Gospel not only in critical argument with enlightenment but also with old Protestant orthodoxy and pietism. For the history of this argument cf. R. C. Schultz, *Gesetz und Evangelium*, 1958.

about Law and Gospel, however, it is not a question of doxological statements of being, nor of statements of doctrine about God's once-for-all accomplished acts in history, but of God's constantly new act towards men in their historical situation at any given time, namely of God's constantly new dual call and working in the historical diversity of the obligations of man and his attempts, whether by libertinism or by legalism, to withdraw from the divine call. Here it is a question of dogmatic statements about the constantly new encounter in which God speaks to men, challenging and giving, and in which man has to answer from his historical position at any given time both words of the divine message.

In view of the difficulties which this theme offers to dogmatic formulation it is not surprising that dogmas about it originated only late, even though the Church actually dealt with this theme from the beginning in sermon, pastoral care and church orders. It is not surprising that many Churches here have not achieved any formal dogmatic decision and that on the other hand the dogmas which have been formulated on this are peculiarly susceptible to disorganization so that more schisms have arisen over just these questions in Christendom than over others. Accordingly controversial theological discussion of these differences is especially in danger of hardening or of slipping into relativism.

How is one to set about the task of translation? It must be kept firmly in sight that dogmatic statements about Law and Gospel are not equally elementary statements with the confession of Christ and even the trinitarian confession which has its seat in the worshipping life of the Church and is repeated in the liturgy. It is rather a question here of dogmatic statements *about* elementary statements of the Church, namely about the proclamation of Law and Gospel. Thus the different dogmatic statements about Law and Gospel are not compared directly with one another, but they must be translated back *into the elementary statements of the proclamation itself* which they are intended to serve.

In this sense these questions can for example be put to the Tridentine doctrine of justification: what does the out-pouring of mercy as a basis for the verdict of justification mean in the proclamation—is the foundation context not resolved in the act of proclamation in the unity of God's justifying act? What do the quantitative statements about the more or less of being justified mean in the listening to God's Word—does each Christian not wholly acknowledge himself in the act of listening to be a sinner, and does he not believe that he is accepted by God as a whole man, as a person? What do *habitus, qualitas, iustitia inhaerens* mean in the listening to the proclamation—is the believer not referred here to the faithfulness of the merciful God who will complete what He has begun in him? What does the rejection of the *certitudo* mean in the proclamation—should not perhaps only the *securitas* be rejected here? What does the description of faith in its connexion with love, hope, etc., mean in the proclamation—is the invitation no less than the demand of God not proclaimed here?

Only in the attempt to translate back in this way are the elementary statements produced which actually determine the life of the Church and which must be compared between the Churches. Doubtless many dogmatic contrasts will lose in sharpness and perhaps even be dissolved in such a translation of the statements *about* the proclamation into statements *of the* proclamation itself. There remains of course the fact that the Council of Trent is silent[1] about the Gospel as the justifying word of action of God and that it made its dogmatic statements one-sidedly in the front against antinomianism, but not with regard to the consciences terrified under the Law.

f) In addition to this we must finally ask whether all the structures of the statement are adapted in the same way so that dogmatic statements about God's speech and action through Law and Gospel can be made. This question can be denied already in principle. For the multiplicity of the structures of the theological statement forms a cosmos in which each one has particular functions and possibilities of statement and in which none can replace the other. The structure of prayer is different from that of witness, that of the doxology different from that of doctrine; it is true that they are all concentrated in the structure of the creed and yet the creed

---

[1] This gap is beginning today to be seen also by Roman Catholic theologians; cf. J. Betz, 'Wort und Sakrament' (in *Verkündigung und Glaube*, Festgabe für F. X. Arnold, 1958, p. 76ff.) and K. Rahner, 'Wort und Eucharistie' (in *Aktuelle Fragen zur Eucharistie*, 1960, p. 7ff.).

does not make the other statements superfluous. Law and Gospel, however, are to be heard and proclaimed, baptism and last supper are to be received and bestowed. Thus those dogmatic statements about the appropriation of salvation are most adequate which remain as close as possible to the structure of the listening acceptance of word and sacrament. The more theological thinking and statements are removed from this structure the greater becomes the danger that the difference between Law and Gospel, on which our salvation depends—whether at the expense of the Gospel or the Law, but mostly at the expense of the Gospel—is weakened or even dissolved in theoretical determination of relationship, that man gets a significance beyond the confession of sins of the believer which competes with God's merciful works, or that even, as in pietism and in Schleiermacher, the statements about God's demanding and bestowing act of salvation will be continuously replaced by a description of the pious frames of mind of man. It remains to observe that in the New Testament scriptures the statements about justification, second birth, new obedience and the fruits of the spirit are made only rarely in general sentences about God and man, but as a rule in the form of testimony, consolation admonition and warning and that a theoretical solution of the contradictions contained in them is renounced. The logically unbalanced New Testament dialectic of indicative and imperative is the adequate form also of the dogmatic treatment of our problem. In this structure can be expressed simultaneously what is to be said in face of legalism and antinomianism. That in the Tridentine structure of description the problem of this determination of relationship cannot ultimately be solved is shown by the history of the dispute between Molinism and Thomism at the turn of the 16th and 17th century, which could until today not be ended by a dogmatic decision but solely by Papal prohibition of the continuation of this dispute.

The ecumenical significance of the Lutheran difference of Law and Gospel lies in the fact that here this theme which is actually central for the Church has been made the content of dogmatic statements and that these statements have been formulated in such direct relation to God's dual speech and action that space is left open for the freedom of God's saving action. The structure of the personal encounter in the Word is obviously not the only one in which the dogma of the Church is to be formulated. For the dogmatic statements about God's message in Law and Gospel it is however the appropriate structure.

VI. APOSTOLIC SUCCESSION[1]

A FELLOWSHIP OF MUTUAL SERVICE

'APOSTOLIC SUCCESSION' generally means the succession and authority of the ecclesiastical ministry, founded on the apostolic ministry which is historically unique, and growing out of it through the whole of Church history. This succession can be described in the following alternative ways:

a) It is the unbroken succession of the laying-on of hands by bishops, beginning with the Apostles. This is sometimes understood to be a matter of pure form without the need of a '*consensus de doctrina*'. This is at least in the thought of some Anglicans, though by no means all.

b) It is the unbroken succession of the episcopal laying-on of hands together with the transmission of the apostolic teaching and order. The Orthodox, the Roman Catholic and to a certain extent the Anglican Churches seem to uphold this idea.

c) It is the unbroken succession of a 'presbyteral' laying-on of hands (by this we mean from pastor to pastor), as well as the transmission of the apostolic teaching and order. Some Scots theologians accept this interpretation.

d) It is the transmission of the apostolic teaching from office-holder to office-holder. In this view the successive laying-on of hands by bishops is considered as non-essential, though it belongs to succession as an important sign. This is how one could describe an interpretation widely held in the Lutheran Church of Sweden. This understanding is also found in some areas of the Church of South India.

e) One can even go further and think of apostolic succession without holding any mechanical view of an unbroken chain of laying-on of hands. One would then simply describe it as the communication of apostolic teaching from one office-holder to the next. This definition is not common, and generally the successive laying-on of hands belongs to the very concept of apostolic succession, whatever way it may be done or interpreted.

[1] Originally publishedin *Encounter*, Vol. 25, no. 1, pp. 50-83.

We should not forget that the doctrine of all the Churches is not just concerned with the ecclesiastical ministry as far as it is built on the apostolic foundation, but mainly with the apostolic Church itself, in all its different aspects.

This apostolic Church, however, is not only the Church of the apostolic age, but also the Church of all ages. It is the whole Church which has been built upon the Apostles' foundation. If then we are to confess with the Nicene Creed that the whole Church is an apostolic Church, we have not only to tackle the problem of the apostolic succession as far as the ministry is concerned, but also the problem of apostolic succession as far as it concerns the Church itself. It cannot be reduced to a concern with the way in which the apostolic ministry can be transmitted from one group or generation to another. It is the whole Church, i.e. each of its members, which is told by St. Paul to be 'his imitators' (I Cor. IV. 16; I Thess. I. 6). The apostolicity of the Church cannot be limited to a historical study of what is meant by the word 'apostle', nor can it be reduced to a succession of ministers. We must deal with the apostolic succession of the Church *and* of the ministry, of the ministry *and* of the Church. Both belong together. We thus describe our theme more closely under the title: 'The apostolic succession of the Church and of its ministry'. The ecclesiological relevance of the question of apostolic succession (in the narrow sense of an unbroken chain of episcopal laying-on of hands) can only be appreciated when these two themes are studied together.

Sections 1 to 4 will deal with the question of Charisms[1] and the ministry, sections 5 to 8 with the Church and the mission of the Apostles. Section 9 will deal with the Church and the ministry. In section 10 we shall draw some conclusions from our study which may help us in our understanding of the apostolic succession.

1. *The Church as a Fellowship of Charisms*

The Church has been built on the foundation of the Apostles, and began with the outpouring of the Holy Spirit

---

[1] The word 'charisms', though not a natural English word, is used throughout this essay as the equivalent of the Greek '*charismata*'. 'Gifts of grace' and 'spiritual gifts' are perhaps the nearest English approximation.

who made all its members into witnesses of the great works of God in Christ. This witness of the prophetic, priestly and royal people of God is similar to a mixed choir, in which the voices sing in harmony rather than in unison. All the New Testament writings witness to the fact that the Holy Spirit has been given to all the members of the Church. The Book of Acts insists particularly on the fact that public witness is the result of the work of the Spirit in all the Church members. But it is Paul who emphasizes especially that the general out-pouring of the Holy Spirit results in a variety of gifts. Thus, each believer has been granted a particular spiritual gift. One and the same Spirit apportions to each one individually as he wills (I Cor. xii. 11, cf. v. 7). We can also refer to the First Epistle of Peter (iv. 10) in which one takes for granted that each individual member of the congregation has received a particular charism. The variety of the spiritual gifts is of such basic importance to Paul, that we could not simply limit the scope of his statements to the Churches in Corinth or Rome or even to the Pauline congregations of the Early Church. No, the variety of spiritual gifts is an attribute of all Churches at all times, in all places. As the 'body of Christ', the Church is an organism with many gifts and duties. Paul has stated this in such general terms, that we cannot make it relevant to one period of history only. It must be taken up into the doctrine of the Church and ministry, even though this variety of gifts may not have been mentioned in the other New Testament writings.

Each believer receives his particular gift from a totally free Spirit. We are not told that the members of the congregations are given their gifts according to a certain pattern. It is true that all have received the Spirit from the moment they first believed and were baptized. The same Spirit is working in and through those who take part in worship and who are members of the Christian fellowship. One can come forward to receive baptism and the Lord's Supper, but the Spirit is completely free to decide which actual gift each individual believer should receive. No mention is made of a particular way according to which one could be assured of a particular gift. We have to allow for all kinds of possibilities: Charisms can be received at the moment when the message of the Gospel is accepted by faith, or at baptism, or by laying-on of hands in connexion with baptism or by a later hearing of the Gospel message or in partaking in the Lord's Supper, or even apart from any special action, as an answer to prayer and supplication. The gifts of the Spirit also appear suddenly when a congregation is in special need and God has pity on it and bestows on it spiritual gifts. The believer should indeed pray for these gifts, and especially in order to receive the greatest of them all (I Cor. XII. 31; XIV. 1).

The variety of spiritual gifts is taught clearly in the list of charisms in I Corinthians XII. 4–20; XII. 28–30 and Romans XII. 6–8, as well as in Ephesians IV. 11. These lists of gifts have to be distinguished from the list of the fruits of the Spirit which we find in Galatians V. 22, for it will be noted that the charisms are distributed among the various members of the congregation, whereas the fruits of the Spirit like love, peace and joy are expected of every Christian. But we should be careful not to make too much of this distinction (compare also the passage from I Cor. XII to I Cor. XIII, and also the verses following Rom. XII. 9, in which love is again spoken of).

In the passage that follows we shall briefly extract the lessons we can learn from the list of charisms which are especially relevant to the question of apostolic succession:

a) It is obvious that we cannot draw up a specific catalogue of spiritual gifts which would be valid for congregations in all places, and we may add, at all times. If we compare Romans XII. 6ff. with I Corinthians XII. 4ff., we immediately notice that over and above the list in Corinthians, Romans adds *diakonia* (in the narrow sense of the term) *paraklesis* (comfort), mercy and understanding. On the other hand, speaking in tongues, healing, miracles, discernment of spirits and '*logos sophias*' are missing in Romans but prominent in Corinthians. It is not that at all times, all the gifts are found in all congregations, but that every individual member of every congregation can expect, at any time, some spiritual gift.

b) In all the lists of charisms, we find some sort of order of gifts, each charism has a certain rank. The specifically kerygmatic spiritual gifts come first: in I Corinthians XII. 8, the word of wisdom and the word of knowledge; in I Corinthians XII. 28, Apostles, prophets and teachers; in Romans XII prophecy and in Ephesians IV. 11 Apostles, prophets and evangelists. As a contrast, we note (and this is very remarkable) that the spiritual gift of the administrator (I Cor. XII. 28), of the leader (Rom. XII. 8), of the pastor (Eph. IV. 11) are mentioned later, after the specifically kerygmatic gifts and even sometimes after the gifts of healing and other services. It is true that in Ephesians IV. 11 the pastors come before the teachers, but they follow the prophets and evangelists.

c) In both the lists of charisms of I Corinthians XII. 28 and Ephesians IV, we find the Apostles first. The Apostles are not adduced here because of their special call (an aspect which is generally emphasized in other passages) but because of their being empowered by the charisms of the Holy Spirit to lay the foundation of the Churches. In fact, the various charisms are concentrated in the person of Paul in a unique way. He is prophet, teacher, miracle worker; he can speak in tongues, has the gift of leadership, etc.

d) It is already clear that we cannot draw too clear a distinction between the different charisms. A prophet can at the same time be a teacher. In Acts XIII. 1 ff., we see how closely prophets and teachers co-operate, as all of them send Paul and Barnabas on their missionary journey.

e) In the lists of charisms we find statements, some of which describe the effect of spiritual gifts and others of which describe the work of particular persons. Thus, I Corinthians XII. 28 begins with vocational designations such as Apostle, prophet, and teacher, going on to mention miraculous powers, gifts of healing, etc. This interchange of vocational designations and descriptions of the effect of the gifts is also found in Romans XII. We learn from the particular vocational designations that the gifts of the Spirit may be given freely by the Spirit but that they do not come and go haphazardly, and neither do they jump casually from one person to the next. On the contrary, the actual spiritual gifts are so constant that it is possible to use them as qualifications of particular persons.

f) One should not overlook the fact that all the charisms serve the Word, that is they are witnesses to the salvation God wrought in Christ, even though some of them (the specifically kerygmatic charisms) come first and others (service and other 'powers and helps') come last. The charisms which are not specifically kerygmatic are also related to the Word, they reveal the image of Christ and may be described as the radiance of the *Logos*. For all the charisms result from the power of Christ; they appear in the power of His name; they are a tangible manifestation of the witness: 'Jesus is Lord'. In the variety of spiritual gifts therefore we find the fullness of the one Christ realized in the congregation, and through the congregation in the world. The variety of charisms can appear according to different patterns in different congregations and at different times, but it is always the manifestation of the one *charis* (grace) of Jesus Christ. He is the head of the body, the bearer and origin of all the charisms and they, in turn, are all ordained to serve Him and are the manifestation of the power of His name, to which they witness either this or that way. Thus, the fellowship of all the charisms exists because all of them are part of the one charis of Jesus Christ. Christ Himself is the real bearer of all those charisms. He is the one Apostle, the one teacher and evangelist, shepherd and minister of the new covenant. He is the leader of His Church because He is the head of His body; He is the revealer of the divine power because He is the origin of all power, miracles and signs of Christendom. The Church is therefore the 'fellowship of the spiritual gifts', for all have a part in the grace of Jesus Christ. *Koinonia* means the part the believer has in God's gift. *Koinonia* is therefore not directly a fellowship in our sense of the word, but means rather a sharing, and in this sharing, the communion of those who share together.

g) This variety of charisms is at the same time the variety of the services which the different members of the congregation can render to each other, all the more since every charism received is a sign of a sharing in the grace of Christ. It is not only for the service of God, but also for the service of the brethren that the gifts are given: 'As each has received a gift, employ it for one another' (I Pet. IV. 10). This mutual service which each renders to the other appears especially when the brethren meet for worship. The worth of each charism is measured according to its meaning for the assembled congregation and according to its edification-value. A charism is to be honoured in proportion to the service it can render to others. This is why love is called the 'most precious way' by Luther when he translated I Corinthians XII. 31. Spiritual disorder and arbitrariness are forbidden by the Apostle, that is by Christ Himself. The spiritual gifts are considered to be valid as long as they are freely and totally subordinated to the Body of Christ, and they are understood to be functions of '*Agape*'. According to the very essence of the Church, the service rendered to the brethren and therefore to the congregation, must also be rendered with all the brethren to the whole world. Every charism is service in the Church and this is at the same time, service on the frontier between the Church and the world.

h) This is why the congregation must make room for the spiritual gifts in its midst. They have to be proved, of course; one has to judge them and discern them according to their use for the edification of the Church; one has to assign values to them; and in some cases, as in the speaking of tongues, one may even have to repress them. False spirits have to be completely excluded. But Paul is always worried lest 'the Spirit be quenched' and his appeal that 'we should earnestly desire spiritual gifts' is a clear confession of his concern.

2. *The Commission to Serve*

Every ministry and service in the Church presupposes a calling and a commission which stem from the Gospel itself. The Gospel calls us to leave the world and become the new people of God, and then it sends this prophetic, priestly and royal people back into the world. All the members of the new people of God are subordinated to the rule of the Spirit by the Gospel and through baptism. The Spirit gives freely; each can receive a particular charism and thus be enlisted in His service. But baptism is the same for all whereas the spiritual gifts which are bestowed on the Christian at baptism, or at a later time, differ. We always pray for one and the same Spirit to come, but it pleases Him to give Himself to everyone in a different way in His free spiritual gifts. Thus a variety of spiritual gifts appear afresh time and again in the Church as a result of the work of the one Gospel and the one baptism. Yet, though each member of the Church has been called by the same word and the same baptism, they all receive a different charism. Thus, in general, we cannot say that the actual charism has been preceded by a particular and specific word of calling. We should rather say that the free spiritual gift of Christ really irrupts into the congregation and among its individual members without a specific word of calling, so that its concreteness must later be recognized as a given reality.

We have now to distinguish between this general vocation to become a member of the people of God and to serve Him, and the more individual vocation to render a *particular* service, a call which gives authority. We have to distinguish the service proceeding from an actual call addressed by the Church which gives the necessary authority for its accomplishment, e.g. the basic service of the Apostle from the variety of freely appearing services and charisms which can come to all believers. In the first case we have an actual word which is addressed to the believer, which meets him and sends him out. It is not only an inner compulsion which drives him to that particular service, but a specific command which is addressed to that individual man, enlisting him to serve in a given situation. Now, all charisms come not from man but from God. But they are effective and manifest themselves by giving an inner compulsion to him that he should engage in a specific piece of service. The task of the commission is to give a tangible word which meets with man, so to speak, from without, remains above him, and continually demands his obedience in the service in which he has been set. Each Christian receives a charism, but not every Christian receives such a specific task. This actual call, ordination, and power can be summarized in the terms 'special commission'. In the Acts of the Apostles we often read about such 'special commissioners' as well as in the Pastoral Epistles; in the commonly accepted Pauline Epistles we hear curiously little about them (with the exception of II Corinthians VIII. 19).

This commissioning of particular Church members for a special service is often spoken of in the New Testament as taking place by the laying-on of hands. It is well known that this was taken over from the recognized Old Testament method of appointment which was continued in the ordination of Jewish scholars. We can therefore surmise that from the very beginning of the Palestinian communities, one finds people being called and ordained by the laying-on of hands, and that this practice really took place even when it is not mentioned in so many words, as in Acts xiv. 23. We have of course to be careful not to imagine that every special calling was accompanied by laying-on of hands, just as we should not think that every statement in the New Testament concerning Church order in a particular congregation or mission area can be extended to include the whole Church.

What particular service was expected of those 'special commissioners' according to the New Testament? They were not commissioned for healing, nor for miracles, nor for the different forms of witness such as the 'word of wisdom' or the 'word of knowledge' (I Corinthians xii. 8). Nor do we hear of the gift of tongues as being imparted through a particular laying-on of hands in the Pauline writings. On the contrary, the details concerning 'special commissions' describe, above all, the service of establishing Churches through mission work and Church leadership, as well as such assistance as may be given in this work. The task of planting Churches through missionary activity and Church leadership corresponds to the service to which the Apostles were being called. They were not charismatic people who came forward voluntarily and to whom the congregation would later say 'yes' and 'amen'; their actual commission came first, before the charismatic ministry. True, they had been called by the risen Lord, but all the later calls came through human beings. In this way, we recognize that all the later commissions are different from the apostolic commission. They are not calls to be Apostles; they are commissions to follow after the Apostles and to continue their ministry.

In this particular commission, we should stress the following key-points:

a) The commission is not simply left to the will of men, even though it takes place through their agency. This is most clearly demonstrated by the election which takes place before the laying-on of hands. The New Testament indicates clearly that the call, the commission and the transmission of the Spirit are in no case at man's disposal, but the commissioners fast and pray, asking the Holy Spirit to come down upon all, not just for Him to fill the one who has been called, but also to fill those who have to do the commissioning. For the recognition of the spiritual gifts in those who are to be called, presupposes in itself the presence of the Spirit who alone can discern between those gifts and recognize them. This presupposition of the Spirit's presence in the commissioners is specially important when the particular spiritual gift has to be asked for through prayer, not just to be recognized as having already been given to the candidate. The guidance of the Holy Spirit is attested as being of paramount importance, as He is calling, ordaining and showing to the congregation the person whom He wants to be sent. This is how the witness of the prophets in choosing has to be understood, in Acts xiii. 1ff., I Timothy i. 18, and iv. 14. Thus, the Spirit indicates charismatically whom He wants to be sent, and also where He wants to be sent.

b) In this commissioning, the word of man and his hands are tools of the Lord who sends. God is calling through the mouth and the hand of the Church as if it were His instrument. This is already the sense we give to the story of Matthias in Acts i. 24ff.: the lot is cast in order that God should choose, and not men. Compare also Acts xiii. 2: the Holy Spirit, and through Him the Lord Himself, is asking for a 'setting apart' and informs the congregation as to the names of those He has called. The prophets and teachers send them off after laying their hands on them, but after that we read again that Saul and Barnabas are sent off by the Holy Spirit. Thus men are but organs, so to speak, as we also see from Acts xx. 28 where it is the Holy Spirit who has commissioned.

c) God authorizes through His call, but two things have to be distinguished in this authorization:

Special commission as a definite acceptance of the service which an already existing charism can render. Compare Acts vi. 3: 'Pick out from among you seven men of good repute full of the Spirit and wisdom, whom you may appoint to this duty'. Compare also the teaching of the Pastoral Epistles concerning the qualities of those who are to be ordained bishops. In these passages, a charism, or according to the Pastoral Epistles at least an aptitude to learn, is already present

o

together with the commission, and this is taken up into the new form of service.[1]

For the special commission, God gives in addition to all this, the particular charism which enables a man to become a shepherd. The call to a particular service gives to the believer, guided as he is by the Spirit of God, because of his faith, the special gift which he needs for the specific service into which God is calling him. The call itself is not a command of the Law but of the Gospel. The Gospel is the power of God, it is the 'act-word' of God. Thus the commission itself becomes also the power of God. It partakes of the essence of the New Testament imperative which builds upon the indicative mood and contains in itself the grace which is necessary to fulfil the command. Thus the laying-on of hands is not an empty sign, but through it we see that what has been commanded by God and asked for in prayer, is appropriated effectively. The laying-on of hands at the commissioning has, however, to be distinguished from other kinds of laying-on of hands which are described in the New Testament, as bringing healing or imparting the Holy Spirit after baptism. But the charism for the specific service into which a member of the congregation is sent is only given by prayer and laying-on of hands, just as in all these other actions, the New Testament shows that what has been asked for is given by a laying-on of hands. 'Ordination was not considered as a simple formality or a symbolic action, but it was an act which mediated the Spirit' (J. Jeremias). This enables us to have confidence in our ordination, and also we look back to an ordination which we have received in the past. It makes possible the comforting assurance: 'I have been called, I have been sent, and this happened through the external word; I may know that this external word is not a word from the Law, neither an empty word of promise, but a word made effective by the Spirit'. The ordinand has the knowledge that his 'ministry charisms' will

[1] The significance of the laying-on of hands, however, should not be generalized, and we should not exclude the possibility of understanding it as an act which mediates the Spirit to the person receiving ordination. R. Sohm made this mistake when he said: 'The laying-on of hands presupposes that the charism which will enable the receiver to be a teacher is already in him. The laying-on of hands is therefore not the cause of the charism but presupposes it' (see *Kirchenrecht*, I (1892), p. 63).

give him the strength to proclaim the Gospel rightly, and he can, in this certainty: 'rekindle the gift of God which is within through the laying-on of hands' (II Tim. 1. 6).[1]

d) Just as the word of men calls people to join the people of God, so it calls particular members of this people to render a particular service. Who is doing the calling? Of course, members of the Church only, but which members? Two lines must be distinguished:

The New Testament writings tell, on the one hand, that those who have been specially called to service and have been sent, have effectively called others and given them a special commission. Compare Acts xiv. 23 where Paul and Barnabas establish elders in Asia Minor, or Titus 1. 5 where Titus, who has himself been called to be a fellow-worker of Paul's (II Cor. viii. 19), is given the task of establishing elders. In I Timothy v. 22, it is said that Timothy, who was himself

---

[1] This aspect has been neglected by research and was driven into the background in the Protestant concept of ordination at the time of the Reformation. This is basically due to the necessary debate with the Roman Catholic concept of priestly ordination prayers. For instance, Luther is reported to have prayed at the ordination of Nicholas von Armsdorf, who became bishop of Naumburg, in clear terms, indicating that in this laying-on of hands, which was accompanied by prayer, 'there is a definite coming and calling of the Paraclete. This calling of the Holy Spirit becomes a blessing; the hands which are laid on the ordinand are blessing hands. This blessing signifies in a visible way, that the ordinand is given strength, courage, and comfort for the carrying out of the ministry which is now on him. . . .' Over and above this particular rite of ordination, it should be generally recognized that, according to Luther, ordination is: 'A confirmation in the presence of the whole church, of the vocation, the effective commission and the blessing to take up a ministry; by it, a person is finally and definitely set up as a minister (by God). Thus the laying-on of hands has not only a judicial significance, but means that a blessing has been given, which comes as a result of the prayer of ordination.' Melanchthon taught as follows: 'The meaning of ordination lies in the fact that the vocation is recognized openly '*de jure*', by other '*ministri verbi*'; Christ himself is thereby calling to the ministry, sends out and blesses through the gift of the Holy Spirit. The laying-on of hands does not only "signify", but also "blesses".' (H. Lieberg, *Amt u. Ordination bei Luther und Melanchthon*, Diss. Erlangen, 1960.) W. Brunotte is less confident in this respect, cf. *Das geistliche Amt bei Luther*, 1959, p. 187ff. An important contribution to the ecumenical discussion is offered by J. Heubach, *Die Ordination zum Amt der Kirche*, 1956. Heubach gives a systematic exposition of the Reformers' teaching and of the neo-Lutheran approaches.

called first, should also ordain with laying-on of hands. It is not quite clear who laid hands on the seven mentioned in Acts VI. 6. According to the language and the syntax the best surmise is: those who have chosen the seven and presented them to the Apostles (there is no suggestion that the subject of the sentence has been changed). But Luke must have meant that the laying-on of hands was done by the Apostles.

On the other hand, the New Testament writings speak also of special commissions which were performed by those who had not themselves been specially commissioned. Thus Acts XIII. 1ff. shows that the commissioning of Paul and Barnabas was done through prophets and teachers in Antioch. We do not read anywhere in the New Testament that prophets are ordained through laying-on of hands. Neither is it likely that the teachers who took part in this particular incident were so ordained. According to II Corinthians VIII. 19, Titus was called by the congregations to be Paul's fellow-worker without any mention being made of office-holders. According to I Timothy IV. 14, Timothy was sent into his ministry through the laying-on of hands by the elders; according to II Timothy I. 6, it is Paul who sent him through laying-on of hands, and we cannot just surmise that the elders who were present at the occasion had themselves been sent into their work by a previous laying-on of hands. There is much to be said for the idea that the elders mentioned in the Pastoral Epistles were ordinary members of the Church, who had belonged to the congregation for a long time possibly as first-fruits who had proved their Christian faith through the purity and blameless-ness of their behaviour, through their works of love, etc., and were therefore specially respected in the congregation. It had not been necessary to ordain them specially to the office of presbyter. According to this conception, the ordination of presbyters mentioned in the Pastoral Epistles would be the ordination of presbyters to become bishops.[1]

[1] This conception has been queried and the position of the presbyter in the early 'pagan-christian' congregation (at least according to the Pastoral Epistles) is far from clear according to German and English theological literature. There are several reasons for this: 'A special problem arises from the fact that in both Jewish and Christian congregations the term 'presby-teros' can mean two things. It is either a sign of age, or the title of a particular Church officer. These two meanings cannot easily be distinguished.' (Cf.

Some have tried to combine these two groups (a) and (b) which we find in the New Testament, so as to say that the election was the prerogative of the congregation while the laying-on of hands was exclusively the task of the ministers or office-bearers. Such a suggestion is far from historically probable. One can however surmise that the congregation at least approved or co-operated in the commissioning by the ministers, or, in other cases, if the commissioning was done by the congregation itself, then the ministers if present at all, would take an active part, or at least give their assent. It follows therefore that the New Testament writings show no interest in the chain of laying-on of hands by Apostles on their fellow-workers and disciples, and by them on the future local pastors (shepherds) of the congregations. Even where we find this chain in fact, we do not find any interest in the actual succession of ordinations, but it is the transmission of pure doctrine which is emphasized (see II Tim. ii. 2). The concept of a guaranteed succession of ministerial charisms which would be conveyed through the laying-on of hands belongs to a much later period, e.g. that of the third century.

3. *The Concept of the Ministry in the Church*

The doctrinal problem of the ministry in the Church has its roots in two facts: first, the New Testament uses different terms to describe the different services which result from special commissioning; second, to found and to lead a congregation in the Early Church was not the prerogative of people who had been specially commissioned to fulfil this task.

The doctrine of the ministry should never miss the point that in the generally accepted epistles, Paul never speaks of a special commission to particular services, except when he speaks of his own calling and when he mentions Titus in the passage we referred to before. We must remember that Paul speaks in these writings, of the congregation as the fellowship of various charismatic services. Nor should we forget that in the Book of Acts and also in the Pastoral Epistles (in which special commissions do play an important role) we do not find any

πρεσβύτερος in T.W.N.T.) One should also consider the possibility that the term did not mean the same thing to the early Jewish and Christian congregations.

emphasis given to the variety of spiritual gifts and services which are bestowed on the individual members of the congregation. It is, however, true that in these writings all Christians are said to have received the Holy Spirit and the Book of Acts insists that the gift of the Spirit results in the witness of each Christian to the world; but even so we miss in these writings the particular Pauline understanding of the congregation as a microcosm of the various spiritual gifts and ministries. This distinction between Paul's and the other author's writings is all the sharper when we discern that in the Pauline Epistles the ministry of leadership (I Cor. xii. 28) and of supervision (Rom. xii. 8) are counted as gifts which appear in the congregation, freely given by the Spirit without reference to a special commission. Here we do not find that it is the commission to minister which is the reason for a demand on the obedience of the congregation in which they serve, but rather the ministry which has already been fulfilled. Thus Paul tells the Corinthians to be subject to the house of Stephanas because: "They were the first converts in Achaia and they have devoted themselves to the service of the saints' (I Cor. xvi. 15). The fact is that when the first converts began to work, they gathered a community and ministered to it, and this is taken by the Apostle to be a reason for the exhortation that one should obey them. One has therefore to reckon that the Early Church expanded through this kind of spontaneous mission work.

These important differences between the ministry of the founder and the leader have often been overlooked. After these had been observed, there was a tendency to overemphasize the difference between them so that charism and ministry were somehow opposed to each other;[1] it became difficult to see that these two different foundations and forms of service in the early church were not mutually exclusive. This is why we have to consider what these two descriptions of the ministry have in common:

[1] This tendency which prevails among quite a few German New Testament scholars of our time, has been given a very extreme dogmatic expression in the ecclesiology of E. Brunner (cf. *The Misunderstanding of the Church*, 1953: *Dogmatics*, iii, 1961). Brunner even transcends the anti-institutional 'spiritualizing' approach of R. Sohm, since he does not even realize the central importance of worship as a basis of development of the Church, its forms and order.

a) The apostolic office is fundamental for all the ministries in the Church. By this we mean the direct calling and authority of those who witnessed the risen Lord with their own eyes. It is fundamental for the ministry which originates from a special commission and also for the ministry which results from the irruption of a charism through a special commission. For faith in the Gospel as preached by the Apostles is a condition for all service in the Church. Over and above this we have in the New Testament writings, a document which shows that the apostolic word had a definite influence even where no special commission to the ministry by an apostle was available. This influence was normative, exhortative, encouraging, and also sometimes acting as a brake on the free expression of certain charismatic ministries (for example, the clear deprecation of speaking with tongues in I Cor. xiv).

b) To consecrate oneself completely to Jesus Christ, the Lord, to believe in the Gospel, and to be baptized are the conditions for every service in the Church, whether by special commissioning or as a result of the free gift of a charism. The foundation for every service (ministry) in the Church is baptism, by which the believer is received into the prophetic and royal priesthood of the Church, which has been called from the world to be sent into the world.

c) It is not only the charisms which appear in the Church without special commission which have their origin in the freedom of the Holy Spirit, but also the ministry which stems from a special commission. For the commission is by no means left to human decision. It is much more those whom the Holy Spirit wants to be called, those who have been indicated by him during the 'probation period', who have to be called. In the actual commission, we find God acting in the freedom of his grace. Those who do the commissioning are simply his tools.

d) It would not do to set the New Testament sayings about charism and ministry over against each other, as if the service by spiritual gifts and the service by special commission could be separated. For the commissioning itself takes place through Christ who has been lifted up and who reigns through the Spirit. The commission is based on the imperative of the Gospel which is the power of God. Through the commission, the task and the power to fulfil it are imparted. The commission gives spiritual authority. Thus, service by special commission is at the same time a charismatic service.

e) One should not try to set over against one another the freely appearing charisms and the ministry by special commission just as if the one was the expression of an enthusiastic tumult, and the other of order, or as if the one was an impulse jumping from person to person and the other a stable power flowing on one person only. Contrary to a widespread misunderstanding, the spiritual gifts do not merely have an ecstatic, and more or less chaotic, character, they do not wander about and change for no reason. One should think much more of stability, a stability which works itself out in a steady service to the Church. It is thus hardly possible to distinguish between the gifts and the deliberately transmitted ministries in their external effects.

f) Both the service rendered through the freely-appearing charisms and the actions of the servants who have obeyed the call, are dependent on the approval and judgement of the congregation. Even the authority which has been given through the special commission does not preclude the possibility of error or of moral failure on the part of the servant. The New Testament warns not only against false prophets or other spiritual aberrations which do not proceed from God, but also against false and self-enriching ministers. Because the Holy Spirit is alive in all the members of the Church, each one who is in possession of a charism has to accept the judgement of the other possessors of spiritual gifts, and especially of those who have received the gift of discerning the spirits (I Cor. XII. 10; cf. XIV. 29ff.).

g) On the one hand, it cannot be said that every charismatic form of service is founded on an actual word of special commissioning. On the other hand it must be remarked that an actual word is imparted to every recipient of a charism, even though he may not have been specially commissioned, because the congregation has to prove and judge his service. This judgement expresses itself in the 'Amen' through which the congregation acknowledges that the witness which has appeared in its midst is truly of the Spirit and thus makes it its own. The congregation renders a public judgement when it says 'Amen'. This 'Amen' does not only mean 'Yes, yes, so let it be', and it is not just a word of man, but it is the judgement of the Spirit who works in the congregation and enables its members to distinguish between true and false spirits. A further word is actually added to the service which is in fact rendered under the inspiration of a spiritual gift: namely the advice given by the apostle or by others, when they challenge the congregation to acknowledge and submit themselves to such men who are actually serving in their midst (cf. again I Cor. xvi. 15). In this case, the actual word is spoken after the charismatic service has been at least begun, and it is added as a word which acknowledges and fosters further acknowledgement. Thus even the charismatic service which comes without a special commission is embedded in the word of God. It is linked with the commission to witness to the world, which concerns every member of the New Testament people of God and is founded on the actual word of the judgement of the congregation and of the others who have been called, through which the Holy Spirit Himself acknowledges this service. The 'amen' of the Spirit is therefore a word which confirms, gives confidence and strength for the continuation of the service.

But in spite of so many features held in common, we should not omit to take certain differences seriously. For there is a distinction to be made between the foundation and the form of the service which was rendered in the early church, in the Pauline congregations on the one hand and in the congregation under the leadership of the Jerusalem Church on the other. There is no indication that a definite order of bishops, elders and deacons existed in Rome and Corinth, when Paul was writing to them, and which would have been based on special commissioning. It is only with the first Epistle of Clement that we find a generalization of the idea of commission, a concept which was later developed by the doctrine of the ministry of the early Fathers in both East and West and of the Reformers, particularly Calvin. But it is just as difficult to argue that the Pauline concept of service in the Church as a variety of freely appearing charisms, can be generalized. One cannot say that the commission is simply a confirmation of the charism which was previously there, or state that it is the sign of the beginning of the institutionalization of the Church. One has much more to reckon with the co-existence of these different foundations and forms of service in the early church. The ministry of 'church founding' and 'church leading' was built on different foundations: sometimes it was based on special commission by an apostle or by others who had been called to serve as church founders and leaders; sometimes it was based on the commission by the congregation or by prominent members of the congregation who had not themselves been specially commissioned; lastly, the service of Church founding and leading could be accomplished charismatically and without special commission.[1]

The doctrine of the ministry can not, therefore, be determined by the generalization of *one* of the different concepts prevalent in the Early Church. The task involved in this doctrine is much more to take the different possibilities seriously, in an attempt to work out an understandable dogma, and to leave room for all of them. A one-sided generalization can be as dangerous as an unhistorical harmonizing, for both methods bring with them the risk of thwarting spiritual life and dividing ecclesiastical units. One has to reconcile oneself to the idea that the dogmatic concept of the ministry in the Church is not, so to speak, 'given' in the New Testament. It can only be the result of a systematic reflection on the statements found in the New Testament.

That the concept of the ministry of the Church is not 'given' in the New Testament, but has to be discovered by dogmatic reflection, is made all the clearer when we realize that there is no consistent concept corresponding to our idea of the ministry in early Christian writings. Sometimes we read of 'elders' as persons who have been specially ordained to this position; sometimes we read of them as the 'older members of the congregation' who are to be respected as first converts, but without special ordination. The order of 'elders' is of Jewish

[1] These are sufficient reasons to say that one could not presuppose historically, that the bishops of the New Testament were all put into their position by apostles and that a chain of laying-on of hands linked the later bishops with the apostles. This has also been recognized by a number of Anglican theologians and by S. Bulgakoff among the Orthodox. (See 'Hierarchy and the Sacraments', *The Ministry and the Sacraments*, edited by Roderic Dunkerley [London: SCM Press, 1937], p. 96.)

and Judeo-Christian origin. Then we read of bishops and deacons, who work out their ministry after a special ordination (Acts xx. 28, Pastoral Epistles, and also Phil. I. 1 where Paul mentions them without closer definition). The bishops and deacons have their origin in the heathen-Christian congregations. One could add that in Acts, in the Pastoral Epistles, in I Peter and in II and III John, the existence of elders is taken for granted, whereas in the generally accepted Pauline Epistles, one never reads of elders. Paul speaks of the gift of leadership (*kybernesis*, I Cor. xii. 28) and of the gift of grace which is at work in those who as leaders take care of the congregation (Rom. xii. 8; cf. I Thess. v. 12). He also writes of those who 'labour' and of the 'zeal' with which many are working for the congregation. But even so, the leaders and the gift of leadership are definitely ranked below the prophets and the teachers. The Pauline concept of '*diakonia*' has generally been translated by the word ministry, e.g. '*ministerium*' in Luther and others. But Paul describes with this one word every form of charismatic service, whether it be the proclamation of the Gospel or whether it be straightforward aid, just as he gives a very wide connotation to the word '*diakonos*' and does not simply limit it to the person ordained to be a bishop's helper.

The Pauline concept of 'steward (*oikonomos*) of the mysteries of God', which is used in I Corinthians iv. 1 to describe the service of an apostle, is used in Titus i. 7 speaking of bishops and in I Peter iv. 10 concerning each member of the congregation. It is therefore impossible once again to take this term as a typical New Testament expression to describe the concept of ministry. In Hebrews xiii we read of 'leader' and of the souls of men over whom account will have to be rendered, but we do not find any description of the way in which they have reached this leading position. Finally, in Ephesians iv. 11, we read of 'pastors' of shepherds of grace, terms which have a christological connotation in the list of the gifts (after the apostles, the prophets, the evangelists and the teachers). The bishops according to Acts xx, 28 and the elders according to I Peter v. 2 are also told to 'feed the flock of God'. In the midst of this great variety of designations used by the New Testament there is none that points, so to speak, to a sacred origin, such as priests or kings.

If we consider all this again, it becomes clear once more that the concept of the ministry is in need of systematic reflection and decision. For in the variety of New Testament definitions of the way the service of Church leadership is to be exercised, we find included all the various possible forms this service can take and ways it can be rendered. This compels any doctrine of the ministry to be broad enough not to exclude fundamentally any of the various propositions which have been used to describe it by the Early Church. Thus the concept of ministry, even more than the concept of the apostolate, is a dogmatic concept, because there is no New Testament equivalent which would possess the same comprehensiveness. This concept of service includes definite facts described by the New Testament, otherwise it would have no dogmatic force; but it includes them through a systematic concentration. For it has to keep the balance systematically between very different historical facts as found in the New Testament, and must therefore leave room for the peculiar dissemination and variety of the services, just as is the case with the dogmatic concept of the apostle's ministry.

The basis which we have chosen for the discussion of the dogmatic concept of ministry is the idea of special commission for service, not the consideration of the freely-appearing charismatic services.

The historical fact that, as time went on, service in the Church was made more and more dependent on a previous special commission, and led to increasing 'institutionalizing' of the works and words of the Churches, cannot at this stage be adduced as a basis for this proposition (cf. e.g., the picture which Paul gives of the Corinthian pattern of Church meeting, with the picture of the form of Church worship given by Justin Martyr in 150 and Hippolytus in 200). For this increasing ousting of the free and charismatic utterances in the Church, could really represent a narrowing and ossification of the idea of service in the Church. On the other hand, it is also impossible to base our argument on the special commission as the ground of our dogmatic concept of service, with the suggestion that the free charismatic utterances soon began to split the Church. Reference to the growth of the Gnostic and Montanist heresies, as well as to the many movements of the Middle Ages and the 'Schwärmer' of the Reformation, are irrelevant. For it is actually just as possible for the specially commissioned minister to fall into heresy as for the Church to be given the watchmen it needs through freely-appearing charisms. But the special commission must become basically more and more important, as the Church finds itself further and further away in time from the Church-founding ministry of the Apostles. The Church can only live if it remains true to the historical Christ, the crucified and risen Lord who is its ever-present master. This means at the same time, that it has to remain true to the witness of the Apostles, who are the elect eye-witnesses of the same Lord. As time went on and one was further away from the Apostles, the tradition of the apostolic message, their teaching and ordinances, had to gain in importance, and so the commission to service which helped this transmission to others was bound also to gain in importance. For after all, everything depends on the fact that the apostolic word will continue to be proclaimed in the Church without falsification, and that all the other voices which become audible in the congregation agree to submit to its authority. We can understand that the Church order described in the Pastoral Epistles has been credited with Paul's authority just because this apostolic transmission is so important. In fact, we cannot exclude the possibility that as Paul became older and saw the Church spreading more and more, he gave his authority and blessing to a Church order which would follow the pattern of ordination and ministry which is found in the Pastoral Epistles; we can come to this conclusion after a careful study of the genuinely Pauline epistles alone. The relationship between Word and Spirit, between the historical uniqueness of God's salvation and the continuity of the saving work of the Spirit (which is at the very basis of church life) finds its proper expression in the insistence on special commission. For the work of the Spirit is to stir the believer's memory; by this we mean that he is always referring back to the unique and historical saving act of Jesus Christ, and in doing this, he points back to the apostolic word, and actualizes this same salvation. Thus Spirit and tradition are not contradictory, far from it, they belong together. Yet at the same time, one should not forget that the variety of charismatic utterances and services which appeared freely in the Pauline congregations, did not remain without the leadership of someone who had, in fact, the authority of a special commission; the apostle was, after all, their guide. The Pauline records are documents which show clearly how the apostle actually worked in the various congregations, encouraging them and exhorting them, giving them praise and warning, in one word, leading them and leaning heavily on his special authority. As this specific leadership and service of the apostle tended to disappear (and, remember, it was most effective even though it was exercised over great distances), the service based upon special commission was bound to gain in importance. This applied also to the service of the holder of charismatic gifts who encountered the congregation with the authority which had been given him, and was not in the same category as the other holders of charisms who were dependent on a later acknowledgement by the congregation.

This is why we understand under the term ministry in the Church the type of charismatic service, which is built on the foundation of a special commission in the midst of the variety of the charisms and services which are given to the Church. This special commission has been transmitted to us by the tradition of the Early Church as a call and commission to the particular service of Church founding and Church leadership, as well as to the service of helping others in this activity. We therefore include in the term 'pastoral ministry' (or ministry of the shepherd) the missionary activity of planting churches and leading them. For in the idea of missionary service, we find already the concept of the service which consists in leading the congregations which are to grow up; again we recognize that the service of leading a particular congregation includes the service of mission to the world around it. Thus, we choose among the many New Testament definitions of the service of leadership, the word 'pastor' (shepherd), because it is less positively fixed, so to speak, 'de jure' than the terms of 'bishop' and 'presbyter' in the whole of Church history, and also because it has undergone fewer changes and has been less narrowed down. The concept of pastoral ministry is thus specially suited to make room for the New Testament variety of propositions in its general teaching about the ministry.

At the same time, however, this concept of pastoral ministry has to remain open to include the Pauline concept of the Church as a fellowship of charisms, and it must make room for the possibility of charisms appearing freely to empower the receivers in the task of Church planting and Church leadership. Paul was always writing from a missionary situation when he recognized the spiritual gifts of leadership, of supervision, and of self-induction of the first converts, without special vocation; it was out of a similar situation that he called the congregations to obey the holders of such gifts. The teaching about the pastoral ministry must therefore take account of the missionary situation which is always present on the frontier of an ordered Church in a given area. If a Christian has been forced by circumstances into a purely pagan society, and there has awakened pagans to the faith through his witness to Christ, has baptized them and has partaken of communion with them, and has done all this in keeping with his teaching and order given by the Apostles, then he has fulfilled the pastoral ministry even if he had not been given authority to render this service by special commissioning before his deportation. He is acting, in fact, in full communion with the Church and its pastors, when he is doing this in the seclusion of a prison camp or of a forced labour camp, and the Church which meets him and his congregation would not dare to withhold recognition of his full pastoral ministry to this congregation. The charismatic service of the Christian is not founded on special commission, but in all cases on the apostolic message of the gospel which the Lord of the whole world wants to have proclaimed to all the world. The dogmatic teaching of the ministry must therefore not exclude any possibility of growth for the Church which has been an actual missionary event in the expansion of the Early Church. Yet these freely appearing services will therefore remain dependent on the 'Amen' of the Church and thus on the recognition by the pastors who have already been called to fulfil their task.

4. *The Task and Form of the Pastoral Ministry*

Just as we cannot find in the New Testament a definite concept which would correspond to the dogmatic concept of the ministry, so it is impossible to get a clear and unified description of the functions of the 'elders', the 'bishops', the 'superintendents', the 'leaders' which have been summarized in this paper under the term 'pastoral ministry' (literally, shepherd's ministry). In some cases we find that the descriptions of the work of the functions remain colourless and shapeless, so that we cannot get a concrete picture of how this service of Church leadership was really fulfilled. In other cases, we see differences which we can by no means neglect. When we study the ministry of the superintendents and of the leaders, who are mentioned relatively long after the prophets and the teachers in the lists of Romans XII. 8 and I Corinthians XII. 28, we find that their ministry seems to have been different from the ministry of the bishops of the Pastoral Epistles; these are clearly servants of the Word, and next to them there seems to be very little room for the special ministry of prophets and teachers. We cannot therefore simply add up the descriptions of the ministry which are scattered in the New Testament in order to determine dogmatically the functions of the Pastoral ministry. We must rather reflect dogmatically and systematically on the nature of the Church which is in need of leadership if we want to gain a clear idea of the question. Furthermore, the very diversity of New Testament statements forbids us to postulate that the conclusions to which our systematic reflection may lead us, will show that these functions were the same everywhere that the pastoral ministry was exercised. It would be far better to start from the premise that the pastoral ministry assumed a different form and emphasis and that its functions were distributed in a different way among the various Church officials in different places.

In our quest for a closer definition of the *functions of the pastoral ministry*, starting from a study of the nature of the Church, we dare not forget that where the New Testament speaks of the 'ecclesia', of the 'people of God' or of the 'body of Christ', or of the 'Temple of the Spirit', it puts at the heart of all these definitions of the Church the community of those who worship God. Thus, the function of the pastoral ministry becomes:

a) The leadership of the worshipping community. By this we mean:

First and foremost, proclaiming the Word and saying the eucharistic prayer in that community.

Making room for the diverse charismatic witnesses during the religious services.

Separating the spirits which do not come from God and also expelling those who fall into gross sins, i.e., exercising Church discipline.

Looking after the material gifts of the congregation, as far as they are not necessary for the common meal so that they can be distributed to the poor and used for other needs within and without the local congregation.

Installing deacons.

b) *The leadership of the missionary advance into the world* which has to start from every meeting for worship. By this we mean:

Calling and baptizing those who are still afar off, in order to gather them into the fold.

Commissioning those members of the congregation who are to serve as missionaries.

These tasks could of course be described in more detail. It is, however, important to note that among all the above mentioned functions, the pastoral ministry is first and foremost a '*ministerium verbi divini*', but that it is surrounded by the diverse spiritual gifts at work in the congregation, all of which are serving the Word, either directly or indirectly.

Neither can we define more closely all the possible *forms of the pastoral ministry* just by adding up the various statements we find scattered and often rather loosely expressed in the New Testament. For here we read of the pastor of a local congregation, sometimes as if he were one person, sometimes as if there were many. We also read of pastors, e.g. Timothy and Titus, who are responsible for the leadership of several churches, and who could therefore be called 'pastors of pastors'. Then we read of pastors who seem to have no direct pastoral link with a local congregation and who carry a missionary responsibility for an area where the church is still to be planted. Finally, we read in the New Testament of pastors and of their helpers ('deacons' in the etymological sense of the term) as well as of other fellow-workers, whose calling was limited in time and who thus were in one sense, 'apostles'; e.g. ordinary Church

P

members who were called to pass on a collection which had been made, and whose calling was ended once they had accomplished their task.[1] Here too we cannot restrict ourselves to general observation, but must infer and deduce systematically the most important forms of the pastoral ministry from our concept of the Church.

a) Every local church is truly 'ecclesia', 'body of Christ', 'Temple of the Holy Spirit'. It is not just a part of the ecclesia, not just a limb of the body of Christ, not just a stone of the temple of the Spirit. Thus the pastoral ministry in each local church is truly the pastoral ministry, it is not lacking in any authority.

b) This understanding of the local church as 'ecclesia', 'body of Christ', and 'temple of the Holy Spirit' does not mean that the churches are independent of each other; on the contrary, it means that all these local churches are in fellowship with one another. For in every local church it is the same Christ who is present and at work. Thus no pastor can remain in

---

[1] From a study of the New Testament it is not possible to presuppose that the threefold ministry (bishops, presbyters and deacons) which prevailed in the patristic Church has its foundation in the early Christian community as a general institution. Here we have one of the greatest difficulties for the Anglo–Catholic and similar teaching about the ministry (see K. E. Kirk, ed. *The Apostolic Ministry*, [New York: Morehouse-Gorham, 1946]. S. Bulgakoff has recognized this clearly within the Orthodox Church: 'The origin of the three degrees of Holy orders as the basis of Church organization is one of the most difficult problems of modern ecclesiastical history. The sources at our command render its solution more or less hypothetical. The most probable conclusion, suggested by historical data, is that the threefold ministry in its present form was not known in the Apostolic and post-Apostolic church of the first century. We find evidences of it at the beginning of the second century at the time of I Clement and the epistles of St. Ignatius, and later (op. cit. p. 95).' Bulgakoff deduces some very important consequences for our understanding of apostolic succession from this, consequences which are rather unexpected within the framework of Orthodox ecclesiology. It is as difficult to prove that the well-known Calvinian division of the ministry was the basic order within the early Church. But it is more important to contrive the systematic disclosure of the wealth of possibilities contained in the New Testament teaching about the ministry, than to try and base one's Church structure on a historic assertion about them. It is important to note that the concept of the Church is fundamental in this respect.

isolation, since he is dependent on the recognition and the fellowship of all the other pastors.

c) In the New Testament, the word 'ecclesia' describes not only the local church but also the Church universal, as well as the fellowship of local churches within a given area. Thus, the pastoral ministry cannot be concerned only with the local church, but carries a responsibility for the fellowship of the local churches within a particular country and, further still, for the fellowship of all the churches in the world. With this concept of the nature of the Church as a premise, we come to the conclusion that there are various forms of the pastoral ministry, with different areas of responsibility, within the one common responsibility of all the pastors for the whole Church.

d) The Church is the growing body of Christ advancing into the world and thus constantly planting new local churches and claiming new areas for the work of the Church. The Church as a whole, as well as the local churches, takes an active part in this growth. The relationship described as a 'mother-daughter' relationship between communities corresponds to the 'father-son' relationship within the pastoral ministry. We thus find a definite order within the pastoral ministry, with a subordination of pastors to 'pastors of pastors'.

e) The relationship between the whole Church and the local churches is not that which exists between any sum total and its components; on the contrary, it is the relationship which exists within a fellowship as common participation in the whole Christ. The relationship between the whole Church and the local churches is not based on an addition, but on an interpenetration, for it is the whole Christ who is present in each local church, and thus the whole Church is truly and simultaneously within the local church. The relationship between the pastoral ministries in the local church, in the wider body covering a definite area and in the whole Church, must follow this pattern. We cannot therefore only describe it in terms of authority and dependence but must at the same time use the idea of the fellowship of those people who exist for each other and with each other. In other words: the injunctions of the 'pastor of pastors' and the obedience owed to him are circumscribed by the commandment that each must be submitted to the other in the Lord.

f) The Church is simultaneously, and in a peculiar way, unity and plurality. The pastoral ministry must therefore appear under this form of unity and plurality too. We can surmise that originally, in the primitive local churches, there was a plurality of serving pastors; it is only later that we find the growth of a monarchical episcopacy (there is no agreement about the existence of this type of ministry in the Pastoral Epistles). But we do not find anywhere in the New Testament any suggestion that one particular person has any power of giving orders to the whole Church. There is no doubt that Peter's particular position within the circle of the apostles is not that of the one who is in charge. He is much more the speaker of the group, and this only during the early period of the founding of the Church.

g) Only then should we consider other differences within the ecclesiastical ministry, as follows:

Certain well-defined functions can be shared out between the pastoral ministries in such a way that one particular pastor hands over to another definite leading functions, so that he obeys him as if he were a 'super-pastor', e.g. the local pastor can relinquish his right to exercise discipline and hand it over to the 'super-pastor'.

Certain diaconal ministries can be established so that particular functions of the pastoral ministry are handed over to members of the congregation who are not ordained pastors themselves, and

Short-term tasks can be given to others, such as visitations or missionary advances and the handing over of collections.

To all these remarks about the form of the pastoral ministry we should add that very early in Church history, theological reflection on the ministry resulted in important differences between theological thinkers. The reason for their differences lies in the way each emphasizes one or the other of the different functions and forms of the pastoral ministry and gave it theological importance. Thus, in the Pastoral Epistles, the function of guarding the pure doctrine is emphasized, whereas in Ignatius' letters, it is the way in which the bishop is actually a representative of Christ, and in I Clement the function of looking after the right Church order. These differences have been continued throughout Church and confessional history. In the Early Church these different concepts were not treated as causes of division within the Church because of their contradictory nature.

It is therefore very important indeed that dogmatic teaching about the ministry should remain open to all the possibilities which are found in the New Testament and that it should not forget that there is a real difference between this and the way in which dogmatics and canon law nail down the same concept. For when a historical decision has to be made as to the definition in canon law of a particular aspect of Church order, it is necessary to make a choice about the actual form this order must take, and this must often be done in the midst of frontal attacks either from a degenerate form of 'freely appearing charisms' or from a devaluation of the ministry itself. But such legal decisions should never be put on the same level as the dogmatic concepts of the ministry, which have always far more width than the legal definitions resulting from the confrontation of the biblical ideas with actual historical situations. The wealth of New Testament definition for Church order is far greater than could be realized by the Church order of any one particular Church.

5. The Concept of Apostolate

If we want really to understand the relationship between the apostolic succession of the Church and the apostolic succession of the ministry, we have first to deal with the apostolate as such. I have however to limit myself in the next four sections to mentioning only such material as may be useful to our particular study. In order to give a proper definition of the concept of apostolic ministry we have to distinguish between two constitutive elements.

The first commission of the twelve Apostles by Jesus before His death was limited in time. After they had fulfilled their task, they returned to Jesus. But then the fellowship of the disciples was broken, in the same way as the fellowship of the old covenant was broken through the disobedience of Israel. It was broken because the Apostles overreached themselves and lacked faith during the passion of their Lord. So it is the appearances of the risen Lord which are the foundation of the apostolate. Indeed, the fact of having been an eyewitness of Christ's earthly life is not a final condition of the apostolate. In any case, Paul spoke of himself as an apostle of Jesus Christ on the sole ground that the risen Lord had appeared to him, though he had never been a disciple of Christ during his earthly life. Thus, the first element in the concept of 'apostle' is to have been an eyewitness of the resurrection of Jesus Christ.

But the actual eyewitnessing is not sufficient in itself to make someone into an apostle. This becomes very clear according to I Corinthians xv. 5ff. If the appearance of the risen Lord had been sufficient ground for apostleship, then all the 'more than 500 brethren' would have been apostles; they certainly were witnesses, yet they did not become apostles. What is of the utmost importance for the apostle is therefore the commissioning by the risen Lord, which has to accompany the eyewitnessing. This commissioning was at the same time a giving of authority. The task given by the risen Lord was not a claim that could not be fulfilled, but at once the promise of a divine fulfilment, the promise of the presence of Christ and of the efficacy of the Holy Spirit.

These two elements, the eyewitnessing and the commissioning by the risen Lord, are the basis for the dogmatic concept of apostle. The pouring out of the Holy Spirit, whom the Apostles received in the midst of the other believers and watchers, was the sign that they were now enabled to accomplish their task.

How were they then to accomplish their task, and what was their function in and for the growing Church?

a) The Apostles proclaimed the act of salvation of which they were eyewitnesses, i.e. the resurrection of the Christ who had died on the cross. This proclamation is not just the communication of the event; it is its manifestation as a divine act of salvation, as a forgiving word to the Jews and the Gentiles, as a kerygmatic advance into ever new conceptualizations and world-views. The manifestation of this 'for you' is at the same time the proclamation of Christ's claim to be the Lord and the warning as to His impending judgement.

b) Faith and fellowship between believers, i.e. Christian communities, sprang up as a result of the proclamation of the

Gospel by the Apostles. The apostolic ministry was comparable with the service of the builder or of the planter. The Apostles did not simply limit themselves to issuing the forgiving word and claim of the Gospel but also gave advice as to the order which should prevail in the life of the communities, including the liturgy and the pattern of common service rendered by the receivers of charisms. They further advised on the co-existence of Jews and Gentiles, marriage, and Church collections. They also appointed those who were to serve as Church leaders, and strengthened the authority of those who were entrusted with congregations.

c) The Apostles were the bond of unity in the Early Church. The unity of the different Churches in the glorified Christ and in the Holy Spirit became historical truth through the service of the Apostles. They witnessed everywhere to the Lord who had appeared to them; they travelled to visit all the churches; they sent messengers and letters to them; they prayed for them and were upheld by their prayers; they organized the collection for Jerusalem. But if the Apostles were a bond of unity for the Churches, then they must have formed a unity between themselves. But the Epistle to the Galatians warns us not to idealize this unity, a danger which was threatening the Church as early as the apostolic times according to the Acts of the Apostles and which was soon to reach its peak in Church history. In that epistle we learn of tensions and real conflicts between the Apostles. But neither should one forget that all agreed they had to seek unity and were committed to it; they knew that there was a real unity already in Christ, a unity which did not consist of a pyramid of subordinates and superiors, but of a fellowship of service. This fellowship was based on the mutual recognition of each other's commission, and we must not underestimate the special role Peter was called to play during the early days of the Church's foundation.

We have now to be quite clear that the concept of apostle which we have been using (and we have also spoken of apostolic *ministry* because it is a service based on a special commission) is a dogmatic concept; no New Testament concept of '*apostolos*' can be found to correspond consistently with our definition. We need not give a detailed account of New Testament statements. It is well known that the Johannine Gospel avoids the use of the term 'apostle' when speaking of the twelve, that Matthew uses it only once or even never in the original text, that Mark has it only once. Luke speaks repeatedly of apostles but it is the twelve whom he so qualifies, not Paul (with the exception of Acts xiv. 14 where Barnabas is also called apostle). On the other hand, Paul himself does not limit the term apostle to the twelve, nor to the twelve and himself. In Galatians i. 19 we read of James and others also, in Romans xvi. 7 Andronicus and Junias are called apostles. The New Testament has no consistent concept of the apostle. We should, however, note that a difference has to be made between the Apostles of Jesus Christ and the apostles of the Churches, but even so we cannot say that there is a single New Testament concept and we have to come to the conclusion that the concept of apostle began at that time to become a dogmatic concept, as it very soon became in the Early Church. The concept of the apostolic ministry describes, however, the central position of the New Testament, otherwise it would not be a dogmatic concept, though it cannot be directly deduced from New Testament statements but has to be the result of a systematic theological study.

But just because this concept describes only the situation normal to the New Testament, it dare not become exclusive but must retain some sort of openness and diffuseness, because the differences in the way the New Testament makes use of the term 'apostle' signifies that the circle of the Apostles was not closed but retained a certain openness. Thus, with Paul the concept of apostle is wide, with Luke it is narrow. The width of the concept corresponds to the fact that the Apostles were surrounded by prophets, evangelists and teachers, and that a clear-cut distinction between all these ministries could not be made. Thus the dogmatic concept of apostle is describing the centre of the New Testament conception of this term, but it should keep an eye all the time on the two sides of the diffusion. Otherwise, the dogmatic idea itself would suffer and lose its historical foundation, since it would no longer see the proper relationship existing between charism and ministry, nor be able to give a convincing argument for the authority of the New Testament canon which does not consist solely of apostolic writings.

6. *The Apostles as Foundation of the Church*

Christ Himself has dealt with the world as its Saviour and Judge, and with the Church as its builder, through the service of His eyewitnesses whom He has called and to whom He has given authority. Christ spoke and acted personally and presently in their words and deeds. They were ambassadors instead of Christ, through whom God exhorted men. The apostle therefore stands where Christ used to stand. This refers also to their suffering: the apostle was a living representation of the suffering Christ in the midst of the congregation and in presence of the world, because he partook of Christ's suffering; because he was a representation of Christ's suffering, he was also the channel of the power of the glorified Lord. Thus the Apostles were representatives of Christ in the world. The witness of the Apostles was the word of God, which could bind and loose; the power of their message was the power of God and the work of the Holy Spirit. The apostolic ministry is therefore an act of God's salvation which can be added to the act of salvation in Christ. Of course it is not added as an independent act, which can be separated from Christ; it comes rather as the act of salvation from Christ's service and ministry, i.e., the ministry of reconciliation. This ministry is however God's special act of salvation, because the act of Christ itself would have remained hidden from the world without the apostolate. The apostolic service is an eschatological act of salvation, which has to be added to God's act of salvation in Christ, inasmuch as the act of salvation on the cross is now breaking into the world through the witnesses of the resurrection who have been called to this task.

The Apostles were not only the builders and planters of the *Early Church*, but they are the builders and planters of *the Church of all times and in all places*. Their ministry is and remains unique. The Apostles are alone in having proclaimed Christ's resurrection in the capacity of eyewitnesses specially called to this task. We may agree that every calling into a ministry of the Church is the work of the glorified Lord, but at any time or place, it happens through the intermediary of human mouths and hands. Thus, because of the historical uniqueness of their direct call by the risen Lord, the Apostles are truly the foundation of the Church, not just of individual congregations, but of the whole Church at all times in all places (cf. Matt. XVI. 18; Eph. II. 20; Rev. XXI. 14). This statement does not mean that there is competition between the Apostles and Christ as the foundation of the Church; for through the service of the Apostles, Christ Himself is the foundation stone, the corner stone and the last stone of the Church.

How far are the Apostles fundamentally necessary for all the rest of the ministry and life of the Church? We must here mention once more the three points which we remarked upon above:

a) *The apostolic Gospel is the authoritative Christian message for the Church of all times.* It corresponds clearly to the definition of it found in those Pauline Epistles recognized as genuine and also in a more concentrated form in the Pastoral Epistles, where one is exhorted to remain true to the teaching of the Apostles. For Paul has spoken of the Gospel as of *his* Gospel, so that we cannot separate the apostle from the Gospel which he proclaimed. Of course it is not only the *content* of the apostolic witness which is authoritative but also the Apostles' *act* of witnessing. To recognize the apostolic claims consists not simply in repeating apostolic words, but in the continuation of the apostolic work in the advancement of the proclamation of God's act of salvation to the world.

b) *The apostolic ministry of Church leadership is also of utmost importance.* Here, too, and possibly more so than ever, we can say it is not only the actual commandments of the Apostles which are binding for all times of Church history, but also their very action creating a Church order. The Church has to follow their example in that it must continually try to find the right pattern for itself in its own way.

c) *The Apostles remain the authoritative bond of unity for the Church in all places at all times.* They bind the Church together not only through their message about Christ, but also through the very differences between them, in their theological description of the message which they proclaim and in their understanding of the Church and of Church order, which we can see from the New Testament writings. For it is just because of these differences that the Apostles are, so to speak, the paradigm for the extent and limits of Church unity. Even the Early Church recognized that all the New Testament writings were within these limits of unity, with all their differences in the gospel narrative, in theological insight, in indications for Church order; otherwise the need for a New Testament canon might not have arisen.

The Eastern Churches, the Churches which came from the Reformation and the Roman Catholic Church all accept this threefold and unique function of the apostolate. There is no contradiction in such an acceptance in principle. The differences only come in later, that is when one asks questions about the origin of the apostolic tradition: Where do we find the apostolic witness?—in the New Testament writings?—in the oral tradition?—or in the contemporary teaching ministry, even when it is not based upon Scripture or upon historically proven tradition? It is then that we get very deep differences because various people have different ways of defining concretely which part of the apostolic teaching is binding and which is not.

7. *The Apostles as Members of the Church*

Paul is our best informant to demonstrate what relationship existed between the Churches and the Apostles. One cannot however generalize the Pauline understanding, because we have to reckon with differences between the Jerusalem conception of this relationship and Paul's. We may, however, make the following remarks from a more general point of view.

The Apostles were together with all the members of the Church 'submitted to the Lord'; they were justified sinners among other sinners and what they were came from grace alone. Indeed, the Apostles had committed specially grievous sin; Peter had denied Christ and Paul had persecuted Him. The apostle will therefore appear with all the other members of the Church before God's judgement seat, and all his works will be manifested. The person of the apostle is nothing, his witness alone counts. The apostle appears therefore in his own judgement as the 'chief sinner', the misfit 'born out of due time', the least of all, as 'buffeted by a messenger of Satan'. The decisive word is: 'Nevertheless I live; yet not I, but Christ liveth in me' (Gal. ii. 20).

The apostle stands over against the Church as a witness

and brings to it all that it has, yet at the same time the apostle stands in the presence of the Lord as a justified sinner and is nothing in His sight. Thus the Apostles, like every other Christian, depend for their life on the witness of the Church to the comfort of God. Their life is dependent on the Churches' intercession, and we read constantly that Paul asks that they should pray for him, so that his work should continue and his sorrow be taken away from him. The Apostles therefore live because of and from their service to the Church. They are dependent on their brethren's material gifts, practical aid and service as well as on the spiritual gifts which the Church bestows upon them for their strength and comfort.

8. *The Service of the Apostles in the Fellowship of the Church*

If the declarations of the last two sections belong together, i.e. if the Apostles are the foundation of the Church as well as its members, then these remarks must have some consequences for the fulfilment of the apostolic ministry. The Apostles act in fellowship with the other members of the Church. This is clear from Acts (e.g. 15) and from Paul's epistles (e.g. I Cor. v. 4). Paul's constant desire to get the 'yes and amen' of the Church as well as his hopes for his fellow Christians' co-operation is characteristic. The Church has also received the Holy Spirit. Thus, just as the Church submits itself to the word of the apostle, so does it have a share in Christ's ministry and in his Spirit, and therefore is empowered and called for to prove everything and judge of all things. But its participation does not only limit itself to proving and judging. The apostle has done his work in the midst of the diversity of the ministries which come to the Church as spiritual gifts from the wealth of the Holy Spirit. Even when the diversity of spiritual gifts is not mentioned in the New Testament, it is quite clear that the apostle does not represent an isolated authority. He is surrounded either by people exercising spiritual ministries, or by elders. Once more we must stress the importance of the diffuseness of the concept of apostle of which we spoke earlier. The Apostles carry out their service surrounded by prophets, teachers and evangelists, who work, at times in more than one congregation (just as they do), and in the midst of a whole complex of '*pneumatikoi*', presbyters (elders) and first-fruits of the local church. Thus, the prophets are also mentioned next to the Apostles as the foundation of the Church (Eph. II. 20); as the prophets are mentioned after the Apostles, we may surmise that the author speaks of New Testament prophets. This aspect of the fellowship of the apostolic ministry with other ministries was also acknowledged by the Church when it collected the various writings for the New Testament canon; we know that some of them did not spring directly from the Apostles.

The apostolic ministry can only be understood properly if we keep our eyes on both, or even on all three, circumstances mentioned above. The Apostles were called before the out-pouring of the Holy Spirit at Pentecost, they received the Spirit together with the other members of the Church and they worked in full fellowship with them. This can also be expressed as follows: The Apostles are lifted up before all the other members of the Church through their call which was issued by the risen Lord, but they live as members of the same Church embraced by the word of forgiveness from all those who have received the Holy Spirit. Finally they work on the Churches and indeed the whole world, being surrounded by the witness of all those who have received the Spirit. We could also say that the Apostles have been called to build and plant the Church, indeed to be the foundation of the Church, but that at the same time they are members of the Church which has been built by the Holy Spirit on the one foundation, Jesus Christ, and are working together with the other members of the Church, for with them they form the Church. It is only those who can bring together these three aspects of the apostolate, which were described in sections 6 to 8, who can really recognize what is meant by the assertion that the Apostles are the foundation of the Church. It is from this that a full understanding of the meaning of apostolic succession can come.

9. *Pastoral Ministry and Church*

The whole Church, with all its pastoral ministries and its charisms, is founded on the Apostles, that is on Jesus Christ, who has given authority to the Apostles as their risen Lord, and who rules the Church through the Holy Spirit as its glorified Lord. Each service of the various ministries and other charisms must prove itself true service taking place in the power of the Spirit when measured according to the fundamental apostolic standard. All that has been said above (5) about the Apostles as foundation of the Church has now to be reiterated for the Church with all its ordained pastors and holders of charisms.

In the midst of the diversity of the spiritual gifts which are given to all the members of the Church, the special commission of the pastor to his ministry has to be understood as a continuation of the special commission of the Apostles. This continuation, however, does not mean that the pastor is commissioned to be a new apostle, but must be understood as a continuation of the service which the Apostles started and founded. The Apostles are unique as having seen the risen Christ and received His direct call; therefore, the apostolate as eyewitness of the resurrection and as the body which received immediate election cannot be continued; it ended with the death of the Apostles. But the task given to the Apostles did not end there. It extends to all the nations to whom missionaries are to go until the end of the world. The commissioning of the Apostles must therefore relate to others besides themselves. For this mission concerns the 'whole' or totality over which Christ has been set as Lord, all people of all countries of all times until the *parousia*. Because of this, other special commissions must essentially be the sequel of the special commission of the Apostles; from the apostolic ministry there flows of necessity the pastoral ministry in its various forms, otherwise the task given to the Apostles until the end of the world could not be fulfilled. All the later commissions come from the glorified Lord, but not directly and not as creating a precedent, but by human intermediaries. This is the very deep difference which differentiates the pastoral ministry of all subsequent ages from the apostolate. We can therefore call the pastoral ministry apostolic, in so far as it is founded on and carries forward the task which the Apostles received, which they did not fulfil before their death and which has not yet been fulfilled. In this sense, the Church itself has at all times been called apostolic according to the Nicene Creed. The distinction between pastoral and apostolic ministry is therefore comparable with the distinction between the individual Christian and Jesus Christ.

The three aspects, of which we spoke above as part of the apostolic ministry, will therefore have to reappear when we try to describe the relationship existing between the pastoral ministry and the Church, all the more because the Church of all ages with all its charisms and pastoral ministries is really founded on the Apostles.

a) *The pastors in relation to the Church.* The pastoral ministry is related to the Church because Christ speaks to the Church through this ministry as its Lord. The pastor meets the Church as Christ's representative, as a good shepherd, in all he does in obedience to the task which he has been given. If he proclaims the apostolic message: 'Be ye reconciled with God', he is like the Apostles, an ambassador for Christ, an instrument through which God Himself is exhorting the Church and the world (II Cor. v. 20). As long as he is proclaiming the apostolic message, the same promise as was given to the Apostles is valid for him: 'He who listens to you, listens to me' (Luke x. 16). The comforting and warning voice of the pastoral ministry may be a human voice, but it is not human comfort and warning that it gives; it is God's voice 'which rings down from heaven' (Augsburg Confession XXV, 3ff.). God Himself is acting in His own power as long as the pastoral ministry addresses the apostolic message to others in the same way as the apostolic ministry used to do. This action of God through the pastoral ministry should vouchsafe real comfort to the pastor as well as to the congregation, in all their human frailty. The same of course is true of God's action in the dispensation of baptism and the distribution of holy communion. It is also true of the action of the pastor when he binds, looses and commissions. Through the leadership of the pastoral ministry, Christ Himself is leading the Church. The good shepherd feeds His flock through the shepherds whom He has called, on whom He has bestowed His gifts and whom He has enlisted in His service. The relationship between Church and pastor is therefore one of 'over-againstness' because Christ Himself speaks through this ministry to the Church, strengthens it and leads it. It is a fact that each charismatic witness and each charismatic service has authority in the Church; for this is the way the Holy Spirit, who is the Lord, deals with the Church. But the charismatic service of the pastoral ministry has a definitely given authority which these others do not have, because it stems from a special commissioning which gives it a special kind of authority. The pastoral ministry is thus different from the charismatic ministry, just because its authority does not derive from the actual exercise of the gift which is then later recognized by the congregation; on the contrary, its authority is actually given, so to speak, in advance, because a special commissioning is understood to have taken place. On the basis that this special commission has taken place, the faithful can have the firm conviction that this brother has been given authority for his service from God. This is why one can meet the pastor with the expectation that God deals through him with the congregation and leads it. Truly, the authority of the pastoral ministry does not derive from the special calling only, but also from the constantly renewed obedience to the call. As soon as the spiritual gift which empowers for the service has been received, then the same can be said as is always true of the outpouring of the Holy Spirit. The Spirit is the gift which has been bestowed upon us, in so far as he is and remains both the Lord who wants ever to be asked afresh to come, and the Lord who is ever ready to give Himself to us. To be in the Spirit is not a quality of man, but the result of the ever-renewed work of the Spirit who acts with the faithfulness of God the renewer. The authority does not therefore simply lie in the historical fact of the special calling, but in the ever-new apprehension of this call, in the ever-new disclosure and stirring up of the charism which has been given through the calling (II Tim. I. 6). But the daily necessity of this obedient apprehension of the authority does not cancel the previously given authority but has its foundation therein.

b) *The pastors as members of the Church.* The pastors are under the rule of the Lord together with all the members of the Church. The minister stands in the midst of his congregation and under the judging and saving hand of the Lord. He is dependent on God's grace and other people's intercession, just like every other man. He too will have to appear before the judgement seat, not despite his calling but because of it and because it brings with it such terrible dangers. To imagine that he has a higher status or rank than the other Christians is sheer nonsense. In truth, the pastoral ministry means just the opposite. For nothing is more humbling than the ministry, and nothing is as overwhelming as the knowledge of one's being the representative of Christ. Ordination is the end of one's own plans, one's own ways, one's own means and words. The pastoral ministry means that Christ will feed His flock through this man whom He has called.

c) *The service of the pastor in the fellowship of the Church.* What we have said about the fellowship of the Apostles and the other Church members in their common service, applies no less to the service of the pastors who came after them. The pastors lead the congregation in communion with the other charismatic ministers. This is true for the pastoral ministry in the local church as well as in regional Church work or even general Church leadership. It is not only true of the fellowship of the pastors one with the other, but also of the fellowship of the pastor with the members of the Church who have not received a special commission, but who have been awakened to serve by the same Spirit. We have once more to remark that the ministry as such is not distinguished from the other charisms by a special expression in the New Testament; there is no word in the New Testament to describe what we dogmatically call the ministry. We must further remark that we cannot show from the New Testament that the services of the pastor are only the result of a previous special commission. Here too we have transitions and a certain diffuseness which cannot be fitted into a scheme of authority and dependence. No, these differences are most effective in upholding the very peculiar structure of the fellowship and in making possible the mutual recognition of each other which is necessary to fulfil the life and service of the Church. Besides, we must not forget that Paul speaks in Ephesians of the superintendents and those who have the gift of leadership as well as of the pastors, after speaking of the actual kerygmatic ministry, and that according to the Didache (which presupposes the episcopal ministry in xv. 1ff.) the eucharistic thanksgiving prayer should be left to the prophets, if some of them should be present (x. 6). In the New Testament therefore, we find that the pastors are

Q

surrounded by 'charismatikoi' and 'presbyteroi', even though we can be relatively certain that there was no college of presbyters with special ministerial functions in the Early Church of the first century, at least not in the Gentile-Christian congregations. On the contrary, we may surmise that there was simply an undifferentiated group of elderly, respected and dignified persons, the first-fruits of the Church. A special calling of the presbyters, and therefore a presbyterial ministry, probably belongs to a later period, at least in the Gentile-Christian Churches. But however it was, we can affirm that the pastoral ministry was, by its very nature, surrounded by the service of the Church, and specially by its witness.

d) The pastoral ministry stands over against the congregation, but again the free charismatic witness in the Church stands over against the pastoral ministry. Christ deals with the congregation through the pastors, but He also deals with both Church and ministers through the diversity of the charisms. The pastoral ministry is therefore in the midst of that mutual service which all members render to each other. The pastor is thus to be surrounded by the manifold work of the one grace of Christ which expresses itself through the services which each renders to the other. The charismatic witnesses of the Church are not simply to be proved one-sidedly by the pastoral ministry, and judged by it, but the converse is also true: the congregation has the task and authority to prove and judge the service of the pastor, just as it does with every free service.

Thus we come to the exciting question of the ultimate authority in the Church: is it the ministry, or is it the congregation? This question is included in the problem which has so often been discussed as to which is first, the ministry or the congregation. It is decisive that the New Testament does not give any answer to this either-or. The pastoral ministry is penultimate too. The ultimate authority can only be Christ who is actually working in the Church through the Holy Spirit. But at the same time we have to say that the Apostles are the authority which has been ordered before the ministry and the Church, for they are the called witnesses of the risen Lord. The whole Church and all the ecclesiastical ministries are founded on the Apostles' ministry. Neither the ecclesiastical ministry nor the Church itself is the ultimate authority, but both must feel responsible to the supreme court which the Apostles proclaimed, that is the Lord Himself. This corresponds to the fact that the Early Church did not define its supreme authority legally, for it did not know of any other than Christ, and even the decisions of the synods were dependent on confirmation by the individual churches. It is amazing to see that even today, the Eastern Churches differ from Rome in their avoidance of a final reply to the question of the supreme authority. According to the understanding of the Eastern Church, councils as well as bishops and congregations can make mistakes. It is only the totality which cannot err. If one asks an Eastern theologian what the organ is through which this infallibility of the total Church expresses itself, he will leave it an open question.[1]

10. *Apostolic Succession*

Apostolic succession cannot mean a continual and extended call to become apostles; it can only signify a following in the Apostles' footsteps, in obedience to those who were the called eyewitnesses of the resurrection of Jesus Christ. This succession can be founded on the general call addressed to all baptized people, or on the special calling to the pastoral ministry.

a) *The apostolic succession of the Church and of each of its members has the following characteristics*:

[1] Thus for instance S. Zankow: 'It is not the ecumenical council as such which is truly ecumenical, but only what the whole Church in the whole of Church history has recognized and confessed to have been a truly ecumenical council. It is only the whole Church which can give a council the aura of ecumenity and thus seal its decisions as infallible. This is why synods and their decisions can only be called infallible, in so far as their witness about the Faith of the Church was infallible. And the decision about this can only come from the Church itself, i.e., the whole Church and it alone' (*Procès verbaux du premier congrès de théologie orthodoxe à Athènes*, ed. Hamilkar S. Alivisatos [Athens, 1939], p. 281). This presupposes the conviction 'that the general conscience of the whole Church is infallible in questions of faith and doctrine. By conscience in this context, we mean the knowledge of the clergy and the laity as a whole, the spiritual leaders and the followers, the directors and the listeners, the masters and the servants, the men and the women who are all members of the Body of Christ and form together the *pleroma*, the totality, the Body of the Church, which alone is thought to be infallible' (J. N. Karmiris, 'Abriss der dogmatischen Lehre der orthodoxen katholischen Kirche', *Die orthodoxe Kirche in griechischer Sicht*, part I (1959), p. 93).

It is based on faith in the apostolic message and on obedience to the apostolic ordinances and warning.

It witnesses to the apostolic Gospel which has been entrusted to every Christian, and it does this in the diversity of the charisms which have been distributed to each one.

It consists in a witnessing and conquering advance into the world, and in the building up of the congregation. Every charism serves for the edification of the Church while taking its place on the frontier between Church and world. In this sense, every Christian has to emulate the Church-building activities of the Apostles and shares therefore in the service of the pastor.

It looks for fellowship with all Christians and all Churches in the world. This character belongs essentially to the apostolic succession of the Church as well as of each individual member of it. For apostolic succession is only there where the Apostles are taken seriously as the bond of unity of the Church in all places and at all times.

b) *The apostolic succession of the pastoral ministry is demonstrated as follows*:

Every pastor is submitted to the example of the Apostles as he preaches, leads and administers.

The pastor's relationship to the Church is like the apostle's; he is the mouthpiece and representative of Christ.

The pastor depends daily on the renewal of God's grace, like all the members of the congregation. Christ's relationship to the pastor is the same as to the Church member.

The pastor feeds the flock in fellowship not only with all the other pastors, but also with the charismatic services which surround the pastoral ministry in the Church.

c) Neither the Churches' nor the pastoral ministry's apostolic succession can be taken seriously unless it continues to express the relationship between the Apostles and the Church as a fellowship of mutual service and of serving the world together. For it is not only the apostolic message and order which are fundamental for the Church of all ages, but also the very structure of the apostolic activity for and with the Church, and this is to be upheld by all pastors in all churches in obedient discipleship.

d) From these fundamental remarks it follows that three

different ways of entry into the ministry must in principle be recognized.

The commission to the pastoral service can be conferred by those who have previously been sent as pastors themselves. This has to be done after they have been given full recognition by the Church or better still with its full co-operation, mainly of members who have not been ordained.

The commission to pastoral service can be conferred through the Church as a whole, namely through those members of the Church who have not been sent as pastors; this can take place after they have been recognized by the ordained ministers, or better still, with full co-operation of the latter.

The recognition by the Church and the existing ministry of such pastoral services as have been rendered *de facto* under the free guidance of the Spirit.

It is quite clear that of these three ways, the first should today have priority and should be the rule. For as the period of time separating us from the Apostles increased, an ever greater importance had to be given to the ministry, and also to a special training for it, if the Church was to keep the pure apostolic tradition. It is right that ordination should now be conferred through ordained people only. Yet we should not exclude the other ways as a matter of principle, for they too correspond to the relationship between apostle and Church and were a means of securing the growth of the apostolic Church. This openness is of great ecumenical importance.[1] Without it we cannot understand many spiritual break-throughs in Church history, whether missionary advances in pagan lands or revivals inside a tired and self-righteous

[1] Though there is much Anglican literature on the question of the ecclesiastical ministry, there is relatively very little about the free charisms; yet we find sometimes a certain readiness to acknowledge that God can act in the Church today as in the Early Church and call individuals to service, giving them authority to fulfil their ministry without the actual co-operation of the Church to do the calling, but directly through the power of the Holy Spirit. It is then the task of the Church to recognize, through its ordained ministry, these freely appearing charismatic services (non-regular ministries) and to fit them into the ordered life of the Church. (Cf. A. Erhardt, 'The Apostolic Succession', 1953, *The Apostolic Ministry* (Scottish Journal of Theology Occasional papers No. 7; Edinburgh: Oliver and Boyd, (1958).)

Church; the resulting divisions within Christianity cannot be healed unless the need for such an openness is recognized.

e) What are we to say then about the apostolic succession understood in its narrow sense as the succession through ordination by episcopal laying-on of hands? It is not the *sine qua non* of the apostolic succession of Church and ministry. It does not produce an apostolic succession and authority which are missing from the other types of ordination. Already during the christological conflicts of the patristic Church, it did not prove to be the unfailing remedy securing the apostolicity of Church and dogma, and this became clearer as Church history unfolded itself. On the other hand, we must see in the episcopal laying-on of hands a *sign* for the apostolic succession of the ministries and the Church. It is a sign which is used to demonstrate that the Church is Christ's Church only when it is conscious of being founded on the Apostles. The succession of episcopal laying-on of hands is therefore a sign for the unity and catholicity of the Church.[1] We should therefore welcome the successive laying-on of hands by bishops all through Church history as a *sign* of apostolicity, and if it is absent, it is right for us to work for its introduction. But this 'signum' must never be dissociated from the 'res' which it signifies, in other words from the traditional teaching of the Apostles themselves. The sign of the apostolic succession can neither replace the necessity of submitting oneself ever anew to the historical teaching of the Apostles, nor devalue the pastoral ministry which exists without the apostolic succession.

f) Whether we feel that these remarks go too far, or not

---

[1] This understanding of the apostolic succession is in many ways not far from the conception of a group of Anglican theologians published in the survey: *The Historic Episcopate*, ed. K. Carey (London: Darve Press, 1954). This study was an attempt to overcome the alternatives which have determined the conflict between the Anglo-Catholic and Evangelical wings of the Anglican communion, for the one considers that the apostolic succession of the episcopate belongs to the *esse* of the Church, whilst the other considers it to belong to the *bene esse* of the Church. *The Historic Episcopate* was quite right in suggesting that the Anglo-Catholic conception was historically untenable, whereas the Evangelical *bene esse* theory is shown to be wanting. Over and against this, we find a new interpretation of the historical episcopate as part of the totality of the life of the Church and a sign of the unity and fullness of the Church which encompasses both space and time (not *plene esse* theory). Cf. in this work the essays by Robinson and Montefiore.

far enough, one thing is extremely important for all ecumenical discussions: we must never separate the succession of the ministries from the succession of the Church; they have always to be considered together. But it is absolutely decisive for the future of ecumenical encounter that we should go beyond the particular theme of succession to a new understanding of the unity of the Church, in taking hold once more of the type of fellowship prevalent in the Primitive Church. This is important not only for solving the problems of Church order, but also for tackling the question of dogma. For, in both these areas, the Primitive Church shows a much greater diversity of thought and definition than is shown in the later history of dogma and canon law, and greater than most would feel to be reconcilable with the future unity of the Church in the midst of the divisions of the churches.

It is only with the regaining of this type of fellowship that we can understand the unity of the Early Church, and what has been scattered during the course of Church history can be brought once more into a new and close unity.

VII. ON THE PROBLEM OF TRADITION

Twelve Theses for an Ecumenical Discussion between
Theologians of the Evangelical and Orthodox
Churches[1]

JESUS CHRIST, the crucified and risen, is the foundation
of the Church. As the appointed eyewitnesses of Jesus
Christ the Apostles are with Him the foundation of the
Church.

2. The Church must at all times and in all places remain
on the foundation of the Apostles. Only as the apostolic Church
is it the one holy catholic Church. Consequently maintenance
of apostolic tradition is laid upon the Church.

3. The apostolic tradition must be present in *all* speech
and action of the Church. In its thrust forward into ever new
domains of the world and in the discussion with ever new
religions and philosophies the Church must proclaim the
apostolic message in new tongues and statements, it must
develop the apostolic confession of Christ and continue in
apostolic prayer, baptism and breaking of bread. In these
historical developments in word and deed it may rely upon
the fact that Jesus Christ is called to mind by the apostolic
tradition not only *historically* but as the risen Lord acts through
the Holy Ghost *nowadays* towards the Church and, through the
Church, towards the world. This is the peculiarity of the
apostolic tradition in contrast to other transmissions of historical acts and sayings. The apostolic tradition is consequently
living tradition, which by its nature occurs in a multiplicity
of historical developments.

4. In the unceasing conflict between Church and world
the apostolic tradition is exposed to danger as a living tradition
in a particular way: the world seizes the Church by false

[1] Lecture given and illustrated on October 27th, 1959, in the Evangelical Academy in Arnoldshain at an ecumenical conference of representatives of the Russian Orthodox Church (patriarchy of Moscow) and the
Evangelical Church in Germany. Trsl. by I. H. Neilson.

doctrines and force not only from the outside but also by the members and groups in the Church who appear in the name of Christ and with reference to the Apostles and strive abruptly to detach the Church from its historical apostolic foundation. In the multiplicity of traditions which refer to the Apostles and their disciples true and false traditions are thus to be differentiated with a constant vigilance.

5. In the midst of the stream of Church life the Church has thus fixed the apostolic tradition in a particular way in the Bible canon, in dogmas and Church orders, so that they determine as constants the diversity of Church life, make known the frontiers of the Church and protect the unity of the Church. The authority of canon, dogma and Church order is based here not on the decision of the Church itself but on the alleged authority of the Apostles, which is recognized by the Church through these their decisions. Thus in the New Testament canon is concentrated on the ecclesiastical deposit of the historical records of the apostolic message, while dogma is the ecclesiastical development of the apostolic confession of Christ, and thus Church order serves to carry on the service with which the Lord charged the Apostles and through them the Church.

The New Testament is here distinguished from dogma and Church order in that the apostolic message is not formulated by the later Church in it but has only been received, while in dogma and Church order the Church recognizes in its *own* words the apostolic authority and binds its members to obedience in view of this authority. Within all other apostolic tradition the biblical canon is consequently emphasized by the fact that we receive in it the *authentic* tradition of the apostolic message (whether in the words of the Apostles themselves, or in the words of the early Christian community) and in this we receive the *authentic* tradition of Jesus' words and deeds.

6. Jesus had not commanded his disciples to write but to proclaim, and Paul wrote his letters not with the purpose of producing a New Testament Bible but merely as a substitute for his bodily presence and for his oral proclamation. According to this basic significance of the *viva vox* a living freedom and great multiplicity of testimony, of prayers, of theologies and of orders is characteristic of the Early Church—a multiplicity

which is also mirrored in the different traditions of the synoptic gospels and the Gospel of John.

At the same time there exist already in the early Christian community definite traditions with fixed wording not only of the words and deeds of Jesus but also of teaching ('kerygmatic'), confessional, hymnal and other liturgical formulas which then in Church history became the point of departure for the quick progress in the stabilization of forms in liturgy, dogma and Church order in general. The more comprehensively this stabilization proceeded, the more the spontaneous testimony and prayers of the charismatics in divine worship retreated in face of the office, and even the sermon and the spontaneous prayer of the officiant retreated in face of what had by then been established textually as the liturgical norm. Finally, the more uniformly, since the beginning of the national Church, one and the same fixture of the liturgy, the confession and the orders were sought after and implemented, the more was the diversity of the living tradition cramped.

The apostolic tradition is theatened not only because it is separated from its historical foundation (the gnostic 'enthusiastic' danger) but also because its living realization is cramped in ever new words of testimony, confession and prayer and in ever new acts of service, and thus its historical diversity, necessary to its nature, is cramped (ritualistic legal danger).

7. The Ecumenical discussion about the dogmatic significance of tradition suffers from the fact that (1) between the historical process of apostolic tradition and the dogmatic concept of tradition, in which thought is given to this process, there is not sufficient differentiation and (2) the same thing is not characterized in the different Churches by the same word 'tradition'.

1. In the religious historical process of the apostolic tradition the most important steps to be emphasized are:

a) The oral tradition of the words and acts of Jesus and the oral proclamation of Christ by the Apostles, supplemented by their letters.

b) The writing down of the words and acts of Jesus, their concentration in different 'sources' and their assimilation in different Gospels, while at the same time the oral tradition of the words and acts of Jesus not fixed in writing continued.

At the same time the oral proclamation of Christ by the Apostles continued in succeeding generations, by whom the apostolic letters were read out even in communities to whom they were not originally addressed.

c) The collection of Gospels and letters, among which was the story of the Apostles, by which the limits of the New Testament canon were not yet closed. But while Papias of Hierapolis had inquired into the oral tradition of the words of the Lord there is in Tertullian, Irenaeus and the other anti-gnostic fathers as good as no further reference to the *concrete* historical tradition of the words and acts of Jesus which are not recorded in the Gospels. The oral tradition of the Lord's words and deeds, which to begin with was continuing alongside the gospels, had evidently been already absorbed *ca.* 200 A.D. in the life of the Church or had been so distorted in agnostic direction that its drift could no longer be reliably ascertained. At the same time the oral proclamation of Christ by the apostles continued, by which the New Testament scriptures have the same valid authority as the Old Testament as basic documents.

d) The demarcation of the New Testament canon as the source of the apostolic tradition—surrounded with the fixing of the liturgy, the dogma and the orders of office, which have developed at the same time as the canon, which should likewise serve the apostolic tradition.

e) After the conclusion of the formation of the canon liturgy, dogma and Church orders develop—surrounded by a growing tradition of interpretation of the scriptures in exegesis, sermon and dogmatic doctrine, in which prominent authority is awarded to individual theologians from the time before and after the demarcation of the canon by the term Church fathers and Church teachers—surrounded as time went on by various ideas and pietistic usages.

f) Each Church actually exists in a tradition, no matter whether it reflects upon it and develops a dogmatic concept of tradition or whether it fails to do this.

2. In view of these many-sided facts is it necessary to explain carefully

a) what is to be denoted by the concept of apostolic tradition:

α) The whole stream of Church life including the ideas and usages of the piety of the people?

β) The stream of Church life so far as it appears in the life and action of the Church offices?

γ) The Bible canon, dogmas, Church regulations, liturgy, Church fathers and Church teachers?

δ) The Bible canon and dogmas or

ε) Only the Bible canon?

b) But if one talks of 'scriptures and tradition' it must be explained whether one understands by tradition only the dogmas, or dogmas, Church orders and liturgies or, besides this, the doctrines of the Church fathers and Church teachers or, besides this, the sayings of the Church officials or, beyond that, the sayings of the piety of the people also.

c) It must then be explained what authoritative rank is to be conferred upon these different components of tradition in their relationship to one another.

8. The position of the Reformation towards tradition is not yet discerned if one bears in mind only its *concept* of tradition. We must rather examine what use it made of tradition *in practice*. With the word 'tradition' almost only 'human ordinances' of ceremonial and jurisdictional nature were characterized by the lutheran creeds in their rejection of medieval corruptions falsely represented as 'handed down by the apostles' (e.g. Apology VII, 38).

9. The Lutheran creeds base their dogmatic statements on scriptural statements, with reference to the dogmatic decisions of the primitive Church which they expressly take over, and with the citation of the Latin and Greek Church fathers. With the dogmatic decisions of the primitive Church their anathemas were also expressly taken over (cf. J. Koopmans, *Das altkirchliche Dogma in der Reformation*, 1955). The most impressive evidence of the significance which was conferred upon the Church fathers is the 'catalogus testimoniorum' contained in the concordance book, the 'catalogue of the testimonies of holy scripture and of the old genuine church teacher'. This collection of quotations of mostly Greek fathers should serve to prove that the concordance book has not 'deviated' from the doctrine 'of the old genuine church fathers' and did not introduce 'new, strange, self-conceived, unusual and unheard discourses'. Consequently in the Lutheran creeds the tradition of the council decisions of the old Church *really* plays a con-

siderable part in addition to the apostolic tradition contained in the Holy Scriptures.

10. In the Confessio Augustana (1530) there exist no fundamental statements about the rank of the authority of the Holy Scriptures, old Church dogma and comments of the Church fathers. But in the preamble to the concordance formula (1580) it is then expressly declared 'that the one rule and guiding-principle, according to which all doctrines and teachers should be judged simultaneously, should alone be the prophetic and apostolic scriptures of the Old and New Testament'. 'Other scriptures, however, of the old and new teachers . . . should not be considered equal to the Holy Scriptures' but be acknowledged only as interpretation of the scriptures, 'as witnesses, whose form has been kept after the time of the apostles and in whose place such doctrine of the prophets and apostles' (from the summary concept, 1f.). The authority of the Church fathers is thus a derived authority. It does not exist beside the authority of the prophets and Apostles but consists in the fact that it serves the preservation, and that means at the same time the actual historical development of the *authentic* prophetic and apostolic message contained in the Holy Scriptures.

This protestant definition of the relationship of the authorities was nothing fundamentally new in view of the theology of the early and medieval Church. Since the fixing of the New Testament canon, tradition had been made valid alongside the scriptures above all as an ecclesiastical understanding of the scriptures, but not as an independent authority existing beside the scriptures. Thus according to Irenaeus and also according to Vincent of Lerin the Holy Scriptures contain the whole doctrine of the Apostles entirely (cf. Geiselmann in the Roman Catholic omnibus volume *Die mündliche Überlieferung*, 1957). Even Thomas Aquinas, who used tradition in large measure, in the fundamental questio 1 of the first part of his *Summa theologiae* made only the scriptures count as the source of theological knowledge. 'The Holy Scriptures enjoyed throughout antiquity and the middle ages such a high esteem that traditions appear no more than an annex in face of it' (Geiselmann, p. 166). The *fundamental* evaluation of the Holy Scriptures by the reformers was not new, but the *critical use* which the reformers made of the Holy Scriptures in the face of corrupt medieval traditions was. In contrast to medieval theology they no longer artificially harmonized scripture and tradition but submitted ecclesiastical traditions to the standard of the Holy Scriptures and purified them by applying this judging standard. The authority of the reformers themselves and that of the Church offices as also all piety and the orders of divine worship remained subjected in the reformation Church to the same standard.

11. The purification of the Western Church tradition by the Lutheran reformation is not to be confused with a biblical purism. Only what evidently contradicted the Holy Scriptures was to be set aside. Much on the other hand was retained which had grown in the course of Church history, without contradicting the Holy Scriptures. In this attitude the Lutheran reformation differs from that of Calvin. The knowledge that the apostolic message is by its nature not to be handed down primarily as a book to read from but in the act of proclamation prevented Luther from overlooking the liveliness of the apostolic tradition in ever new historical words and deeds of the Church and from scorning what had grown in Church history. Beyond Luther, Melanchthon then made the early Church tradition in contrast to the medieval fundamentally valid as true interpretation of the scriptures and with the scriptures represented the consensus of the old Church—also for the sake of its age—as the basis of Church unity (cf. O. Ritschl, *Dogmengeschichte des Protestantismus*, Vol. II, 1908, p. 193ff.).

12. It is to be understood from these assumptions that the theologians of Tübingen in their correspondence with the ecumenical patriarch Jeremias II proceeded from the conviction that the Church of the Lutheran reformation has the same faith and is just as apostolic a Church as the Orthodox Church of the East. For they recognized the early Church's dogmatic decisions as proper interpretation of the scriptures in face of the false doctrines of that time and held fast to them and were at the same time certain, in face of the Western false doctrines of their time, to have taken a position which was just as much in accordance with the scriptures as that of the early Church fathers in their different historical situation. With this new

beginning with the Holy Scriptures as the 'one rule and guiding-principle' in the knowledge that the apostolic tradition takes place primarily by the *viva vox evangelii* we are enabled to understand anew the differences of Church tradition which have arisen in history and to perceive again in the midst of different historical developments the one apostolic foundation.

PART III

ENCOUNTER IN COUNCIL

R

I. GOD'S PILGRIM PEOPLE[1]

I

THE CHURCH is on the way between the first and second
coming of Jesus Christ. It is on the journey towards its
Lord who is coming again. It does not know all that will
befall it on this way through the world. But it knows for sure
that at the end of this way the Lord stands as the conqueror of
the world and of all conflict. Then he will gather his own from
all lands and peoples and times and hold the great Banquet
with them. Then, after all conflict and strife, there will be *one*
flock and *one* shepherd. When the apostle Paul wrote: 'For now
is our salvation nearer than when we believed' (Rom. XIII. 11),
this word is all the more true today: The second coming of
Christ is nearer than ever before. Christ will come to redeem
his people.

But let us not forget: The Lord will come not only as the
redeemer but also as the judge, and indeed not only as the judge
of the world but also as the judge of Christendom. 'We must
all appear before the judgement seat of Christ' (II Cor. V. 10).
Then the Lord will say to some: 'Come, ye blessed of my father'
—and to others: 'Depart from me, ye cursed' (Matt. XXV. 34,
41). Then he will carry out a separation which goes much deeper
than all the separations which we people on earth undertake.
In face of the separation of the last judgement the dissolutions
of the Church are only provisional and in spite of all their
seriousness lack eschatological finality. For the separation which
Christ will undertake goes through *all* Churches. None of the
Churches assembled here can count on remaining undivided.
The Lord will then say even to those who have eaten and drunk
before him and listened to his word (Luke XII. 26f.), even to
those who have prophesied in his name and done great deeds:
'I never knew you: depart from me' (Matt. VII. 22f.).

[1] Lecture delivered on August 17th, 1952, at the opening session of the
third World Conference for Faith and Church Order in Lund. Trsl. by
I. H. Neilson.

245

But who then will be saved? The poor in spirit, the hungry and thirsty (Matt. v. 3, 6). those who longingly watch and wait (Matt. xxv. 1ff.)—the restless who know that in this world they are wholly in a foreign country and that they have no resting place here—those who yearn and await the solution of all problems from the coming Lord alone. Christ, however, says to the rich, the satisfied, those who laugh, those who have homes and are loved in this world: 'Woe'! (Luke vi. 24ff.).

We are gathered here as divided Churches. But before us all stands the Lord who is coming again, whether we are mindful of it or not. We are all already in the net which He has cast out, even if this net has not yet been drawn out of the sea and we still think we can swim around gay and free in the water. But the net is drawn out of the water with certainty and the good and bad fish will be separated (Matt. xiii. 47ff.). However much at variance we may yet be, we are actually one as those inescapably enclosed in *one* net and as those delivered to the *one* Lord and fisher.

II

This judgement is not only a future one but goes already to large parts of the world and broad areas of Christendom. I am thinking here of the mighty historical catastrophes and the persecutions which God has permitted to overtake many of our brethren. For them, with the growth of forces tied to an anti-Christian world-view and their demand for obedience which claims the whole man, God has already let the eschatological testing and sifting time begin. In these troubles and in the temptation given with them to save one's own life by the renunciation of Christ's claim to be master and by the surrender of the brethren, divisions of utmost gravity are now already occurring. Here the Lord has already taken his fan in his hand and put the Churches on this fan to separate the wheat and the chaff (Matt. iii. 12).

The result of this separation which occurs in catastrophes and temptations can be foreseen just as little by man as the result of the separation on the last day. Then it can be seen that great and proud Churches which seemed to stand there firmly knit together, fold up like a pack of cards and only a small part of them holds firm in temptation. Communities who have the

reputation of being alive turn out suddenly to be dead (Rev.
III. I). Leading men in the Church at whom Christians were
wont to gaze sudddenly have no resolving word of comfort and
instruction for their flock. Then separations and transformations
of a wholly unforeseen nature are accomplished. The first
become last and the last become first.

At the same time, however, the partitions which stand
between the denominational Churches become strangely transparent. In temptation there takes place a revaluation and transformation of the standards by which the divided Christian
communities have measured one another hitherto. The great
came out of the small, the significant out of the insignificant,
the *one* out of the many. Much, however, of what was tradition-
ally considered as great and significant and designed to separate
the Churches now appears as small and insignificant. For the
gaze of those who withstand temptation and remain in temptation with Christ, the sole head of the Church and the world,
is radically drawn forward. The past sinks in the revolution,
there remains only the view of the coming redeemer and the
yearning call for the coming of His kingdom. Thus in prison
cells and forced labour camps and on the way to executions
today the community of the divided brethren becomes reality,
as Vladimir Soloviev saw in his vision of the anti-Christ. Thus
Christ gathers his one people even now in the midst of the
divisions of this age.

This unity of God's people is experienced everywhere where
it makes an appearance in great difficulties, as a reality bestowed by God, namely as the reality of the present Christ.
Whoever experiences it can perceive in it not only perhaps a
desperate evasion or an extravagance conditioned by the un-
usualness of the situation, but it is to him an undeniable divine
reality.

III

It is all the more astonishing how little the fact that this
developing transparency of the traditional ecclesiastical partitions affects the rest of Christendom. It is true that it thinks
with sympathy of the persecuted Churches. But the themes and
questions peculiar to it are here as a rule quite different from
there. Even the treatment of confessional problems is different,

namely much more determined by historical tradition than there. With all sympathy one can only in a very restricted way place oneself in the situation of those brethren let alone draw conclusions from it for one's own situation.

But it is even more astonishing how quickly that experience of the unity of God's pilgrim people fades in the case of many when the period of persecution has ceased. After the order of the Church had been continuously disturbed in the catastrophe they often only too naturally go back to the earlier order, seek guiding principles for the reconstruction in their own past and thus at the same time restore the old separation of the denominational Churches from one another.

But can that experience of unity be so lightly passed over? Can it be disposed of with the hint that it is here a matter only of an exceptional situation, of emergency measures and of quite unusual experiences? Why then is the same thing not true of 'normal' situations as in those borderline situations? Have we forgotten that alienation, misunderstanding and lack of peace is the normal situation of the Church in the world, and recognition of the world and peace with the world the anomaly? In this world the Church is always in a frontier situation and often enough times of persecution were less dangerous to it than the pact of peace with the world which respects and guarantees the historically developed state of the church. 'Beloved, think it not strange concerning the fiery trial which is to try you, as though some strange thing happened unto you: But rejoice, inasmuch as ye are partakers of Christ's sufferings; that, when his glory shall be revealed, ye may be glad also with exceeding joy' (I Pet. iv. 12f.). Even in affliction real experiences will be had and hope will be strengthened which will not come to nothing (Rom. v. 3ff.).

Christendom will have to learn in its attempts at unification of these their poorest and yet richest brethren, of these their most despised and yet by God most honoured members. Even though their mouth is shut their way is an audible testimony. Even though this way is often concealed from us they are visible before God as his true people. We must learn from them to tear away the view of the past and look forward to the coming Lord. This is the only direction in which the view of the tempted is still sinful. The movement forwards, however, is also the direction of the whole early Christian testimony. Hastening forward in this direction we must look at one another with new vision.

IV

In the past few years there has often been talk of a crisis in the work of the Commission for Faith and Order. Is this assertion valid?

If there is a crisis here it does not at all events consist in a lack of *interest* in the theme 'Faith and Order'. This interest has rather developed quite considerably in the course of the twenty-five years since the conference at Lausanne. Think, for example, of the transconfessional liturgical movement and of the interest awakened likewise in the sacrament, the office and in the problem of tradition.

It is also not possible to talk of a lack of *results* in the work so far. The divided Churches have learnt in the course of this work to know one another anew and see one another with new vision. They have reached a clear understanding of where they agree and where they are different, in which what they have in common has often been recognized as surprisingly overpoweringly and unforgettably great. The unmitigated alienation of the Churches from one another is today to a great extent overcome.

There is also by no means a lack of further tasks. Decisively important themes like Christology and eschatology are still waiting for a thorough consideration. The same is true of many questions of pneumatology, in particular the problem of the unity and diversity of the charismata of the body of Christ. Moreover important points of view appropriate to the further elucidation of problems already considered are still waiting for a methodical application; think, for example, of the significance of the anthropological and philosophical presuppositions of the ways of thinking in which the different Churches make their statements of faith. Indeed the more the Churches have drawn closer to one another the more comprehensive becomes the task which they see is set.

If there is talk of a crisis in the work for 'faith and order' this cannot, however, be based on the fact that this work is allied to the other work of the conferences of Stockholm and Oxford since 1948 in the World Council of the Churches. For the work of the study-section in Geneva, which has grown out of the 'Life and Work' movement, has become in so gratifying a measure a truly theological work intent on a biblical foundation that it and the commission for faith and Church order are supplementing each other as well as possible.

In spite of all this, however, there must be something genuine in it if many are speaking of a crisis today. At all events the work for 'faith and order' is, it seems to me, in a crisis in relation to the method used hitherto. This method was above all that of a methodical and comprehensive interconfessional comparison, in which the attempt was made to work out a maximum of common interest. After it had led first of all to surprising results in far-reaching agreements, it made, with increasing exactness of application, the existing differences and contrasts more strongly known than was the case in the enthusiasm of the first awakening of the ecumenical movement. That cannot be otherwise because this comparative method is a statistical method. It presupposes a certain finality of the characteristics of the different Churches, which can be compared with one another, and considers the Churches as a static form. It does not reckon with changes and demands no sacrifice on the side of the participating Christian communities. Thus this method as such does not ultimately take one further on the way to unification, even if one will never be able to do without it.

Moreover ecumenical work is meanwhile placed in a crisis by what God does today to the divided Churches in many lands. This goes far beyond the result of even such a careful comparison. God himself placed the work for 'faith and order' in a crisis—and indeed at one time through the new community which originated among our most oppressed and persecuted brethren, and at another by the awakening of the young Churches which resolved to 'forget those things which are behind' and 'reach forth unto those things which are before' (Phil. III. 13), which leave historical traditions behind them and strive for unity, which is in accordance with the one Lord who came to us. Here changes do in fact take place. Here traditional peculiarities are sacrificed. And these sacrifices turn out to be the receipt of riches—they turn out to be so gladsome that they cannot even be called sacrifices.

The crisis in the work for 'faith and order' might consist in the fact that the vanguard of God's pilgrim people seems today to be further ahead than the state of our considerations. In face of what is actually taking place today in many countries in the impetuous seizure of the goal offered by God our work so far appears to many theoretical and slow and too backward-looking.

V

In this criticism we must not of course overlook the fact that the Churches assembled for the world Church conferences have already taken an unprecedentedly revolutionary step forward. And indeed this has taken place in the often repeated ceremonious declaration of their unity in Christ. After Lausanne, Oxford and Edinburgh they again professed in Amsterdam: 'We praise God and thank Him for the mighty deed of His Holy Ghost, through whom we were led together and through whom we recognise that we are one in Jesus Christ in spite of our separations' (Report of the first section). This testimony of the unity of the Churches in Christ was an advance of the greatest importance. What happened here?

Is this proclamation of unity only a rhetorical statement which is to hide the disgrace and shame of the disunion of Christendom? No.

Is it only the expression of a hope and does it only name a goal to be reached? No. The answer to this question has been given already in Oxford: 'Unity in Christ is for us not only a goal which we set ourselves. It is a reality, which we know from experience' (Message to the Christian Churches). It is a present reality. But in what sense is the unity a present reality?

Is it present only in the denominational Church, to which the individual delegates at the time belong? No, for it is testified by all together as 'our unity'.

Is this unity visible to everyone? Is it an empirical reality in the strictest sense? No, not that either, for the Christians who testified their unity in Christ here belong to separate Churches and further have no community of the sacrament together.

Is it then a rhetorical statement? No. The testimony of unity is the testimony of faith which springs away from what it sees and clings to Jesus Christ who is the one Lord over and above all our separations and beyond all our comprehension, who rules over his people and deals with them in the present.

The acknowledgement of our unity in Christ in spite of our evident separation is a statement of faith of a similar kind as the testimony of the death of our sinful body in baptism. 'Know ye not, that so many of us as were baptized into Jesus Christ were baptized into his death?' Know ye not 'that our old man is crucified with him, that the body of sin might be destroyed, that henceforth we should not serve sin'. 'Reckon ye also yourselves to be dead indeed unto sin, but alive unto God through Jesus Christ our Lord' (Rom. vi. 3, 6, 11). All this is true, even if we do not see it. As people who have been baptized we are dead to sin, even if we acknowledge ourselves daily to be sinners and have every cause to pray daily to our father in heaven: 'Forgive us our debts'. As the belief that we are dead to sin with Christ in baptism goes beyond our visible sins—as we are sure in our faith in the crucified Lord that we sinners are righteous before God, so we are sure that in spite of all divisions we are one in Christ. And as the certainty of having died to sin is founded in the baptism we have experienced, so the certainty of unity is based in the experience which we have had in our encounters, namely in that we have heard the voice of the one good shepherd out of the mouth of those gathered with us, over and above all divisions, comforting and admonishing. In this mutual Christian testimony is expressed the fact that we are baptized into the same Christ.

VI

Even this recognition of unity can lead to the crisis of ecumenical work. For God's invisible act of mercy will always take shape in the life of the man pardoned. The indicative of the divine act of salvation always brings with it the imperative which demands obedience in face of the act of salvation. If in baptism we have died with Christ we must 'walk in newness of life' (Rom. vi. 4). 'Shall we continue in sin, that grace may abound? God forbid. How shall we, that are dead to sin, live any longer therein?' (Rom. vi, 1f.). To want to remain in sin as baptized men would be not only an anachronism but a grievous sin. But the same thing that is valid for the individual baptized man is also valid for the baptized community: are we to wait in separation so that the unity becomes stronger? How could we want to live in separation, who have recognized and admitted our unity in Christ? It has already been absolutely and rightly declared in Lausanne that 'we can never again be the same as we were before' (Call to Unity).

Have we really become different from what we were before?

One cannot always declare unity again anew and at the same time persist in separation. The indicative of the recognized unity contains at the same time the imperative to achieve the unification. It is not permissible to seek to find the unity of the Churches only in the mutual *faith* in unity. To be content with this would be a docetic concept of the Church and an illegitimate spiritualization. For the body of Christ is always a simultaneously visible communion of his members in word, sacrament and ministry.

One cannot, however, take comfort from the fact that the diversity of our Churches, the organically developed riches of the body of Christ, is according to the Pauline statements about the diversity of the gifts of the spirit. We are not permitted to equate this diversity with the divided churches today. For the Church as the body of Christ is constituted by the community of the body of Christ in Holy Communion. But where the communion of the sacrament is missing there is not organic diversity but disorder and shame.

But we can also no longer fall back upon the separate denominational Church. For we cannot forget that we have met brothers from other Churches, that we have recognized that we are members of the *one* Church.

And in the ecumenical movement itself we are all placed in a crisis by this very admitted unity. Without effective progress in the union the repeated declarations of unity before Christendom and the world are not worthy of credence. Without realization of the unity bestowed on us this act of mercy of God becomes an accusation. The beatifying recognition of unity itself places us then under God's judgement.

It is not disputed in these statements that there are also amongst those who call themselves Christians separations which *must* be carried out in obedience to God. Then it is a question of eschatological separation between Church and pseudo-Church, between the dominion of Christ and the dominion of the powers of corruption which are disguised as Christian; then it is a question of eternal life and eternal death. But it is certainly to be disputed that in all the existing dissensions of Christendom today it is a question of this last unavoidable separation.

VII

Let me break off here and return to the starting-point of the lecture.

The Church is God's pilgrim people. In this world it is on the way towards its returning Lord. It does not know everything that will befall it on this way. But it is certain that the Lord is going to meet it in order to gather his own who are scattered in the world, so that they may live united with him in eternal glory.

Let us hasten forward on this way and *not stand still*. Let us look forward and not be caught gazing at the present. Let us tear our gaze from the visible separations which we have not yet conquered and look firmly to the one Lord whom we are going to meet. In looking forward, in awaiting the coming judge of the world and the redeemer, we will perceive the provisional nature, the lack of finality of many things which separate us.

Let us hasten forward on the way, not stand still and also not look *backwards*. Let us live in expectation, instead of sticking firmly to the past. Let us tear our gaze from the one-sidedness, which has often become so rigid, of the consideration of those historical events in which the schism of the Churches was accomplished. Let us direct our gaze to the much deeper separation which the returning Lord will accomplish in all Churches and to the unity in the eternal glory which he will then bring about. In looking forward the past emerges in a new light and many problems which formerly seem insoluble are solved.

Let us hasten forward. Only in the expectation of the second coming can we understand properly the Biblical testimony of the first advent of our Lord. For the whole New Testament message directs us forwards, and only in hastening on do we submit to it in the proper way. Only in hastening forward can we understand it properly. Only in the expectation of the returning Lord do we have communion with the Lord who came in the flesh. For the crucified Lord knocks as the returning Lord on the house we have built, in which we have hidden ourselves from God and the brethren and barricaded ourselves in against them, while he says: 'Behold I stand at the door and knock: if any man hear my voice, and open the door, I will come in to him, and will sup with him, and he with me' (Rev. III. 20).

II. CHRIST THE HOPE OF THE WORLD[1]

I

WHENEVER we ask about the future of the world, we come immediately and unavoidably in the New Testament to the announcement of the end of the world: 'The fashion of this world passeth away' (I Cor. vii. 31). 'And the world passeth away, and the lust thereof' (II John ii. 17). The New Testament further announces that great tribulation shall befall the world before it finally does pass away: war and hunger, the disintegration of all community, mass destruction and natural disasters are to be expected. We are told to watch for such things to occur. Wherever, then, the coming of Christ is spoken of as the *Hope* of the world, the end of the world is always spoken of, too.

Against this proclamation of its end, the world defends itself by means of its own hopes. Even among Christians, many have grown deaf to the proclamation of the world's end. They dismiss it as mere Judaic-apocalyptic thinking. Yet it is clear that today people are afraid that humanity is doomed. The world's own hopes, therefore, have become especially tenacious. Everywhere the thoughts and dreams of men are filled with the visions of the horror that may be waiting for us. Men fear that we shall see the return of the destruction of two world wars in even greater and more horrible forms. Men see before them the possibility of ruined skyscrapers and annihilated cities. The further development of the atom bomb has opened before our eyes in a very clear and concrete way prospects of the end of humanity and the breaking asunder of the earth. It is just because it has made so much progress that mankind has reached the point beyond which it must not go.

There is an essential difference, however, between the fears

[1] This is the official text of the speech given on August 15th, 1954, at the opening plenary session of the Second Assembly of the World Council of Churches in Evanston, Illinois, U.S.A. Originally published in the *Ecumenical Review*, Vol. vii, 1955, p. 127ff.

of modern men and the New Testament proclamation of the end of the world. Today we are afraid of men who may misuse the power entrusted to them and unleash horrible destruction upon the world. We fear the atomistic powers of nature over which we may easily lose control. But in the New Testament the calamities of the last days are not merely human misdoings nor are they the consequence of human frailty. They are rather the activity of God Himself. In the New Testament it is *God* who will bring the end of the world. It is from God's throne that the orders go out, that send the apocalyptic riders over the earth (Rev. VI. 1, 3, 5, 7). They are the vials of the wrath of God which shall be poured out upon the earth (Rev. XVI. 1ff.). God has given mankind 'over to a reprobate mind to do those things which are not convenient' (Rom. I. 28). The end of the world is the day of divine judgement.

We are also told that God has given over to Jesus Christ this judgement over all human arrogance and presumption. Christ will come as the judge of the world. He will break in like a thief in the night (I Thess. v. 2). He will pounce upon the world like an eagle on a dead carcass (Matt. XXIV. 28). The appearance of Christ will mean the end of the world. Then 'All kindreds of the earth shall wail' (Rev. I. 7).

How then dare we speak of 'Christ the Hope of the World'?

If in our thinking about this subject we place the emphasis on the preservation of this threatened world, then we shall miss the point of our Assembly theme completely. If we expect Christ to insure this world so that men may continue undisturbed their pursuit of liberty, may carry on their business, and seek an improvement in their standard of living, then Christ is not the hope of the world, but rather the end of all the world's hopes, for Christ is the *end* of the world. The name of Christ is taken in vain if it is used as a slogan in this world's struggle for its own preservation.

The decisive question is not how can we manage to avoid wars and disasters, but rather how do we stand in *God's* eyes. Our real threat does not come from men, 'powers' or the forces of nature, but from God whose judgement no man can escape. The hidden root of our fear is fear of God, God who will bring to nothing the pride of this world. The important question is this: Is there any deliverance from God's judgement?

II

We have no right to speak of Christ as the hope of the world unless we humble ourselves before God and recognize Him as the judge of the world. Surely, we have deserved God's judgement. We have not given God the honour which is His due. We have thought only of ourselves when we should have served our fellow-men. We have too often remained silent when our voices should have been clearly heard. We have too often been afraid when we should have loved and judged when we should have forgiven. The unrighteousness, oppression and bloodshed which we have begotten defy description. The history of the Church itself is not just a hymn of praise to God, but is again and again a scandal. 'We have sinned, and have committed iniquity, and have done wickedly, and have rebelled, even by departing from thy precepts and from thy judgements' (Dan. ix. 5). 'If thou Lord shouldest mark iniquities, O Lord, who shall stand?' (Ps. cxxx. 3).

Only when we have repented and confessed that we have wasted our life in God's sight shall we ever know Christ as the hope of the world.

Christ who is our hope is the Christ who was *crucified*. Look upon this man hanging on the Cross of Golgotha, crowned with thorns, despised, rejected. Look upon this man with the disfigured body and the bloody countenance. Here is the perfect picture of all human misery and shame. Hear from His lips the cry, 'I thirst'. 'My God, my God, why hast Thou forsaken me?' The good religious people have denounced Him. The government has condemned Him. All His friends have now forsaken Him. But the deepest depth of His misery is that He is forsaken by God, abandoned before the Judgement Seat of God. Yet this man Jesus Christ is not dying there for His own sin: 'Surely he hath borne *our* griefs and carried *our* sorrows' (Isa. liii. 4). 'For he was wounded for our transgressions and bruised for our iniquities' (v. 5). God 'has made him to be sin for us who knew no sin that we might be made the righteousness of God in him' (II Cor. v. 21).

He who was judged *for* the world will appear as judge *of* the world. It is the same Christ who has borne the sins of the world who comes again into the world. He who died for the world intercedes at the throne of God for those who cry unto Him. It is to the crucified Lord we must cling and in the crucified Lord that we must hope. Only through faith in Him will we find salvation at the Day of Judgement and will we, in spite of our sins, be judged 'not guilty'. For God has made Him who was crucified our righteousness.

He who was crucified would not be our hope, however, had He not also risen from the dead. God has raised from the dead Him who was crucified. In this act, God declared Himself for Jesus Christ; 'This man alone died without sin. This is my Son.' God delivered Him from the bonds of death and set Him down in that life which is not bound by the limitations of this world. He is the new man. God has made Jesus Christ the victor over all His enemies, has lifted Him up and has 'given unto him all power in heaven and earth' (Matt. xxviii. 18). Christ is the Lord of the world, but Christ has not kept this victory for Himself. As He died for the world, so He rose again for the world. He conquered the powers of sin and death that those who believe in Him might become victors too. He was the first who opened the way to life that many might share with Him in this life. The Risen Lord had just escaped from the bonds of death when He returned to His own, to those who had forsaken and even betrayed Him, and appeared to them, and greeted them with 'Peace be with you'.

Let us then place our hope in one who was crucified—in one who rose again. He is our victorious brother who will come again to judge the world. He is the first-born of the new creation, who will bring this world to an end. The conqueror of all suffering and sorrow will come. He will come to raise His own from the dead as He Himself was raised, to make His own victors as He Himself is victor. He will gather together a new humanity whose Head He is and then will appear the new creation.

Jesus Christ then is the hope of the world not because He guarantees the preservation of this world, but because He liberates us from all the binding ties of this world. Christ is the hope of the world because He calls men out of the world. He gathers together from every corner of the earth His people whose members are strangers in this world and whose citizenship is in heaven. Christ is the hope of the world only in so far as the world no longer remains the world, but is transformed through

s

repentance and faith. Christ is the end of the world with its joy and its sorrow and for just that reason He is the world's hope. For as the world passes away, He will bring to birth a new creation.

III

Christ then comes again into the world as its redeemer and as its judge. We cannot rightly hope for him as Saviour unless we also look to Him as judge. At the same time, we cannot rightly fear Him as judge unless we also expect Him as Saviour. When He comes, He will accept some and reject others. He will raise up some to life and some to death. To some He will say, 'Come ye blessed of my Father,' and to others 'Depart from me, ye cursed' (Matt. xxv. 34 and 41). He will smash the rule of the mighty, the rich and the self-contented and all their unrighteousness. He will destroy the comfort of the satisfied, the happy, and those who are at home in this world. But the poor in spirit, they that mourn, they who hunger and thirst after righteousness, the peace-makers, and those who watch longingly for the day of His Coming—all these He will save (Matt. v. 3 and Luke xii. 35).

This future separation is already *happening* now. By the preaching of the Cross, God is already putting to shame the wisdom, virtue and power of this world, and saving the foolish, the unworthy and the helpless: 'And base things of the world, and things which are despised, has God chosen, yea, and things which are not, to bring to naught things that are' (I Cor. i. 28).

Even now, the coming redemption is taking place through the Gospel. Even now, the faithful are in this world being acquitted before the future judgement. Through baptism and the Lord's Supper, the believer participates even now in the power of the coming resurrection. He who is born again to a living hope through the Holy Spirit, is even here and now a new creature. So through the Gospel here in this world Christ is gathering His people to live together with Him in the new life. In the Church, the coming new creation is already a present reality. 'Therefore if any man be in Christ, he is a new creature: old things are passed away; behold, all things are become new' (II Cor. v. 17).

For this reason, the days in which we live are the last days. In His resurrection, Christ has broken through the limitations of this world and has been raised to become Lord over the world. All men and all powers are subject to Christ whether they know it or not and whether they recognize Him or revolt against Him.

When He returns, He will make His victory apparent to every eye and bring to an end all the revolt of this world.

This world's time then is tightly hemmed in by the victory of Christ. It is quite impossible to break out of this encirclement. Into this hopeless situation comes the call of the Gospel through which the world is bid to recognize its Lord. These are the last days: 'Today if ye will hear his voice, harden not your hearts' (Heb. III. 7).

That these are, in fact, the last days seems to be disproved by the fact that nearly two thousand years have passed since the coming of Jesus Christ. Many people no longer believe in the promise of His future coming. But the length of time is no refutation of His promise. It is not a sign of God's weakness, as if He could not if He wished bring to fulfilment what He has promised through Jesus and the Apostles. Rather, this time in which we live is the time of God's patience. God wills that many shall be saved. This time in which we live is the time of the Church, of the growing body of Christ. But when the body of Christ shall have grown to full stature, when the number of the elect shall have been completed, then shall the world pass away and then shall the new creation appear as from a hiding-place.

IV

What does hoping in Christ mean? Hoping means not sleeping, but watching with the utmost alertness. Hoping means not just dreaming, but waiting with utter soberness. Being sober does not mean using the cold calculation of this world, but rather waiting for the coming Christ. Hoping means not growing weary but carrying on our work with the most intense expectancy. From the time of the Apostles until our own day, it has not been paralysis, but action that has characterized the life of those in whom Christian hope dwells. For we know not the hour of His coming.

What then are the actions born of Hope?

The first act of hope is the preaching of the Gospel to the whole world. The World Council was right to choose Evangelism for the theme of the Assembly's Second Section. Because God redeems through the Gospel alone, those who hope are bound by the command of the Redeemer to preach that Gospel. As He has freed us from the binding ties of this world, so He sends us back into the world to call others likewise to freedom.

This commandment binds *everyone* who hopes in Christ. No one can keep the hope silently for himself without losing it.

This commandment makes us *debtors* to *all* men, for God wills that no one shall perish.

This command means *denying* the so easily assumed advantages of our own nationality and cultural traditions. Even more, as so often has been the case in the history of missions in the past, we must become Jews to the Jews, Gentiles to the Gentiles, and weak to the weak in order to win them over. Only by emptying ourselves can we become servants of Christ (see I Cor. ix. 19).

The command of God the Redeemer requires of us the greatest *speed*. We do not know how much time we have left.

It is furthermore of the utmost importance that we should preach the Gospel in truth and purity. Those responsible for the preparation of the Second Section here at Evanston have been mostly concerned with the *methods* of evangelism. But the whole Assembly must concern itself with the *content* of evangelism. At stake here is the message of God's judgement of the world and of salvation through faith in Jesus Christ alone.

The spreading of this message seems difficult indeed, for the world does not want to hear about its own end; for it the preaching of the Cross is indeed foolishness. And yet at the same time, the preaching of the Gospel is infinitely easy and full of unspeakable joy, for it is not our task to bring the world to Christ's feet. God long ago has put the world under Him. We only have to tell the world who its Lord already is. It is not up to us to save men. Christ wants only to use our witness that He may speak through it and do His saving deeds Himself. We cannot engender faith. Only the spirit of God can do that.

V

The second action born of hope is accepting responsibility for the just ordering of society. It was right therefore that this theme was made the basis for discussion in Sections III to VI of the Assembly.

Those who wait for the coming of Christ know how patient and long-suffering God is. They know how He sustains the world in spite of its own arrogance and in spite of the fact that it stands already under judgement. He causes the sun to shine on the just and on the unjust. He keeps alive both believers and non-believers. He sustains not only Christians, but also pagans and anti-Christians. To all of these, God the Preserver gives time to decide for Jesus Christ.

For this reason, those who hope are also under the orders of God the Sustainer. God demands that we take responsibility for the preservation of all human life regardless of whether that life be Christian or not, that we take responsibility for all men, regardless of their nationality, race or social status, and He also demands that we accept responsibility for their freedom. For God sustains men in order that they should make, under Him, a responsible decision. Accepting the obligation for the maintenance of life and freedom means taking responsibility for justice and peace on earth—peace among men, classes, races, peoples and nations. And it means having an active concern, in the fullest sense of that word, for the right ordering of society—not only in individual well-doing, but also in law-making, etc.

The orders of God the Preserver bind *every man* who hopes in Christ. He is never justified in abdicating this responsibility to statesmen.

These orders also make us *debtors to all men*. He who hopes in Christ has no right to limit his well-doing only to the circle of the like-minded.

Furthermore, this commandment requires that we *renounce* the privileges we so easily take for granted and it forces upon us the need for acting *quickly*. Now for the first time in their history, the nations have the task of creating a new world order for mankind and for this the old order appears quite inadequate and is breaking down.

The Christian has no right to remain aloof from the struggle between political programmes and secular hopes. The world wants immortality for itself and looks to its own programmes for salvation. Because the Christian is freed from utopianism by his expectation of the Lord's coming, he owes it to the world to bear the witness of sobriety, of cool-headedness. His is the task of showing what mankind's real situation is and of cutting through the prevailing fog of propaganda. Because the Christian is by faith set free from all legalism, he can never be satisfied with any kind of general scheme. He will have to speak up whenever political principles enslave men and wherever existing laws are used to justify or conceal unlawfulness. He will stand for such action as is required by the concrete historical situation. Because the Christian is saved by the sacrifice of Christ, he will in the struggle for a just order be selfless in defence of his own interests, but demanding and adamant in his concern for the enslaved, the hungry and the forgotten. Because he has experienced the patience of God, he will oppose with all his strength the use of weapons for mass destruction and will seek peace and understanding even when these seem utterly impossible of attainment. Because he hopes in Christ, he will be fearless in the face of all the threats of this world.

Yet, in all this, we must never forget that peace on earth is not peace with God. The justice of this world is not in itself justice under God. Freedom on earth is not real freedom and this life is not eternal life. Our striving for a just order in society does not bring in Christ's Kingdom on earth nor does it fashion the new creation. Christ's Kingdom enters only through the Gospel; the Communion of Saints is the new creation.

But God the Sustainer commands us to accept the responsibility for the preservation of this world until the Day of Judgement. In spite of its arrogance and self-rightousness, this world is nevertheless God's creation. It is for this world that Christ died. And it is God's will, while He lets the world disintegrate, to bring His creation to its goal which is the new creation.

These commands of God as Redeemer and God as Sustainer cannot be separated from one another. The preaching of the Gospel and the acceptance of our responsibility for the establishment of justice on earth are both actions born of hope and love, and, therefore, service under God. But these two activities are related to each other in a particular way. One follows the other and we must not confuse them. We do not preach the Gospel in order that the world may be preserved. Rather we accept our responsibility for the preservation of the world in order that many may be saved through the Gospel. God preserves this world in order that through the Gospel salvation may be offered. He does not offer salvation in order that the world may be preserved. We do not preach the Gospel in order to bring about earthly justice. On the contrary, we try to establish justice in order that we may preach the Gospel. It has always been the great temptation of the Church for people to misunderstand this fact. It is also a temptation for the World Council of Churches. Let us never forget that the Lord has said: 'Heaven and earth shall pass away, but my words shall not pass away' (Matt. xxiv. 35).

VI

Will our actions born of hope be successful?

We today are fighting on a different battle front from that on which the Apostles fought. The old paganism is passing away. We are faced with a new kind of post-Christian man. He has heard the Gospel. He has been set free from the binding ties of this world and from submission to gods and demons. He has heard the words: 'All things are yours. The world, life, death, things present, and things to come' (I Cor. iii. 21f.). But he has separated his new freedom from submission to Christ. He has usurped the control of nature. He has himself set about to establish the eternal Kingdom of Peace on earth. He no longer waits for Christ to come. This freedom which is derived from Christ, but which is cut off from Him, weighs heavily upon the peoples in our own time, destroys their own religion, and pushes the tensions between East and West to the point of complete cleavage. Such freedom threatens life. for freedom when it is severed from duty leads to the use of violence, and the struggle of such free men for the establishment of a world order leads only to horrible destruction. When they remember the effects of two world wars, when they look at the post-Christian and anti-Christian powers about them, when they consider the possibilities of a third world war fought with atomic weapons, many people are filled with fear and inactivity because for them all activity seems pointless.

And yet we are told, 'when these things begin to come to pass, then look up, and lift up your head, for your redemption draweth nigh' (Luke xxi. 28). 'When ye shall hear of wars and rumours of wars, be ye not troubled for such things must needs be' (Mark xiii. 7). For those who hope in Christ the tumult of this world is a sure sign of Christ's coming. The world would not tremble if He were not the victor. The wintry gales that are now howling over the world are the signs of the coming spring-time. The sicknesses of our time are the birth pangs of the new creation.

So we ask again, will we be successful if we accept our responsibility?

The Gospel is now being preached to all nations on earth. At the same time, Churches in our day are being so oppressed and persecuted that the persecutions of the Early Church seem almost trivial in comparison. For the Gospel's sake, many have been deprived of their freedom, imprisoned and even put to death. Many in order to save their lives have denied the Gospel and have fallen away from the faith. Mission stations and whole Churches have disappeared. Proud Churches have been maimed and now live in modern catacombs.

Here also, it is true: 'For such things must needs be' (Mark XIII. 7, Rev. I. 1). There is no other way for the Church but the way of her Lord: 'Through suffering to glory'. Judgement must begin at the house of God (Pet. I IV. 17). God winnows and sifts His Church through persecution in order to test it, and to purify it: to separate the wheat from the chaff. But he who submits to the powerful hand of God and takes up his cross soon realizes that Christ has long since taken it up for him. Through their suffering, believers are united with Christ. Through their humiliation, their imprisonment and their death, the crucified Christ becomes visible in the world and demonstrates the power of His resurrection. Those are God's most beloved children to whom He grants to praise Him not only with the songs of their lips but also with the sacrifice of their lives and so to bear witness to Christ. Their defeat is in reality their victory. It is not the powerful privileged Church which the world recognizes but the helpless, suffering Church which reveals the glory of Christ. It is the Church which dies with Christ that is the Church triumphant.

Dare we, then, ask whether we shall see the results of our actions? The question itself is born of hopelessness.

We do not know what results our evangelism and our struggle for a just society will have in this world, but we know the most important thing we need to know—that our work 'is not in vain in the Lord' (I Cor. xv. 58). Christian hope does not depend upon what our eyes see of the results, whether they be successful or unsuccessful. It is not by chance that we find in the New Testament that the words of hope are closely tied to words which describe the trial through which Christians must go (Rom. v. 3f., Rom. viii. 18f., I Pet. i. 3f.). Christian hope is based on Jesus Christ alone. Therefore, it can never be confounded. For that reason, Christian hope always looks for the best from God and is tireless in its struggle against the powers of darkness: 'If God be for us, who can be against us?' 'He that spared not his own Son—how shall he not with him also freely give us all things?' (Rom. viii. 31f.).

This is not the hope of the world; it is the hope of the Church To this hope, the Church must call the world.

VII

Is this truly the hope of all of us? Is our faith really 'the victory that overcometh the world' (I John v. 14)?

We have gathered here as separated Churches. To be sure, the historical divisions of the Churches are only to a very small extent due to differences in eschatology, but that does not mean that the separated Churches really live in Christian hope. For where hope dwells, there the existing differences and separations of the Churches appear in a new light. And we are filled with shame that through our disunity we deny the unity of the body of Christ and so make it quite easy for the world to cast aside the message that Christ is its only hope. 'Our unity in Christ and our disunity as churches' is rightly therefore the theme of the first section. But at heart this theme is in reality that of all sections of the Assembly.

If hope were really alive within us, then we should have less fear of men than fear of God. Then we should be less concerned for the preservation of our confessional traditions and more concerned how we appear before God: 'For we must all appear before the judgement seat of Christ' (II Cor. v. 10). On that day a separation will take place which goes deeper than all the separations and all the divisions of Christendom, a separation which is ultimate. Then it may be that many of the Churches will receive this judgement: 'Because thou art lukewarm and neither cold nor hot, I will spew thee out of my mouth' (Rev. iii. 16).

If hope were really alive within us, then we should know that it is not only the world which will pass away, but also the outward form of the Church. Then we would see clearly the provisional nature of our ecclesiastical activity, of our Church order and even of our dogmatic formulations. The Church too will be transformed. In the new creation there will be no temple, for 'the Lord God Almighty and the Lamb are the temple' (Rev. xxi. 22). Then we shall not only believe the Word; we shall see God face to face.

If hope were really alive within us, we would rejoice less in the untroubled existence of our denominations, less in their security and preservation. We would instead rejoice because the Gospel is being preached and men are being saved through faith from the binding ties of this world: 'Christ is preached, and I therein rejoice' (Phil. i. 18). And our greatest glory would be the chains and suffering of our brethren of all confessions all over the world.

If hope were really alive within us, then we would not stand looking back but would rush forward towards the Lord. We would not be so much in love with the history of our own confessions, of our own denominations, but would see Christ at work all over the world. The walls that divide the Churches are quite transparent to those who look ahead.

If hope were really alive within us, we should be able to distinguish much more clearly the non-theological factors which divide the Churches. These are only important when the Church clings to the world and tries to get from the world the security which Christ alone can give. Here I stop.

But let us remember: we have all come here from Christ, from His death, from His resurrection. We are all going towards Christ who will come as judge and Saviour of the world. He is behind us and before us. He is all around us. As He who has come and as He who will come, Christ is here now among us.

Let us give Him the glory and put aside all whereby that glory is hidden from the world.

III. CHANGES IN PROTESTANT THINKING
ABOUT THE EASTERN CHURCH[1]

WHEN Adolf von Harnack in his *History of Dogma* (especially Volume II) and his *What is Christianity?* published his very critical and disparaging views on the state of theology and spiritual life in the Eastern Church, he directed his remarks not only against the Eastern Church of relatively recent centuries but also against those doctrinal decisions of the ancient Church which the Reformers had expressly retained and which the Churches of the Reformation felt had always bound them to the Eastern Church. (Harnack singled out particularly the decisions on dogma taken at the councils of Nicaea, Constantinople and Chalcedon.) Harnack's opinion was of course not representative of the Reformation Churches as a whole but only of the liberal wing known as 'neo-Protestantism.' Alongside of the neo-Protestants, who felt themselves to be fundamentally at variance with Reformation teaching and with the Lutheran Orthodoxy that followed it, there was never any lack of energetic protest in the Protestant Church—also at the turn of the century—against this neo-Protestant separation of the Church from its foundations in the ancient Church. Nevertheless Harnack's theses exercised a great influence upon Western thinking, and the Eastern Church was probably never regarded so critically and considered so strange as in the first two decades of this century. This is all the more true when one considers that Roman Catholic writers such as Bonomelli (*Die Kirche*, 1902) and Konrad Lübeck (*Die christlichen Kirchen des Orient*, 1911) seemed to share Harnack's view that the Eastern Church was torpid, ignorant and at a generally low level (cf. Friedrich Heiler, *Urkirche und Ostkirche*, 1937, p. 555f.).

This situation has altered profoundly in the past thirty years.

First, the world pricked up its ears when the persecution of Christians in Bolshevik Russia began to be known. A Church

[1] The basic thoughts of this thesis were delivered in a lecture to the Theological Academy in the Troize-Sergijewo-Monastery at Sagorsk near Moscow on March 31st, 1958. Trsl. originally published in the *Ecumenical Review*, Vol. XII, 1960, p. 133ff.

which could produce thousands of martyrs could not possibly be so torpid and moribund as it had been charged with being.

Then there were the many encounters with Orthodox emigrants—theologians and lay people—and with the Orthodox refugee congregations who gathered together with a loyalty that was as great as the distress in which they found themselves. The liturgy and piety of the Eastern Church began to exhibit in the Western world, quite unexpectedly, a vitality hitherto unknown.

But this impression of the Eastern Church upon the West remained at first on the sensuous and aesthetic level and did not yet signify that the West's conception of the Eastern Church as strange and unfamiliar had been breached and understanding produced. Such a break-through did come, though, when the Protestant Church in Germany also began to suffer oppression and persecution; liberalism's *Kulturprotestantismus* ceased to be a live option for the German Church, which was forced to rethink its positions. In the struggle of the German Church with National Socialist ideology, historic confessions and dogma took on new meaning, and in the struggle with the encroachments of a totalitarian power the ministry appeared in new perspective. In the midst of hostile attempts to crush the congregations of the Confessing Church, the services of worship where the Church gathered together assumed a new significance; and the more arrests increased and congregations, pastors and many individual Christians were cut off from one another, the more the unity of the Church, which in Christ is the same in all places and in all times, entered into the forefront of Christian thinking, hopeful and living. Then the walls separating the various confessions became peculiarly transparent. Christians began to hear the consoling voice of Jesus Christ, the one good Shepherd, speaking to them from many confessions where up till then they had not been accustomed to listening for it. At the same time the liturgy and the creeds of the ancient Church assumed new vitality in the worship life of Christians. In the awakening liturgical movement they experienced the unity of the Church as they appropriated words of confession, praise and petition, the same words in which the Church, from the earliest times onwards, had been united through the centuries as it confessed His name and praised and called upon Him. The connexion which the ancient Church saw between dogma and liturgy again began to be manifest.

The result was a new view of the Eastern Church. Precisely those elements which neo-Protestantism had criticized appeared in a new light. This could be illustrated at various points. Here I will confine myself to a few remarks on dogma in its relation to liturgy. I will seek to shed light upon the change in Protestant understanding of the Eastern Church by referring to a certain, very important structural element of that Church, one of which many discussions of the Eastern Church's decisions on dogma do not take adequate account. In understanding another Church it is often more illuminating and of greater significance to perceive the structure *underlying* and at work in the doctrine, order and life of that particular Church than to dwell upon the *details*.

1. One of the chief indictments brought against the development of dogma in the Eastern Church is that of Hellenization; more specifically, it has been charged that in the Eastern Church the Gospel suffers from an over-exposure to alien elements and that there is a syncretistic synthesis of Christian faith and pagan philosophy. Critics have had in mind particularly the appropriation of the ontological, metaphysical and 'physical' concepts of Greek philosophy in the formulation of the doctrines of the Trinity and of Christology. Between this Greek mode of thought and that of the Old Testament and of Jesus—which is Hebraic—there is a real difference which cannot be overlooked, and the Hellenization in the ancient Church goes far beyond anything found in Paul, who pushes forward into the Hellenistic sphere. Moreover the Eastern Church made no secret of its Greek heritage nor was it ashamed of it.

The neo-Protestant critique of this state of affairs overlooked, to be sure, the fact that among the various possible responses of faith to the message of God's act of salvation there is one—attested by the New Testament writings and, indeed, present already in the Old Testament congregation—which bears a clear affinity to ontological statements and prompts to the use of ontological concepts. This is doxology, as we find it from time immemorial expressing itself, with almost an inner necessity, both in public worship services and in the prayers of the individual. Doxology rests upon and also praises God's act of salvation; but it goes beyond praise of God's act of salvation to praise of God Himself who is the same from everlasting to everlasting. God cannot be contained within His act of salvation on our behalf and on behalf of His Church and the world. In the freedom of His being, which is the same from everlasting to everlasting, He has carried out the work of salvation and He wishes man to praise not only His work but also Himself. Doxology is addressed to God, and yet God is here as a rule not addressed as 'Thou', as He is in other prayers, but as 'He', who is from everlasting to everlasting. In the doxology God is also not implored to do this or that but is praised in His eternal glory, holiness, might, power and wisdom. Thus we find in the biblical doxologies, again and again, statements about God's being, His nature and His qualities. For example, Rom. IX. 5: 'God who is over all be blessed for ever'. Or the song of Rev. IV. 8, in part a quotation of Isa. VI. 3: 'Holy, holy, holy, is the Lord God Almighty, who was and is and is to come!' Or: 'Amen! Blessing and glory and wisdom and thanksgiving and honour and power and might be unto our God for ever and ever! Amen' (Rev. VII. 12).

Dogma in the Eastern Church is quite apparently determined to a large degree by the structure of doxology, for its dogma is determined by the structure of the credal confession of the service of worship. This confession is directed not primarily to the world but to *God*; it not only bears testimony before men but is offered to *God* as the Church's sacrifice of praise. Thus the decisions on dogma of the councils of Nicaea and Constantinople are direct credal confessions for use in the service of worship, and if the Christological decision of Chalcedon was not itself formulated and employed as such (the introductory words no longer read 'We believe' but 'we teach that it is necessary to confess') yet it is most intimately related to the credal confession of the service of worship, seeks to serve the same and still bears the unmistakable marks of hymnic and doxological style. If one understands the nature of doxology, then it can come as no surprise that the ancient Church drew upon ontological concepts from Greek metaphysics when formulating, developing and interpreting its dogma. The statements of doxology about God's being, nature and qualities were, in the nature of the case, a step in that direction; but in addition it was precisely Hellenism, its language and its mode of thought, that constituted the historical terms in which doxology had to express itself; and it was the Hellenistic environment to which doxology had to be interpreted.

But this need by no means signify syncretism and an over-exposure of the Gospel to alien elements. There is abundant proof that the Greek philosophical concepts employed in the dogmas of the ancient Church were subjected to thorough-going correction and profound transformation; and, further-more, that precisely the salient concepts of pagan thinking were turned to magnificent service in witnessing for the faith. In other words, the process initiated by Paul in taking the Gospel to the Hellenistic world was continued in the history of dogma in the ancient Church.

2. The Eastern Church is also charged with never having fixed any dogmas on man and his relation to grace, as was done in Western Christianity in connexion with Augustine's battle with Pelagius and his followers and then, again, at the time of the Reformation and afterwards; that is to say, dogmatic decisions on the questions of original sin, freedom of the will, etc., are lacking in the East. The cordial reception and even vindication which Pelagius met with in Palestine, and which Julian and even Coelestius experienced for a time in Con-stantinople, and the faint response in the East to the condemna-tion of Pelagianism by the Council of Ephesus were an early cause of Western mistrust of the East on this point. Even today one still meets Orthodox theologians who recognize Augustine as a gifted writer of the Church but not as a Church Father.

One cannot of course overlook the fact that the Eastern Church was not really interested in giving a dogmatic definition of sin and in determining what capacities the sinner still pos-sesses apropos of his relation to grace. But once one has recog-nized the basic doxological structure of the dogma of the Eastern Church, then its reluctance to express itself on anthropological dogmas can come as no surprise; for it is characteristic of doxology that man recedes into the background. Even if the confession of faith begins with the words 'we believe' or 'I believe', yet as a rule the words 'I' or 'mine' or 'we' or 'our' do not occur again. It is rather *God's* deeds on behalf of the world and the Church which are confessed. Indeed, in the pure doxo-logy the words 'I' and 'we' do not occur at all, not even in an introductory formula; it is only God who is mentioned: 'Holy, holy, holy is the Lord of hosts; the whole earth is full of his glory' (Isa. vi. 3). In the service of worship here on earth it is of course man who initiates the doxology. And God's saving work on his behalf is the reason why he praises and worships God. But in the act of worship the eyes of the believer are directed wholly away from himself to God; there are no sidelong glances at himself or the relation between what God has done and what he himself has done. In doxology God is all in all—it has no other content but God. The lack of anthropological dogmas in the Eastern Church is, therefore, partly a consequence of its approach to dogma, namely, the fact that its dogma is determined by the credal confession of the service of worship.

Now of course theology cannot get along without making statements about man. Such statements are abundant in the Old Testament and in the New. In reality, the writings of the Eastern Church Fathers also contain an abundance of thinking about anthropology. The way in which they insist upon the freedom which man still possesses is striking (an emphasis entirely foreign to Augustine and the Reformers), as is their extensive appropriation of Greek and philosophical anthropology with but little modification of it by biblical anthropology (cf., e.g., John of Damascus' *Ekdosis*, II, 12–24). The anthropological statements of Eastern theology were not elevated into explicit dogmas about man, however, and this should not be regarded as something wholly negative. The Church's Christological and Trinitarian pronouncements differ fundamentally from its anthropological ones in so far as God's act of salvation in Christ has been carried out once and for all and the Triune God is the same from everlasting to everlasting. But man lives in history, subject to change and transitoriness, his self-understanding undergoing continual alteration. Man is torn this way and that by false concepts of human nature—libertinism and determinism, individualism and collectivism, and many others. First this side and then that has deceived him as to his true nature. It is in this situation that man is called to believe in God's decisive act in Christ and to praise Him for it. Thus anthropological dogmas are of necessity exposed to the vicissitudes of history to a much greater degree than are

Christological dogmas, and it is obvious that numerous severe crises have arisen and many schisms have been engendered in Western Christianity precisely because it attempted to give to such historically conditioned statements about the relation between sin and grace the full authority of dogma, statements which had digested the anthropological thinking of that particular age and had succeeded in addressing men where they actually *were*, with a call to repentance and faith. But do such anthropological dogmas still speak to the members of that particular Church a hundred or two hundred years later?

3. Another charge made against the Eastern Church is that for over a thousand years doctrinal development has been at a standstill, even though during this time a great number of new questions have arisen in Christianity's intellectual environment and within Christianity itself, questions that the Church should have undertaken to answer in new doctrinal decisions. There was already, at the Council of Chalcedon, a decided disinclination to formulate new dogma and had it not been for the wishes of the emperor it is quite unlikely that anything would have been forthcoming. This disinclination grew steadily stronger with the passage of time. 'It was not only the innate traditionalism, common to all religions, which was opposed to change; it was also that concern for the ritualistic treatment of dogma which resisted change and suffered hurt with each new doctrinal formulation' (Harnack, *Dogmengeschichte*, 2nd edition, 1909, Vol. II, p. 443). 'It is only when one observes how the doctrinal controversies were—of necessity—always controversies about words which clamoured for inclusion in the liturgy that one realizes they were bound to awaken mistrust . . . The doctrinal controversies of the seventh century were in reality only an insignificant epilogue which merely gave dogma the deceptive appearance of being possessed of independent existence' (ibid. p. 444). According to Harnack, the mystagogy of the Eastern Church gradually brought doctrine almost to the point of extinction (p. 443). Its mystagogic theology stifled dogmatics and usurped its place (cf. also p. 511).

The reasons why the development of dogma in the Eastern Church atrophied at an early period are of course many and various. The Arian controversies in the decades after the year

T

325 and the monophysite, monergist and monothelite controversies in the centuries after 451 certainly had severe reper-
cussions, particularly in the Eastern Church. Another reason is
that the Eastern Church was deprived of the freedom to make
further dogmatic decisions by the emperors, for whom the
unity of the Empire was of first importance; then in later times
the assembling of an ecumenical council comprising all the geographical areas where there were Orthodox churches was a
practical impossibility. But in the transition to a traditionalistic
and scholastic mode of thought, there was also an unmistakable
atrophying of the original vitality and strength of Greek systematic theology. In the midst of all these different historical
factors, another extremely important one—that had an in-
hibiting effect upon the further formation of dogma—is the
connexion between dogma and liturgy. It would certainly be
misconstruing the situation, however, were one to call attention
only to a liturgical formalism of *words* and a mistrust in the
Eastern Church of every move to alter *words* or add new ones.
That the Eastern Church ceased dogmatizing shows rather that
it wished to retain—and did retain—precisely the same *structure*
of dogmatic statement as that employed by the ancient Church
when it began to develop dogma, namely, doxological confession offered to God by the congregation when gathered for
worship. The Eastern Church was concerned not only about
retaining the *wording* of historical and now commonly used formulations; it also remained loyal to the *structure* which the
ancient Church's approach to dogma assumed, i.e. a structure
in which credal confession is at once the sacrifice of praise of the
service of worship and doctrine binding upon the worshippers.
For this reason one cannot make the unqualified statement that
dogmatic theology in the Eastern Church was stifled and replaced by mystagogic theology; rather, the dogma of the ancient
Church was from the very beginning an inherent part of the
service of worship. But if this basic doxological structure of
dogma is kept in mind, then it becomes clear that it is quite
impossible to make statements about the sacraments, about
Church and State, natural law, etc., along the lines of those we
find in the doxological confession of faith. For the nature of
doxology is such that although it treats of the sacraments, the
Church and therefore the world and the contention between the

two, yet the content of doxology is not the sacraments as such, nor the Church and the world as such, but the Triune God who is operative in and through them all. If dogma is approached as a doxological confession of faith—and if this approach is then maintained—then within the resulting doxological structure one will not find dogmas on the sacraments, the Church and the State as such. Interest is rather in the actual celebration of the sacraments, in the actual life of the Church in the world and therefore in the fixing of the liturgical and legal order in which this is all effected and within which the true credal confession is offered to God.

This tenacious loyalty of doctrinal development in the Eastern Church to its doxological beginnings cannot be simply regarded as a weakness, for it has meant that the Eastern Church has retained two important virtues which can become of increasing ecumenical significance. Let me explain what I have in mind.

a) If the Eastern Church did not make dogmatic decisions on a number of matters acted upon by Western Christianity, this does not mean that the Eastern Church was simply silent on these matters. Instead of expressing itself on the sacraments in the form of *dogmas* it drew up *liturgical* and *canonical regulations* for the celebration of the sacraments; that is, it by no means left the sacraments at the mercy of human whim and caprice. The same is true of ecclesiology. The significance of the fact that the Eastern Church was very hesitant about formulating dogmas on the sacraments and the Church, and instead expressed itself on these subjects mainly in the form of regulations for the ordering of Church life and the celebration of the sacraments, is that in the history of dogma in the East a very definite danger was rid of much of the potency it possessed in the West. I mean the danger that dogmatic thought may separate itself from the actual *event* of God's saving activity and imagine that by taking thought it can arrive at a vantage point from which it is possible to grasp in theory and, to a certain extent, calculate and balance off against one another the co-operation between God and man, divine grace and the human will, God's sacramental gifts and the earthly elements (water, bread and wine), the invisible and the visible Church. That in the Eastern Church there is not such a cleft between dogma and piety, as there is to some extent in the West, is a virtue. There is no doubt but that some problems in the history of theology, in the East as well as in the West, have arisen only because theology became detached from God's saving activity in the celebration of the sacraments, in the life of the Church, etc. To a certain extent these are problems which one may describe as being merely apparent, because they are no longer concerned with receiving and witnessing to God's gracious acts but with the theoretical explanation of those acts. In Western Christianity, however—in contrast to the Eastern Church—many theological problems of this sort were made the subject of *dogmatic decisions*; and since these dogmas deal with questions which are no longer directly informed by the reception of and the testimony to God's gracious working in the congregation gathered for worship, it is little wonder that the dogmas formulated in response to these questions diverge, both from century to century and from Church to Church. Although the Eastern Church has also reflected upon such problems, it has in large measure refrained from *dogmatizing* about them; and thus it has been more respectful of the mystery surrounding God's gracious work than has the West.

b) If the development of dogma comes to a standstill, this can be a weakness. It would be so indeed if a Church where this had happened were to content itself with the mere repetition of its traditional dogmas, neglecting to interpret and relate them to new historical situations. It would also be a weakness if such a Church were to attempt, simply by means of analogies based on existing dogmas, to come to terms with problems in those areas where no decisions on dogma had been taken. Thus some Eastern theologians have attempted to clarify the problems connected with Holy Communion through the use of analogies based on the doctrine of the Incarnation, or when considering the problem of Church and State they have drawn analogies from the doctrine of Christ's two natures. This method fails to bring out fully the uniqueness of Holy Communion or of the relation between Church and State. But reluctance to formulate dogmas is not, in itself, any more a weakness than a steady, sanguine advance towards new and ever more intricate dogmas is necessarily a sign of spiritual and theological strength. It could very well be just the opposite, for, as the history of dogma in the Roman Church shows, dogmas which are continually increasing in intricacy and detail prove in time to be so cumbersome that theological thinking becomes increasingly hampered in its movement and loses its broad catholicity. Dogmatizing that limits itself to the Christological and Trinitarian centre of the Christian faith, however, gives full scope to the unfolding of the riches available in Scripture, riches which are waiting to be utilized in a vigorous missionary thrust into the spiritual and intellectual situation of the Church's present environment. Sometimes the development of a 'wealth' of dogmatic decisions of increasing refinement may be a denial of the fullness of biblical truth and so prove to be in reality not wealth but poverty. On the other hand, an apparent 'poverty' of dogma may be in reality a form of wealth, because being centred in Christological and Trinitarian dogmas it discloses the fullness of biblical truth and thus promotes the unhindered development of catholicity in theological thought and in the Church's witness.

If, now, one attempts an appraisal of the history of dogma in the Eastern Church from these two points of view, then it becomes evident that the Eastern Church, precisely because of its peculiar reluctance to formulate dogmas, possesses very great and, in many respects, unique ecumenical possibilities. Ecumenical discussions in past years on problems of faith and order have shown again and again that we must approach the dogmas dividing the Churches by going back to the place these dogmas occupy in the life of the Churches, especially in the Church's liturgy and in its preaching and teaching. The further dogmatic statements become removed from their setting in the service of worship, the more difficult it is for divided Churches to come to any agreement about them. Conversely, it has been the often quite astonishing experience at ecumenical conferences that these same Churches, despite their dividedness, were able, in common acts of worship, to pray with one another and to receive from one another the proclamation of God's mighty acts of salvation. In that the Eastern Church in its dogmatic utterances has retained the closest ties with the service of worship, it has in a very special way also retained the possibility of explaining its dogma from its setting in the worship service. Thus it assumes a central position midway between Churches (such as the Roman Church) which have come to the point where their frequent dogmatizing has proved divisive of Church fellowship, and on the other hand the extreme wing of Protestantism which rejects every tie of dogma (a principle that sets it off from Rome *and* the Reformers). In saying this, of course, everything depends on whether present-day Orthodoxy can muster the spiritual and theological strength and versatility to make use of its mediating position in such a way that it applies what it has inherited from Athanasius and Cyril—in the terms and concepts of the first centuries of the Christian era—to the concrete problems of the 20th century, and in terms which this century understands and employs. The same is true, however, of any Church which is in possession of a heritage of dogma deriving from the past—it is true, therefore, also of the Lutheran Church.

4. What we have said would be incomplete if we did not also call attention to various other ways—besides the liturgical way of Orthodoxy—in which faith responds to God's redemptive act in Jesus Christ.

Since in Christ God has revealed his love for the world, therefore we are to love in return. The response of love to God's love manifested in Jesus Christ is twofold: love of God and love for one's neighbour. Since God's love comes to us in the world which proclaims His love in Christ, we should respond with love in words addressed, first, to God in prayer and, second, to our neighbour in witness.

In *prayer* faith responds to God, addressing Him on familiar terms as 'Thou'. In Christ God has addressed me, a lost sinner, reaching out and rescuing me and bestowing His gifts upon me. Prayer gives me the opportunity to respond to Him, in Jesus' name, to thank him and call upon Him in the certainty that He will hear me and answer me, and not only me but His whole Church and yet within this Church also me. Among the various types of prayer, *doxology* occupies a special place, with the 'I' and 'we' of other kinds of prayer retreating into the background and God being addressed as a rule in the third person instead of the second. Furthermore, instead of God's succour being implored, he is praised for his wonderful works and worshipped as God from all eternity.

Faith responds in *witness*, the believer addressing his fellow-man and proclaiming to him God's act of salvation. Witness too is response in the name of Jesus. The believer assures his fellow-man that the same salvation which God has accomplished in Christ for the believer He has also worked 'for you'. The believer cannot hoard the Gospel which he has received—it is an urgent Word that forces its way into the world, laying hold of men and widening its outreach as it goes. It is the exalted Christ, the Lord, who through the Gospel is establishing possession of the world over which He reigns. When the believer witnesses, he addresses concrete individuals in their particular historical situation. His witness enters of necessity into the thought and language of that particular age, into the self-understanding, the world views, the concepts of God, the hopes, the morality and the immorality of those to whom the Gospel is to be pro-claimed—it participates in all the vicissitudes of history.

Among the various ways of speaking the Gospel to our fellow-men the special nature of doctrine should be stressed. Here the 'I' of the believer addressing his fellow-man, face to face, recedes into the background. Doctrine does not speak directly to a person, asuring him that salvation is 'for you'; it is not prophetic proclamation in the here and now. In the New Testament, doctrine (*didache*) is primarily transmission of the tradition that has been received regarding God's saving acts in history, done, once and for all, in Christ on behalf of the world. Doctrine tells about people in the past, but also about man and the world in general. It is therefore more strongly inclined to a fixed form of expression than is personal witness. Its 'objectivity' distinguishes it from such witness in a way similar to that in which doxology is distinguished from prayers of petition. Doxology and doctrine are both responses of faith but the structure of doxology differs from that of doctrine and the two should not be confused with one another.

The original act in which the believer responds to the Gospel which he has heard, the act in which he subjected himself to the Lordship of Christ, is the *confession of faith*. In the confession of faith not only does it become clear that prayer and witness belong together but that prayer, witness and all the various forms of the response of faith converge in the confession in a peculiar way and there find their focus. The confession of faith is directed to God and yet it is at the same time witness before men. The confession finds the believer both acknowledging

Christ as his Lord and joining in the Church's witness to Christ before all the world. As a rule the confession of faith does not employ explicitly either the 'Thou' addressed to God or the 'you' addressed to one's fellow-man; instead, it praises—before God and in the presence of men—God's act of salvation. In the confession of faith the self-surrender of the believer is so complete that not even the very fact of that surrender—indeed not even the person of him who surrenders himself—receives any mention, unless it is in the words 'I believe' or 'we believe'. Thus, in the 'objective' statements of the confession of faith the peculiar structure of doxology and doctrine are also uniquely recapitulated.

All these basic forms of Christian response belong together—and necessarily so—in the life of the Church and of the individual Christian. Not one of them can be relinquished without distorting the others. It is God's will that the response of faith express itself precisely in this sort of variety.

Dogma is rooted in confession. The history of dogma began as the history of the confession of faith, first of all of the confession made at baptism and in the service of worship, and then of the consensus—understood in this sense—of the Church. Since, now, the various forms of the response of faith are recapitulated in the confession of faith, it came about that in the history of dogma first one of these forms and then another—the doxological, say, or the kerygmatic—played a decisive role. Modifications of these forms resulted where dogma was no longer formulated as a confession for the service of worship, or as an expression of adoration or of witness, but as teaching concerning the proper *way* to confess, adore and witness. A further modification resulted where dogma no longer pointed out what one *was* to believe, confess, praise and testify to, but instead was limited to defining—in the anathema—what one must *not* believe. The element of separation from the world, which is always implicit in the original act of confession, became the explicit and, not infrequently, the sole content of dogma. In addition, a modification in the form of faith's response—one with grave consequences—was bound to result from the fact that from the 4th century onwards the various confessions of faith used in the various Churches were increasingly replaced by *one* confession, so that to be one in faith no longer meant the mutual and harmonious acknowledgement of one another's confessions but the use of one and the same form of confession. Modifications of this sort, which in themselves should not be approached with any preconceived notions, must be kept in mind when comparing the dogmas of various periods of the Church's history, or when comparing the dogmas of one Church with those of another.

What all this signifies is a difference in the structure of the dogmatic utterances of the Eastern Church and those of the Church of the Reformation. It is true that in the *worship life* of both Churches all forms of the response of faith are very much in evidence: prayer and doxology, witness and doctrine, and all of these recapitulated in the confession of faith. But in the historical development of the Eastern Church, *dogma* was determined primarily by the doxological element in the confession of faith while in the Church of the Reformation it was determined by the kerygmatic element. The Church of the Reformation did, of course, hold with conviction to the creeds of the ancient Church—both as dogma and as an essential part of the liturgy. Its own dogmatic utterances, however, were expressed not in doxological confessions but in ones which (like the Augsburg Confession) were addressed, *corum Deo*, to the emperor and the empire. Thus in the Augsburg Confession *docere* means, as a rule, to preach, to proclaim, to testify; and in Melanchthon's Apology for Augsburg, Article IV (*De justificatione*), there are whole passages in which the effect is that of pastoral comfort and assurance and evangelical preaching. As a result, none of the confessions of the Lutheran Reformation were produced for the liturgy of the service of worship nor was any of them incorporated into the liturgy. Later, in the development of 17th-century Orthodoxy, this structural modification had this result: *doctrina*, even when the word no longer signified preaching itself but teaching about what was to be preached, still addressed itself primarily to the sermon and did not develop into mystagogic theology.

In these differences in the form of faith's response, there are not as yet any necessarily irreconcilable antitheses between the two Churches—but such *can* develop. On the Orthodox side, that could conceivably happen if the ontological structure of its doxology were made into the predominating pattern of its theological thinking in general and of its anthropology in particular. That would call into question not only the historical nature of man but also the contingent character of God's acts of salvation. On the side, in the Church of the Reformation, the same kind of thing could happen to the pattern of witness, of pastoral assurance, of personal encounter with God and thus the I-Thou correlation of encounter be absolutized, to the exclusion of all other forms of theological statement. For this would be calling God's deity into question, since God is, after all, not contained within His act of revealing Himself to man in an historical encounter; indeed, it is in this act that He reveals Himself as the one who is the same from everlasting to everlasting. But if either of these forms of theological statement not only receives special emphasis but is also carried to extremes, and made the one and only pattern of theological thought, then false alternatives and antitheses divisive of Church fellowship arise. Then it is no longer only separated Churches that confront one another but also ontological and personalistic philosophical systems; held captive by such, one group of Christians is then incapable of regarding the dogma of another group of Christians as a 'confession' of Christ.

In present-day ecumenical contacts between Churches, we are confronted by the task not only of comparing the differences in dogma which exist between us, but also reinterpreting them by tracing them back to their roots in the act of confession of faith. Then we must recognize the function of different statements of dogma within the variety of the multitude of responses which God demands of us.

IV. THE SIGNIFICANCE OF THE EASTERN AND WESTERN TRADITIONS FOR THE CHRISTIAN CHURCH[1]

WHETHER a Christian community accepts the principle of tradition or not, the fact remains that every Christian inherits a definite historical tradition. Inner necessity has given rise to a variety of different traditions. Already in the books of the New Testament we find different versions of the sayings and acts of Jesus, and different forms of the message being preached by the Apostles. For the message of the one Christ had to be unfolded within the contemporary environment of Jewish, Greek and Gnostic thought. Different traditions were bound to develop when the Gospel was carried farther afield to other nations, and further decisions had to be taken on questions of doctrine and order.

Variety of tradition is an enrichment, as long as fellowship is maintained between the different traditions. They are then manifestations of the catholicity of the Church. For catholicity does not consist merely in extending the Church geographically, but also in variety of witness, of prayer, of theologies, of ministries and of charismata. But when fellowship ceases to exist in the Lord's Supper and in the mutual recognition of ministries, the difference between the traditions becomes a stumbling-block. The traditions begin to withdraw into isolation, to harden in their attitude to one another, and thus to cripple the Christian Church's missionary task to the world.

Differences between the Eastern and Western traditions began to appear already in the early history of the Church, in liturgy, in theology and in the concept of the ministry. Ignatius of Antioch argued on different lines from Clemens Romanus; Irenaeus on different lines from Tertullian. Moreover the Eastern and Western traditions themselves were not fixed factors; both traditions contained many differences, and they overlapped geographically and with regard to their content, to their

[1] Address delivered to the Central Committee of the World Council of Churches, Rhodes, Greece, August 20th, 1959. Published in the *Ecumenical Review*, XII. 2, 1960, pp. 133–142.

mutual enrichment. These differences constituted a wealth of tradition, which is still an enrichment to us all today.

These differences did not continue to be a mutual enrichment, however. As the unity of the Church began more and more to be expressed through uniformity of worship, dogma and ministry, on the model of the legalism of the Roman Empire, the variety of traditions came to be regarded as a defect. The more the geographical structure of the Church coincided with the provinces of the Roman Empire, the more the Church districts (with their different local traditions) were drawn into the political quarrels between the Eastern and Western provinces, and the more the different Church traditions came to be regarded as conflicting. When finally the schism occurred between Eastern and Western Christendom, its primary cause was not the difference in liturgical and theological tradition, but the involvement of the Church order with political forces and with the political order. It was only then that, for the first time, differences in liturgical and theological tradition began to be considered as divisive. Christians began to regard one another not only as schismatics but even as heretics, and to treat one another accordingly. This found its most monstrous expression in the Fourth Crusade of Western Christendom against Constantinople, and in the Crusades undertaken by the German order of Knights in the Baltic area not only against the pagan Slavs, but also against Orthodox Christians. These events weakened the resistance of the Eastern Church in its struggle against the Turks and Mongols with very grave consequences, and left their mark for centuries upon the subconscious minds of Christians, until nearly every difference between Churches (even the question whether leavened or unleavened bread should be used for Communion) came to be regarded as a cause of division.

In spite of all this, during the last four hundred years it has become increasingly difficult to speak of a rigid cleavage between the Eastern and Western traditions, for various reasons. At the time of the Reformation large geographical areas of the Church in the West broke away from the specifically Western traditions, i.e. from the Papacy, and founded their faith afresh upon the teaching of the Apostles and the dogma of the Early Church. Although the Reformation Churches are not united with the Eastern Church, they have never separated from it.

They have merely inherited the old division between East and West. Both Luther and the professors in Tübingen who began corresponding in 1573 with Jeremiah II, Patriarch of Constantinople, spoke about the Eastern Church in full assurance that they were united with it in the same faith. And although later on it came to be recognized that the Eastern Church has more in common with the Roman Church than had been supposed at that time in Germany, nevertheless it is since then that the strict opposition between the Eastern and Western Churches was broken through in the thinking of the Church of the Lutheran Confession and of the Church of England. The schism between the Eastern and Western traditions is no longer strictly geographical either. Today there are Orthodox Churches in the West and Western Churches in the East. Moreover many of the Western and Eastern traditions have become transformed by the stormy events of world history. Although Kartaschov (the Paris Church historian) tries today to apply the Eastern concept of the symphony between Church and State to modern democracy, and the Moscow Patriarchate recognizes the authority of the Communist state, that symphony is no longer the tradition of the Eastern Church. And although the Pope concludes Concordats with sovereign states, that is no longer administration of the two swords in the sense of Boniface VIII, although this claim has not been retracted in principle. If one speaks today of the opposition between East and West, one means something different from the divergence between the traditions of the Eastern and Western Churches.

The opposition between the two traditions is less rigid today, because the hearts of many people both in the East and in the West have been touched with God's Spirit, so that they feel ashamed about the division of Christendom, and long for unity. Through our divisions we are again beginning to realize the wealth that lies concealed within the differences between the two traditions. If the question of the importance of Church traditions arises, therefore, it no longer suffices today to stress the importance of *our* tradition for the other confessions (as was done for centuries). We have begun to realize how important it is for us to recognize the positive value of the *other* tradition.

I therefore intend to speak primarily about the importance of the Eastern tradition for Western Christendom. As the basic structures of the Christian traditions are often more essential than the liturgical, dogmatic and legal details, within the brief space of this paper I will indicate three basic forms of the Eastern Church which, in my opinion, are of special importance for Western Christendom.

1. In the worship-service of all Churches, God's great acts in history and the promise of the coming redemption are expressed through Scripture reading, preaching, the Lord's Supper and prayers. But in no Church are the pronouncements made in the worship-service so strongly determined by the form of the hymnology and the doxology as in the Eastern Church. In its Canons, Stichera and Troparia the Gospel of the day is developed in ever-new forms of praise. Praise is offered not only for God's act of salvation (related in the Bible) but to God Himself, who is the same for ever and ever in the one glory of the Father, the Son and the Holy Spirit. The message of God's act of salvation in history is drawn into the worship of the Eternal God and His Christ, so that this act of salvation is experienced in the liturgy as if it were actually taking place among the congregation. In the doxological attitude, the lapse of time between then and now disappears. The same applies to the lapse of time which separates our life now from the coming consummation. In praising Christ's victory on the cross and in the resurrection, and in the adoration of the Eternal Trinity, the glory that is to come is experienced as a present reality. The worshippers are translated into that glory, and the menace of the material world grows dim. In no other Church does the liturgy so triumphantly unfold the victory of Christ with its implications for the whole cosmos, or laud and magnify in such a rapturous way the presence of the New Creation that is to come. The liturgy of the Eastern Church resounds with the eschatological exultation with which the early Christians celebrated the Lord's Supper.

2. It is against this background that the special form of the dogma of the Eastern Church must be seen. All Churches have dogmas; even those Christian bodies which reject all dogmas as such share common convictions. Dogmas may be expressed in widely differing forms. But it is characteristic of the Eastern Church that its dogma has not become separate from its liturgy, but is formulated as a liturgical statement. It is expressed in

the worship-service as a statement of faith and doxology. It is the doxology also which produces the ontological statements characteristic of Greek theology (not to be confused with domination of the Gospel by metaphysics). The Early Church's formulations of the dogmas concerning the Trinity and concerning Christology were an integral part of the worship-service, or at any rate statements made for direct use in praise and worship. Unlike the Western Church, the Eastern Church has always had an aversion to separating its dogmatic statements from the liturgy; it has never turned them into binding dogmas isolated from the doxological framework. Hence the confessional writings of the Eastern Church which were drawn up during the quarrels with the West in the 17th century (for example, the 'Confessio Orthodoxa' of Peter Mogilas and the 'Confessio Dosithei') never received the same authority as the dogma of the Early Church. While adhering strictly to the dogma of the Early Church, the Eastern Church, therefore, in principle left open opportunities for free theological thought. In the Western Church such opportunities did not exist, because its dogmas were fixed in a much more rigid form.

3. Another point to be noted in the Eastern Church is the special relationship between Church and ministry. In spite of its emphasis on hierarchy, this relationship is not merely one of higher and lower grades, because it is enclosed within the framework of fellowship. The relationship between ministry and congregation is also one of fellowship. This is apparent both in the worship-service and also in the fact that the supreme authority in the Eastern Church is not a single dignitary but the Ecumenical Synod, and that the decisions of the Synod are not valid unless they receive the confirmation of the Church members. By renouncing any legally secured supreme authority with complete jurisdiction over the whole Church, the Eastern Church shows a more reverent attitude than the Roman Church towards the free action of the Holy Spirit, which cannot be hampered by any order of ministries. Jesus Christ is honoured as the sole Lord of the Church, and this leaves room for a number of different autocephalous Churches. For the incarnate Son of God, as the ascended Lord, wishes to permeate through the Holy Spirit the historical reality of every nation and language. The unity of the Church is a fellowship of Orthodox Churches.

In accordance also with the doxological nature of its worship-service and its dogma, and with the congregational form of its Church order, the Eastern Church has always interpreted its relation to the State mainly as a spiritual service, but has never sought to possess secular authority itself. In its conception of the symphony between Church and State, the Church has affirmed its spiritual power by renouncing all secular power.

The question may be asked, of course, whether the reasons why the Eastern Church has not developed in the same way as Western Christendom were not merely external. The reason why the Eastern Church has not developed its dogmas to the same extent may be ascribed to the fact that it was unable to hold any more Ecumenical Councils, owing to political up-heavals. It may be asserted that it is a fellowship of autoce-phalous Churches because the Patriarch of Constantinople was unable to prevent the formation of national Churches, despite all his efforts to do so; and that the Patriarch did not become a secular potentate (like the Pope) because between the 5th and 8th centuries no political vacuum arose in the East as it did in the West. But it is absolutely clear that the resistance to these trends was due not only to external political events, but also to strong opposition from within the Eastern Church itself, because they were contrary to its nature.

In the Western Church the basic forms are different. It is true, it also has the 'Hymnus'; but it gives first place to the concrete promise of salvation, not to the hymnic portrayal of God's glory. The Western Church also worships the eternal glory of God; but the statements about His eternal nature receive less emphasis than the recognition of His powerful influence here and now through Word and Sacrament. The Western Church also has the certainty of the actual *presence* of the glory that is to come; already now, through the Com-munion, we participate in the Great Sacrament in God's future Kingdom. But the Western Church realizes more strongly that the world is not yet glorified, and that an interval of time sep-arates us from the glory that is to come. The Western worship-service imparts not so much a sense of being removed from this world through a mystical experience of 'heaven on earth', but rather a call to give service to the world. In the Western Church the 'voluntarist' features in the representation of God have always been stressed more than in the Eastern Church; and in the Reformation Churches the crucial point is that God speaks afresh to every age of history, and that the Christian must obey Him within that concrete situation.

This explains why the Western Church did not confine itself to the dogmas of the Early Church, but proceeded to take further decisions on dogma as new problems and dangers arose. And these decisions were not only in the field of doxology. The Western Church fixed a large number of dogmatic pronouncements concerning man, concerning grace, concerning the relation between human and divine action in salvation, and so on. The Reformation Churches did not place their dogmatic statements within the setting of the worship-service either; they fixed them in the form of confessional writings whose purpose (in contrast to scholastic theology) was not theoretical dogma but preaching. The form of these dogmatic statements was therefore determined not by ontological relations, but by the personal encounter between God who speaks and gives and man who hears and receives.

Moreover at a very early date the interest of the Western Church was directed more towards the practical and legal problems of Church life, while the speculative theology of the Latin Fathers before Augustine did not reach the level of the Eastern Fathers. This basic attitude in Roman thought then developed in the West into an increasingly legal concept of dogma, of penance and grace, and of Church order, culminating in complete centralization (in the Papacy) and the struggle to dominate the world. The Reformation opposed this with its teaching concerning justification by grace, the distinction between the Two Kingdoms, and its concept of Church unity as a fellowship of Churches.

People with these Western concepts have often spoken of the 'weakness' of the Eastern Church. In this circle I need not mention the criticism to which the fellowship-form of the Eastern Church is subjected by the Papacy. For on this point the Reformation Churches are on the side of the Eastern Church. On the other hand the Western Churches regard it as a weakness in the Eastern Church that it has clung to the dogmas of the Early Church, and fixed no further dogmas (with equal authority) when confronted by fresh theological and ideological

U

questions later on. But above all the Western Churches regard the Eastern Church's concentration on the holy liturgy as a way of eluding responsibility in the world, and its hymnic emphasis on the eschatological presence as tantamount to abandoning this world to its own devices without attempting to influence society or promote justice. Does the Eastern Church seriously realize that obedience to God implies something more than witness and worship, but also demands active efforts to promote justice and freedom in human society? For it is not only as our Redeemer, but also as the Sustainer of the world, that God requires our obedience! Similar questions have been raised by members of the Eastern Church themselves, and not only by Vladimir Solovyev.

When considering these questions we must in all justice take due account of the fact that for hundreds of years the Eastern Church was unable to exercise any influence upon its environment, because it was living under the oppression of Arabs, Mongols and Turks. Furthermore, while recognizing the dangers inherent in the basic forms of the Eastern Church, we must not assume that it is *bound* to succumb to these dangers. In my own view these dangers can be avoided.

Every dimension of Church life is concentrated in its liturgy in such a way that the Eastern Church has not only been protected during times of oppression; from this focal point it can also constantly receive fresh power to push out into the world. This is proved by the history of its missionary efforts. The doxological exultation of the Eastern Church need not mean abandoning the world to its fate; like the eschatological exultation in the hearts of the early Christians when they met to celebrate the Last Supper, that joy has echoed far and wide. It was, in fact, through this exultation that the joyful message penetrated into the hostile world. The actual Presence of the *Eschaton* has always had tremendous power to transform men. It is true, the Eastern Church interprets its ethical task in the world to be the transformation and sanctification of men rather than the passing of new social and legal ordinances. But where there is a genuine renewal of men and women to faith, love and hope, this is bound to have an effect on the social order.

Nor is it true that by retaining the doxological structure of the dogmas of the Early Church, the Eastern Church was less well equipped to confront the questions that confronted it later on. The Eastern Church carefully studied the question of anthropology, the doctrine of grace, and Augustine's theme of 'God and the soul'. There is proof of this, not only in the speeches of Symeon, the new theologian (ca. A.D. 1000). But in contrast to the Western Church, the insights which arose from such discussions and which had a great influence on the Eastern Church were not raised to the status of binding doctrines. They found reflection and expression instead in liturgical texts, in instructions for sanctification, in forms of piety and of course in didactic writings. Owing to the fact that (in contrast to the Western Church) many of the insights of the Eastern Church have not been fixed as legally binding dogmas, in spite of its close link with the Trinitarian and Christological dogma of the Early Church, it has remained basically freer than many Western traditions. There is therefore no reason why it should inevitably become ossified in traditionalism. The spiritual power which springs from its liturgy would lead us rather to expect it to tackle the great problems of our time and to make an active, independent contribution towards their solution.

On the other hand the Western Church must bear in mind that the very points on which it has gone much further than the Eastern Church have been the cause of far-reaching divisions. The more it abandoned the fellowship form and centralized the Church order, the more the priesthood of all believers protested, even going so far as to question the ministries altogether. As its dogmas became separated more and more from the worship-service, and the more it proceeded to formulate and impose theoretical tenets concerning the doctrine of man, the relation of nature and grace, and other doctrines, the more new claims arose for recognition as dogmas (as the tide of history brought new self-knowledge and new experiences of grace). And in the West the more the presence of the eschaton in the worship-service was complemented (or even replaced) by political sermons on contemporary themes, the more the Church was dragged into secular divisions. The more the Western Church tried to bring uniformity and legal obligation into all these questions, and sought church unity in unity of formulas, the more divided it became.

Every Church tradition is exposed to its special dangers,

especially if it claims to be exclusive. But the basic structures of preaching and doxology, of historic-personal and of ontological statement, complement one another; the expectation of Christ's return also complements the assurance that he is already present here and now. I am therefore convinced that on essential points the Eastern and Western traditions complement one another, and can warn and protect one another against the specific dangers inherent in their respective positions. The importance of the Eastern tradition for Western Christendom must not be underestimated. It may also help us to examine from a fresh angle the differences between the Roman Church, the Reformation Churches, and the free Protestant groups. In my view it is therefore absurd for the West to want to proselytize within the Eastern Church. The Western Church should be restrained from any such projects already through respect for the fact that the Eastern Church not only survived centuries of oppression by Mongols, Arabs and Turks, but also that during the 20th century it has suffered the bloodiest persecution ever experienced in the history of the Christian Church, and in face of that persecution has shown a spiritual strength which has strengthened the whole of Christendom.

I have particularly mentioned the importance of the Eastern tradition for Western Christendom. As I myself belong to a tradition derived from Augustine and Luther, this may seem paradoxical. I could really have spoken much more convincingly about the insights and impulses which spring from the Reformation, which in my opinion are of tremendous importance for the Eastern Church. For in my opinion it is an undoubted fact that some important and essential pronouncements contained in the message of the Apostles are less developed in the Eastern Church than in the West. But during the course of the centuries the different Christian traditions have become and still are so estranged from one another, that the *first* step must be for each of us to try to understand the importance of the *other* tradition. Our *first* question must be what fruits of the spirit we can perceive in *other* traditions, which are based on the common foundation of all Churches, namely the message of the Apostles. Our task today in the Eastern and Western Churches is to do this better than the medieval councils did; their major concern was to impose uniformity of dogma and centralize the legal order of the Church. But we must also do better than the 16th-century correspondence between Tübingen and Constantinople which soon developed into a quarrel about the principle of tradition and reached an impasse. Our main concern must be to discover the spiritual wealth concealed in the different traditions, and to seek the unity of the Church not in uniformity but in a fellowship of different traditions.

V. THEMES OF THE SECOND VATICAN COUNCIL FROM THE EVANGELICAL VIEWPOINT[1]

1. *The Ecumenical Task of the Second Vatican Council*

IF one looks at Church history so far in the 20th century the persecutions of Christians and the ecumenical movement stand out as the two most important events. Just as the persecutions of Christians in this century have in size left the old Church ones far behind so has the ecumenical movement all previous searches for the unity of Christians. That both events took place in the same period is not accidental. One will of course not be able to explain the synchronism simply by saying that by being mutually threatened and consequently through fear the separated Christians moved closer together. Rather did the steadfastness of Christian faith in suffering begin to develop in the persecuted churches such an illuminating power that the other Churches could not shun the impression that there the same Christ is at work on whose mercy they themselves lived. Thus there arose through the martyrdom of the Orthodox Churches in the years after the Russian revolution a completely new understanding of the Eastern Church, which had previously been thought fossilized. Thus in the time of the national-socialist oppression the partitions between the Catholic and the Evangelical Church also became in many places transparent. Beyond these particular causes the ecumenical movement had its roots in the knowledge that nothing calls in question the Christian message of salvation for the world so much as the disunity of the Churches.

Thus the divided Churches began to open for one another, there was a new attempt at a brotherly union and at the mutual adjustment of Christian witness. In the midst of the shame about the divisions there arose a joy in the particular spiritual gifts which fell to the share of the other Churches in their liturgy, in

[1] Published after the first session of the Second Vatican Council in April, 1963. Trsl. by I. H. Neilson.

their doctrine and in piety, and the urge for a mutual share in what is entrusted to each Church by the Lord. This movement began at the turn of the century in world missionary circles, led after the First World War to the first World Church Conferences in Stockholm and Lausanne, then in 1948 took on legal shape in Amsterdam in the constitution of the World Council of Churches, with which the International Missionary Council finally united in 1961.

From the beginning this movement was not only a Protestant one but was also most warmly welcomed and promoted by the Eastern Church. It is true that the Russian Orthodox Church in consequence of the Bolshevist oppression could not take part in the first World Church Conferences and after the Second World War the Orthodox Churches in Jugoslavia, Bulgaria and Rumania were also to begin with prevented by the Iron Curtain from taking part. But since 1961 these Churches together with the Orthodox Church in Russia are also members of the World Council, so that it embraces all Christian confessions —with the exception of the Roman Church.

The Roman Church was until recently very restrained with regard to the ecumenical movement. It is true that from the beginning it was invited to take part but it had refused these invitations and warned its own members about this movement. This happened with particular pungency in 1928 in the encyclical 'Mortalium animos'. The Roman Catholic theologians who wanted to take part as unofficial observers in the World Church Conferences in Amsterdam and Evanston were forbidden to do so, and all non-Roman Churches who assembled in Evanston were termed sects in a pastoral letter from the bishop responsible. Many Roman Catholic theologians who in those years stood up for ecumenical problems were distrusted in their orthodoxy and the ditches in face of the other Churches were made deeper by Pope Pius XII both by his encyclical on the mystic body of Christ—whose limits were equated with those of the lawfully constituted Roman Church in a more emphatic way—and by the dogma of the bodily assumption of the mother of Jesus into heaven.

It is important to remember this early history in order to appreciate the change which came about under Pope John XXIII. The proclamation of the second Vatican Council as an ecumenical one was, it is true, widely misunderstood in so far as according to Roman understanding every council of the Roman Church is ecumenical, no matter whether it is occupied with a rapprochement with the other Churches or not—because the Roman Church considers itself to be the exclusive true Church. But this council, is, however, also ecumenical apart from this in so far as it is adjusted to other Churches. Thus Pope John XXIII with regard to the council established the secretariat for the furthering of the unity of Christians, which does its work under the excellent guidance of the German curia Cardinal Bea and has continuously gained in significance. Thus this Pope also allowed Roman Catholic observers to take part in the assemblies of the World Council of Churches and invited the World Council and all denominations to delegate observers to the second Vatican Council. These observers were then afforded most generous insights into the activities of the Council, and between them and the Secretariat for Unity there developed a very frank and lively exchange of views, which extended also to numerous theologians of the Council and bishops. In these exchanges, criticisms by the observers of proposals before the Council were explicitly sought and received serious attention. Everyone who had encountered Vatican circles in previous years affirms that under Pope John an astonishing change in atmosphere took place. The Pope acted here doubtless from quite elementary impulses of longing for unity with all who bear the name of Christ.

It is evident that this ecumenical change is not assessed in the same way on both the Catholic and also on the evangelical side. On each side three groups can be distinguished which correspond to one another in certain respects:

There are certainly Catholics, especially in Rome and in purely Catholic countries, who noted the Pope's ecumenical interest with head-shaking and only accepted it out of dutiful obedience. This acceptance is perhaps eased for them by the consideration that after the recent successful enrolment in the World Council of the Orthodox Churches we mentioned the Roman Church appears isolated in the eyes of the world and that in view of this the presence of Orthodox and Protestant observers at the council could be interpreted as something like an ecumenical assembly of the other Churches round the Pope.

These Catholics meet other Christians with an emphatic but cool politeness.

Then there are others who enthusiastically leap over the deep differences that exist and the history of the separation of the Churches and think that all problems are solved by the Pope's turning to the divided brethren. They talk of the end of the counter-reformation, while they expect from the magnificent spectacle of the council assembly such a far-reaching impression on the rest of Christendom that in it the longing for unity with Rome and with the Pope as the head of all Christendom becomes irresistible. They meet the other Christians with an all-embracing certainty of victory.

But there are also those who know about the seriousness of the grounds for the split and about the obligation to conscience of the Christians separated from Rome and feel the existence of the other Churches as a real question for the Roman Church. They have no firm conception how unity can be brought about, but in brotherly frankness they ask first about the truth by which the others live and testify to them the truth by which they themselves live. Here true encounters take place and ecumenical judgements grow which have the promise of bearing fruit.

One must of course not imagine that these three groups can be statistically demarcated. The course of the council has rather shown in an impressive manner that the boundaries are moving. It was not the first two but the third group which grew larger in the course of the council and only from it is a true rapprochement between Rome and the other Churches to be expected.

Corresponding attitudes can also be distinguished in the Protestant camp:

There, are on the one hand, the suspicious who do not forget the counter-reformation and the rejection of the ecumenical movement by previous Popes. They see in the new ecumenical change only a continuation of the old Roman policy of subjection by other means, as the political resources of power have been taken out of the hands of the Roman Church in most countries. They judge the Roman Church according to its most backward appearances and misjudge what has resulted in the way of a new start in the so-called 'new theology'.

On the other hand there are naturally also in the Protestant camp some enthusiasts who, with flying banners, leap over the existing differences. They expect from the Roman Church concessions which are illusory and develop programmes which attain neither the reality of the Roman Church nor portray the connexion with the Evangelical Church community.

But in between there is the crowd of those who are attentive without illusions, who take seriously the ecumenical impulses in the Roman Church and see themselves genuinely questioned. Here begins a frank questioning about what Christ is doing today in the Roman church. Here one tries to meet the Roman Church in a similar way to what has been experienced in the ecumenical movement for decades with other Churches, and here many a genuine brotherly exchange is achieved.

On the Protestant side too these groups can naturally not be understood statistically. But obviously the third is on the increase. Characteristic of this is also the public intercession with which many communities of the Evangelical Church have attended the opening of the second Vatican Council.

But however one judges the groups and their ecumenical attitude within the Roman Church one will still be able to say that the Roman Church has recognized the ecumenical task and set about it. Likewise one will be able to say of the other Churches as a whole in spite of all differences that they have taken notice of and welcomed the new ecumenical alignment of the Roman Church.

If, then, with impatience of scepticism, questions are put about the results so far of the second Vatican Council one must not forget that it needed centuries of long growth before the non-Roman Churches achieved the measure of communion as it is exhibited today in the World Council of Churches. Likewise ecumenical thought will need a time of growth in the Roman Church. It would also on that account be unjust to judge the first period of the council negatively on account of the lack of definite resolutions, as only the beginning of the council has taken place here. That the discussions and the formation of the theological fronts in the first period of the meeting were able to follow in such freedom and that such motions as were executed very conservatively and less ecumenically were criticized and put aside is to be judged much more positively.

Just as premature are the attempts to say already what will

be the final results of this council. For at the moment it is not even known which themes, namely which of the motions of the council, originally about 70, will finally be dealt with and given recognition by the drafting of decisions. Also one cannot foresee how the struggle between the conservative and the ecumenically forward-thrusting powers, which appeared so impressively in the first period, will finally work out. In many respects the start of ecumenical questioning in the first period of the council resembles the situation at the beginning of the ecumenical encounter at the time of the World Church Conferences in Stockholm in 1925 and Lausanne in 1927. It was a spring of opening impulses and hopes but still no harvest. The impulses were strong, but still very much unelucidated. They created a new atmosphere and with it the hypothesis for the work of succeeding decades, but they were not the anticipation of the results of this work.

And yet more should result from a careful observation of the first period of the council than these moments of a change in atmosphere, placed mostly in full publicity in the foreground. It seems to me much more significant that in an attentive analysis of the events so far apart from such less comprehensible moments of new impulses an ecumenical method stands out which can be of great significance for the future. I say 'can' for the discovery of a method does not yet say anything about whether and with what logical consistency it will then actually be applied. The discovery and the handling of a method are just as much two things as the discovery of a path and the taking of the path and finally the persistent progress on this path. In spite of this the perception of a method is already more than only a good intention and a vague hope. It is much more a programme. If I understand correctly six methodological standpoints have so far emerged, which are becoming significant for the tackling of the ecumenical task by the Roman Church.

1. Contrary to many expectations which had been awakened by the first proclamation of the council the Pope did not convene any council for union, no council, that is, in which the representatives of the divided Churches have to negotiate with one another about union and bring it about. He rather made the theme the inner renewal of the Roman Church—a renewal which the Roman Church has to carry out in self-examination.

Thus the Roman Church did not appear in this council, as in the invitations to the first Vatican council, with challenges to the other Churches, but it deliberated the challenges which it must put to itself for its own renewal and for proper service to the world. The call to repentance with which the Pope introduced the council is in accordance with this attitude. In fact self-examination in repentance must be at the beginning of every ecumenical encounter.

2. Even though the second Vatican Council consequently takes place as an internal council of the Roman Church without representatives of other Churches having seats and votes in it, its work should not be introverted but take place with regard to the other Churches. It must constantly be observed how the Roman Church and the theme of its council is represented in the eyes of the other Churches, how the formulations of the texts of the council are understood by them, and offensive statements should, whenever possible, be avoided. This challenge includes the necessity to study the other Churches more closely, to free oneself from the polemical and one-sided prior understanding of them which has grown up historically and to push forward to a genuine understanding of their present reality. All this means the entry into a dialogue between Churches which neither records nor disguises the differences—a dialogue which serves understanding and the state of becoming understood. Observers would be invited to this dialogue in which frankness in criticism of the motions of the council would be expressly asked for by them.

3. In connexion with the inner renewal and alignment to non-Roman Christendom it is repeatedly demanded by the Pope that a new form of statement (modus enuntiandi) must be found for the decisions of the council. In this he is thinking above all of a pastoral manner of speaking, that is an ecclesiastical language which addresses present-day man directly—in place of the abstract form of statement of the traditional neo-scholastic dogma of sin. With this demand facts are at the same time taken seriously which have become increasingly important in the scholarship of the different Churches independently of one another, namely the significance of the philosophical conceptions and the forms of thought and statement by means of which the divided Churches have made their theological

statements. There are differences of dogmatic formulations which are not differences in faith but only differences in the form of statements of faith. Thus there results the necessity for a translation from one form of thought and statement to the other and from one conception to the other. Only then can the essential agreements and differences which exist between the Churches be determined. Moreover the return of such analyses and translations to the elementary statements of faith in which every Christian lives, namely the statements of prayer, confession and witness, is decisive. These are also the statements with which the pastoral address demanded so intensively by the Pope has in a particular manner to do.

4. It is thus of fundamental significance that so far in the course of the council a distinct tendency became evident to open the uniformity of the Roman Church in the direction of the diversity of ecclesiastical life. This tendency appeared in the order of the Mass with which each session of the council began in the church of Peter. The Mass was by no means celebrated only in the Latin form, which is almost generally widespread in the West and is the custom in Germany also. As well as it other still only locally used Latin liturgies, as for example the Ambrosian-Milanese one, gained acceptance, but so too did Greek, Slav, Coptic and Arabic liturgies in great variety. Moreover, the services of the oriental united Churches were conspicuous because in contrast with the Latin Masses they were linked with a communion, in which the sacrament was administered to those present in both kinds, that is with bread and wine. In that a place was given to all these rites, which are in general in use somewhere within the Roman Catholic Church, and thus at the same time to different vernaculars, one was again reminded of the truth often overlooked by Rome that Catholicism properly understood is unity in diversity. Even though this was made evident at the council first of all only for the rites this could still mean a fundamental switching of position with consequences beyond those affecting the rites. The old Church was before the progressive national ecclesiastical and then especially Roman uniformity a union of very differently ordered Church territories. Various regional confessions of baptism and Church orders were valid in it side by side. Decisive for the unity was not the same dogmatic or legal ecclesiastical formula but mutual recognition

and indeed recognition that here and there in different forms and with different formulas one and the same Lord is known and served.

5. Of fundamental importance is also the fact that in the course of the council there began a distinct movement from curial centralization in the direction of the joint responsibility of the bishops for the whole Church. This movement had been promoted by the Pope himself in that he gave the council fathers freedom for the formation of judgements and groups and thus made possible a council, which, in contrast to the previous councils in Trent and in the Vatican, is determined not only by the confrontation of Pope and curia on the one hand and bishops on the other, but by three poles, namely Pope, bishops and curia. Moreover, the tendency here to give the bishop's colleagues of the individual countries or areas greater authority and thus to let the unity of Church direction appear stronger than the community of bishops corresponds to the tendency of diversity in unity which I spoke about in the previous section. Even though it is until now only a matter of a beginning in this direction it is still of fundamental importance in so far as the old Church had for many centuries understood its unity as communion but not as obedience to a central court. This understanding of the old Church has been kept in the Eastern Church and in the Reformation Churches till the present day, while the bishops of the Roman Church, especially after the first Vatican Council, appeared, when seen from the outside, to be often only the executive organs of the central papal-curial authority.

6. Finally, the repeatedly given explanation that this council is not to create any new dogmas is methodologically important for the ecumenical dialogue. This naturally does not mean any restriction of a further development of theological thinking or even of the ideas of piety. But dogma is distinguished from all this by the fact that it raises a generally binding claim and excludes from the communion of the Church everyone who does not submit to this claim. Since the Roman Church created dogmas with a wider scope than any other Church and strengthened the ditch between itself and the other Churches the renunciation of this council of the proclamation of new dogmas would express the fact that this ditch is not to be made deeper and that discussion with the other Churches over and

above the ditch is to be taken seriously. One can, for example, hope that in spite of the insistence of a group of bishops on further mariological dogmas the council is practising reserve.

That these six methodological standpoints have appeared in the preparation and in the course of the council so far seems to me of great significance. Their appearance is hopeful because they are in accordance with the methodological standpoints which have also been prominent in the history of the World Council and have stood the test here. It is not as if the Roman Church had taken them over from there, but rather that they appear wherever a genuine urge for Christian unity presses for elucidation. It is true that the six standpoints cited are not alone sufficient for the production of unity but they are still the first important indications of the way laid upon all Christians for a brotherly union.

2. *Scripture and Tradition*

In the second Vatican Council the ecumenical self-disclosure of the Roman Catholic Church with regard to the other Christian Churches proceeds in the first instance in an indirect way. For the tasks of the council are not negotiations of union with other Churches.

This ecumenical orientation which is, to start with, only indirect brings with it the idea that among the themes, for whose treatment the so-called schemata, that is the motions for the decisions of the council, have been worked out during the time of preparation for the council, are many which are of a quite internal Roman Catholic nature. This is true, for example, of the arrangement of the dioceses, the questions of the benefits and the ecclesiastical administration of wealth, of the stipends of the mass and of many affairs of order. More significant for the other Churches are the liturgical questions, as divine worship in each church is the centre of ecclesiastical life and therefore in the order of divine worship there are preliminary decisions for the dogmatic understanding of the Church, of the office, of the general priesthood of all believers and so also for the understanding of the divided Churches. Over and above this, however, there are also those themes which have directly as their subject the relationship between the Roman Church and the other Churches. The evangelical public thinks moreover

above all of the problems with which the practical living together of Catholic and evangelical Christians is burdened and
the ecumenical good will of the Roman Church is untrustworthy to many; above all, the practice of mixed marriage, the
practice of missions in Evangelical Church spheres and the
curtailment of religious freedom in states in which the Roman
Church has the upper hand. But these problems can in my
opinion be relatively easily solved, and indeed even without a
council, since neither an adjustment of existing dogmatic
obligations nor new dogmatic decisions are necessary. More
weighty than these practical problems are on a long-term view
the fundamental questions of a dogmatic nature, a decision
about which then yields a norm for practical behaviour. Of the
greatest significance is, for example, the dogmatic definition of
the nature of unity and the boundaries of the Church: what does
the name of brother mean, by which the non-Roman Christians
are today addressed by prominent members of the Roman
Church? What kind of communion with Christ and the Roman
Church is conferred on them by this? Depending on how the
decisions of the council turn out, the nature of the way forward
will be settled for a long time for the corporate life of the
Churches. The really dogmatic themes of the council are to be
taken the more seriously, as according to Roman Catholic
understanding no dogmatic decision, once taken, can be altered
again.

It is not possible here to go into all the themes whose treatment has been prepared beforehand by schemata. It is the less
possible here to go into the text of the schemata themselves, in
so far as it has been given up till now to the council fathers and
the observers; for it is of a confidential nature. But it is certainly
possible to go thoroughly into some of the themes of the council
and indeed in the manner in which they are presented in
the present theological situation. I will confine myself here to
the themes, scripture and tradition—Christ, the Church and
Mary—the unity and the boundaries of the Church. In each
case it is a question of themes of a fundamental nature, on
whose treatment by the council the future relationship between
the Roman Church and the rest of Christendom will in a particular manner depend, and indeed I will begin with the theme
scripture and tradition. What are we concerned with here?

With the invitation to non-Roman Churches to send council observers the Roman Church requested an ecumenical dialogue and the other Churches accepted this invitation. But these standpoints do not alone suffice. Joint statements must be added about the standard which the partners in the discussion acknowledge in common and on which they can mutually address one another. If such a set standard is lacking the dialogue soon becomes, in spite of the most friendly intentions, merely an opposition of self-representations: I am thus, and I am thus— and each demands of the other: become as I am. Without a mutually acknowledged set standard each dialogue soon ends in monologues. The theme 'scripture and tradition' deals with this common standard.

All Churches agree that they profess Jesus Christ, the crucified and risen, as their historical basis and present Lord. This profession includes the acknowledgement that the Apostles as Jesus' appointed eyewitnesses of his words and deeds, his suffering and his resurrection are of lasting, fundamental significance for all ecclesiastical doctrine. For there is no other approach to the historical event of Christ than that about the message of the historical eyewitnesses. A final normative force is thus conferred on apostolic doctrine by all the Churches. Only the apostolic Church, i.e. that remaining on the foundation of the Apostles, can be acknowledged as the true Church.

But it is a source of dispute between the Churches where this normative apostolic doctrine is to be found. The question of the 'sources of the revelation' is disputed, as the wording of the corresponding scheme of the council puts it. The answers of the Roman Church 'scripture and tradition' and of the Evangelical Church 'the Holy Scriptures alone' are here opposed to each other. If the reformers had made the Holy Scriptures valid as a critical standard in the face of definite doctrinal developments and abuses of the Roman Church, the Tridentine council decided in face of this that the apostolic doctrine was to be ascertained from both the Holy Scriptures and the oral tradition. It is true that the council distinguished fundamentally within tradition between the tradition of the apostolic doctrine and the tradition of ecclesiastical decisions, but as it did not state concretely what is apostolic and what only ecclesiastical tradition, this doctrine was understood on the evangelical side as the self-justification of the Roman Church, namely as a defence of their mistakes and abuses of the claim of the divine word. This contrast became most critical recently by the erection into dogma of the bodily ascension of Mary. For on this point both the Holy Scriptures and the tradition of the first five centuries are silent. This view of piety arose only late. If in spite of this it has been proclaimed as a dogma necessary for salvation and as an apostolic doctrine, the doctrine of the historical apostolic foundation has, according to the evangelical view, been here dissolved, and the religious consciousness and teaching profession of the Roman Church has itself become the standard. Even the Eastern Church rejects this dogma.

Without more ado it is clear that such different answers to the question about the so-called sources of revelation necessarily also bring in their train very different doctrinal statements with regard to contents, whether it is the doctrine of faith and works, or that of the number and nature of the sacraments, or the adoration of Mary and the saints, etc. But how can an ecumenical discussion be conducted here if the normative presuppositions of this discussion diverge? Must the discussion not then proceed without result?

However logical this train of thought may appear we must not overlook the fact that in Church history very often the reality of the spiritual life does not correspond with the logical consequences from previous decisions on principle. Rather is it an important fact that almost simultaneously with the most acute stage in the post-Tridentine clash of positions new impulses in the question of the sources of revelation emerged both in evangelical and in Roman Catholic theology, which made the ecumenical dialogue become more intensive than in the time previous to it. These newly arisen impulses must be seen clearly even if the existing boundaries cannot be overlooked. What are the factors by which the ecumenical discussion received new stimulus?

1. The first thing to be mentioned here is the intensive and fruitful encounter and co-operation between evangelical and Catholic biblical scholars. After Catholic exegesis was freed by the biblical encyclical of Pope Pius XII from the narrowness of an anti-modernistic tutelage for genuine historical research it progressed in a very noteworthy manner. Because this

encyclical was emphatic in laying down as a task the examination of the historical meaning of the scriptures, that is of what the authors of the biblical texts wanted to say themselves, the same methods and the same problems have resulted in the Catholic sphere as in the evangelical biblical research. These problems are no longer concealed from the outset by later ecclesiastical interpretations and by reinterpretations having recourse to ambiguities in scriptural meanings. By the joint application of historical-critical methods an astonishing measure of agreement has resulted in exegesis and indeed also in the understanding of those texts whose interpretation was very much disputed in centuries gone by by evangelical and Catholic theology. This is partly true even of the understanding of the Pauline doctrine of justification. It is particularly significant for the ecumenical discussion that by exegetical work both in evangelical and in Catholic theology the great diversity of New Testament statements has become evident more clearly than ever before—whether the statements about the significance for salvation of Jesus Christ, or those about faith and works, or those about the order of the Church. For this diversity within the New Testament signifies at the same time a diversity of beginnings for later theological and ecclesiastical developments. It is true that this Bible scholarship has not remained undisputed in the Roman Church; thus strong attacks have recently been directed against the Papal Bible Institute by conservative Roman circles. But the awakening of historical exegesis could no longer be stopped. Thus the Bible *really* came to have an astonishing importance in the Roman Church without the fundamental relationship of scripture and tradition having been altered.

2. But even the relationship of scripture and tradition has been thought over anew in Roman Catholic theology, and the swift interpretation of the Tridentine decision according to which apostolic doctrine was to be derived partly from the Holy Scriptures, partly from tradition, has been questioned by very notable historical investigations. Here we might indicate particularly the important works of the Tübingen theologian Geiselmann. He attempts to interpret the Tridentinum so that both the Holy Scriptures and tradition contain *the whole* of the apostolic doctrine, that consequently the apostolic doctrine of

the Holy Scriptures is passed on in tradition and interpreted. Even though Geiselmann's interpretation of the Tridentinum is disputed historically there still remains to consider that the early fathers wanted to be theologians of the scriptures alone and that even Thomas Aquinas and other teachers of medieval scholasticism acknowledged only the Holy Scriptures as the source of ecclesiastical doctrine. This too has been worked out more recently by Catholic research workers in a most impressive manner in relation to the post-Tridentine definition of the relationship of scripture and tradition. It is true that one can ask critically whether and how far Thomas was really an exegete—but it is first of all essential for the relationship *in principle* of scripture and tradition that he *wanted* to be one. Even if these more recent examinations of the concept of tradition have by no means generally succeeded in the Roman Church they have still created a new ecumenical situation for discussion.

3. Even in evangelical theology the treatment of the problem of scripture and tradition has recently been put in motion. On the one hand by the knowledge that oral traditions are at the root of the New Testament scriptures. On the other by the statement that at the beginning of the Reformation stood not the principle 'only the Holy Scriptures' but 'only the apostolic gospel'—not the letter, but the living message of Christ thrusting into the actual historical situation. This proclamation of the Gospel which is continuing throughout the centuries can, however, be termed tradition, so that even in the evangelical sphere the apostolic doctrine is passed on by scripture and tradition. For the rest, it is known to our present-day historical thinking more clearly than to early generations that even in the Evangelical Church traditions have solidified which stand in the way of the development of many New Testament approaches.

With these new questions and insights in evangelical and Roman Catholic theology the problem of scripture and tradition is naturally not yet solved. To say the least, the Roman Catholic and the evangelical traditions themselves are not the same. Moreover, there is no agreement in the important question whether, in what radius and by whom the Holy Scriptures can be used as a critical measure against the tradition of the Church. But doubtless a notable loosening up in the whole state of the discussion has ensued, and it has become clear that both sides are wrestling with the same problem.

4. But the ecumenical dialogue has not waited till these problems were solved. Just as the separated Churches determine the relationship of scripture and tradition so they still have the same Bible. It is read out everywhere in divine worship, sermons on biblical texts are delivered and in theology people argue from the Bible. And even if as well as the Bible tradition or even later piety and its self-expression has within the Roman Church been validated as the source of the revelation by those who teach, yet at least the demand for freedom of opposition between all that and the Bible holds fast. Thus it is obvious that in the ecumenical dialogue from the Bible should be the point of departure as the *real* common factor and that from it, in the diversity of statements and beginnings contained in it, to interpret anew the different traditions and also the different dogmas of the divided Churches. At the same time the historical method is no less important in the discussion about dogmas than in the examination of the scriptures. For the dogmas are properly understood only if the historical situation and the concepts conditioned by history are understood, in which in the face of new problems and threats, such as the apostolic era did not yet know them, and consequently in new words, the apostolic faith must be known. Even if in this effort with the Bible as the *real* common factor nothing is yet decided about the question of principle, 'only the Holy Scriptures' or 'scripture and tradition', a genuine dogmatic discussion between evangelical and Roman Catholic theologians has nevertheless got under way here—in a similar manner as it has already existed for quite a long time within the World Council between the Evangelical and the Orthodox Churches.

5. These discussions have proved themselves not only as auspicious from the human angle but also as fruitful, and indeed more than to begin with could be supposed. Many misunderstandings of mutual doctrine, at times centuries old, were put aside. Much common property, which lay hidden under differing terminology, was brought to light. Many one-sided attitudes in the dogmatic positions, conditioned by struggle, were perceived, and this is indeed true not only on the evangelical but also on the Roman Catholic side. Within Catholic

theology the break-through of thought concerned with Heils-geschichte in place of one-sided ideas on being, and the under-standing of the gospel as an operative word and a divine act of grace in face of a one-sided sacramentalism must be welcomed as the fruit of such encounters. On the other hand there exists every occasion for evangelical theology to be called by Roman Catholic theology to a new serious approach to the early Catho-lic beginnings in the New Testament. From these first results there are doubtless still further fruits of the ecumenical dialogue to be expected in the future.

Nevertheless all this must not be overrated. However sig-nificant and hopeful these events are they have their limit in the dogma in force in the Roman Church. The dogma is considered according to Roman understanding in its entirety as something that cannot be corrected, and all dogmas, whether they are more or less central, are considered as binding in the same strict degree. If one considers in addition that no Church has erected such a range of its doctrine into dogma as the Roman Church then it is clear from the outset that the possibilities of discussion in the Roman Church are less and the walls shutting them off are incomparably higher than those between the Eastern Church and the Churches of the Reformation. The non-Catholic will do well not to disregard for a moment this frontier of the Roman Church in its dialogue with other Churches. The Pope also sees himself committed to this frontier of dogma. A unifica-tion of the divided Churches therefore appears hopeless as long as the Roman Church holds fast to this demand in its entirety. For many of its dogmatic decisions are too little in accordance with the scriptures and too time-bound and their Tridentine and post-Tridentine dogmas are in particular too polemically one-sided and too little Catholic in the true sense, that is, too little in accordance with the fullness of the apostolic truth, for them to be accepted by the whole of Christendom.

But it would likewise be wrong to under-estimate the positive events previously mentioned. For we must not overlook the fact that within these Roman frontiers is possible a greater diversity of theological thinking and also a more intensive struggling of different theological tendencies with one another than one generally accepts from outside. In spite of holding fast to the dogma not inconsiderable changes in the interpretation of the dogma, new accentuations, new questionings, and also new perceptions are possible, and the longer one concerns onself with the Roman dogma the clearer it becomes that many possibilities have not yet been utilized which are left open by the dogma in spite of its so far-reaching fixation. Thus even in the Roman Church, in spite of its being tied to dogma, much can change in the activity of ecumenical dialogue. Even if such changes in themselves do not suffice for the union of the divided churches they can yet lead to the elimination of vexations and over and above that to an opening and to a brotherly relationship between the divided Churches, so that it becomes clear to the world that Jesus Christ is the one and same Lord whom the different Churches serve in different ways.

It should have become clear what eminent significance the council's theme, 'The Sources of Revelation', has for the relationship of the Roman and non-Roman Churches. Much will depend on how the decisions on this theme turn out. On the evangelical side one will wish above all that the vital qualities of Catholic biblical scholarship, and a new dogmatic and historical consciousness deriving from it, should establish themselves— but at least that their scope for development will not be curtailed.

3. Christ, Mary and the Church

We had established in the previous section that the ecumenical discussion between divided Churches can proceed fruitfully only if it proceeds with the acknowledgement of a common standard. Now all Churches refer to the fact that they are built on the foundation of the Apostles and consider themselves to be the apostolic Church. If the Churches want to come out of separation into unity again they must prove themselves under the common standard of the apostolic doctrine and try to understand one another afresh. Only with the acknowledgement of this common standard is the ecumenical discussion ultimately meaningful.

Now the Apostles are of course not themselves the foundation of the Church but only as the witnesses of Jesus Christ. Christ is the sole foundation and Lord. Only as the eye-witnesses of the words and deeds, of the death and resurrection of Jesus Christ and as the proclaimers of this Christ as the present and coming Lord have the Apostles a lasting normative significance for the Church of all times. Likewise neither the Bible nor tradition is in the true sense the source of the revelation. Jesus Christ is that alone, in whom the truth and the life of God has appeared. Only as original testimony of this divine act of revelation are they of normative significance. The question of Christ is thus decisive for the ecumenical dialogue.

Just as each Church raises the claim to be apostolic so it also raises the claim to be in communion with Christ and comes face to face with the other Churches with this claim. This claim can be expressed in different ways: the Evangelical Church considers itself above all as the community of believers in Christ and of those justified by Christ. The Roman Church emphasizes in a particular manner over and above such a community the identity of Christ and the Church and understands the Church as Christ himself living on in history. Their mariological statements point in the same direction. For the Roman Church worships Mary not only as the mother of Jesus but conceives her at the same time as the archetype, representation and embodiment of the Church. Because it gives Mary increasingly Christological titles of honour, as for example that of king, and because it wants to give others, these titles are simultaneously allotted to the Church, whose archetype Mary is considered to be. With the mariological statements also the unity of Christ and the Church is emphasized.

The promise of the Lord to the Church is in actuality valid: no one shall tear it from My hand. A Church in which Christ does not live and work through the Holy Ghost would not be a Christian Church. But at the same time we must not overlook the fact that the New Testament statements about the relationship between Christ and the Church are very diverse and that each is of fundamental significance for the relationship of the divided Churches. In the midst of all the statements is the confession that Jesus Christ is the Lord of the Church. As Christ's body the Church is the fullness of the present working Christ and in this sense identical with Christ. But the head of the body is alone Christ Himself, not the Church, and as this head Christ stands out against the Church. As the community of the believers in Christ the Church is the community of those justified and sanctified by Christ and is thus united with Him. But the Christ who gives Himself is at the same time the admonishing, commanding and warning Lord who as opponent of the Church demands the obedience of its members and judges disobedience. In the sovereign title of Christ the moment of judgement is also contained. But this moment is all too easily overlooked by the divided Churches in their behaviour to one another. There is such emphasis on unity with Christ that it goes beyond the usurpation of the name of Christ. There is a self-assurance in the Churches which prevents them admitting that Jesus Christ not only draws them in mercy to Himself as Lord but also calls them in question. In the ecumenical dialogue, however, this element of challenge must be clearly perceived.

Let us begin with some quite elementary New Testament considerations. However diverse, conflicting and bewildering the different traditions and Churches within Christendom are side by side and face to face with one another, they are still all together surrounded by two great acts of God, which they can by no means escape. In one of God's acts all Christian communities actually originate, no matter whether they recognize the truth of it or not, and they are all going towards the other act of God, no matter whether they are expecting it or not.

1. All Christian Churches originate in God's act of salvation, which is accomplished in the birth, the activity, the death and exaltation of Jesus Christ. In this act of salvation God manifested His love to the world. Christ bore the sins of the world. All men are placed under the promise of mercy. In this event of salvation human piety has been radically refuted and the opposites of piety and Godlessness have been reversed with breath-taking severity. The pious, the righteous rejected Jesus; the sinners accepted Him. The pious considered that Jesus was a sinner and brought Him to the cross. But the crucified thief was the first to perceive the victory of Jesus on the cross. In fact Jesus appeared not only to save but to judge: the saviour of sinners and the judge of the righteous. God justified Jesus, killed as a sinner, in the resurrection from the dead and placed him as Lord over His people and over the world, and indeed so definitively that nothing can be added to His existence as Lord.

Are we Christians sufficiently conscious of the offence of this our origin when we boast of salvation? Or have we diminished and made harmless this offence in the traditions of our Christian piety and adapted to the ethical and religious needs of man and the ease of action in worldly self-assertion?

2. All Christian Churches are moving towards the coming appearance of Jesus Christ. The apostolic message proclaims not only the Christ who has come but also the coming Christ. It proclaims that at the end of the ways of all men the Lord stands as conqueror over the world and over all its conflict. For he will gather his own from all lands, peoples and ages and hold the great communion with them. Then after all conflict and strife there will be *one* flock and *one* shepherd. Christ will come to redeem His people. But let us not forget: the Lord will come not only as redeemer, but also as judge, and indeed not only as the judge of the world but also of Christendom. Then the Lord will say to some: 'Come, ye blessed of my father'—and to others: 'Depart from me, cursed' (Matt. xxv. 34, 41). Then He will accomplish a separation which goes deeper than all separations that we men are occupied with on earth. In face of this separation of the last judgement even the divisions of the Churches are only temporary and in spite of all the seriousness with which they are taken lack any eschatological finality. For the separation which Christ will accomplish at the end of the world affects all Churches. None of them can count on remaining undivided. Even to those who have eaten and drunk with Him and have heard His word, even to those who have prophesied in His name and done great deeds, the Lord will then say: 'I never knew you: depart from me (Matt. vii. 22f.). Who then will be saved? The poor in spirit, those that hunger and thirst (Matt. v. 3, 6), those who watch and wait with longing (Matt. xxv. 1ff.), the restless who know that they are wholly strangers in this world and that they have no resting place here, the yearning, who await the solution of all problems solely by the coming Lord. To the rich, the satisfied, the laughing people, those who live and are loved in this world Christ says 'Woe, woe' (Luke vi. 24ff.). The one great net of the Lord has already been cast and all Christian communities, however disunited they may be among themselves, are already caught

in this one net which the Lord will one day draw from the floods of world history in order to arrange the fish.

Is Christendom conscious of the coming Lord? Is it wakeful in the expectation of its coming Lord? The Church has become older than the Apostles had expected. Christendom has not ceased to mention the coming again of the Lord in its confession of faith. But the spirit of expectation and the hastening and running towards its Lord has ceased in many places. Has Christendom not held on firmly to this earth? How far does it still see itself as the pilgrim people of God in a world that is coming to an end? Or has it again become a part of this world with the heavy load of its long history?

3. Is it not one-sided to speak with such emphasis of the challenge posed to Christendom by the first and second advent of Jesus Christ? Christendom does not exist in an empty space between the first and second advent, but in a space filled by the activity of Christ. Christ is the present Lord in the Church. Christ not only faces the believers critically, but they are his body and thus an insoluble part of himself. If he lives in the Church He is active through the Church in the world. All this is indeed to be acknowledged with full emphasis.

And yet Christ and the Church are not simply identical. The Church is His body, but never at the same time the head of the body. He alone is the head; Christ does not simply come up in the existence of the Church, but living in it He is simultaneously its opponent, its Lord, also its judge. Thus the Holy Ghost too is not simply identical with the Church, but living in it He is simultaneously its opponent, indeed its judge and indeed not only the judge of individual Christians but also of whole Churches. Thus the Lord admonishes the community in Ephesus through the spirit: 'Repent! . . . or else I will come unto thee quickly, and will remove thy candlestick out of his place, except thou repent' (Rev. II. 5) and the Lord calls to the community in Laodicea: 'Because thou art lukewarm, and neither cold nor hot, I will spue thee out of My mouth. . . . Be zealous therefore, and repent' (Rev. III. 16, 19). 'He that hath an ear, let him hear what the Spirit saith unto the churches.' These intimations of judgement are valid not only for individual Christians but for whole Churches.

4. That Jesus Christ is not only the confirmation but also

the challenge to the Church becomes clear in another way too if we look at the New Testament statements about the relationship of Christ and Mary.

All Churches revere Mary, the virgin mother of Jesus, as the human agent whom God took into His service in a unique way for the accomplishment of His work of redemption, namely in order that His son become a man. They worship Mary at the same time as the chosen member of God's race which this taking into service in faith confirmed. The magnificat 'my soul praise the Lord' in which this affirmation is expressed has remained a flourishing hymn of praise in all Churches.

This veneration is not only a reminder of the past fact of Jesus' birth, nor only a reminder that according to the account of the Acts of the Apostles Mary waited after Jesus' resurrection with the Apostles for the descent of the Holy Ghost. For the Church on earth knows that it is surrounded by the throng of the perfected and praises God in the invisible communion with the members of God's race who have preceded it in faith. Thus the Churches revere Mary in praising the one redeemer with Her, the prophets, the Apostles and all the perfect, the one redeemer who came from Mary's womb and by whose mercy Mary lives with all the faithful.

At this point we must of course by no means overlook the fact that according to New Testament testimony the affirmation of faith for Mary during the public activity of Jesus did not remain obvious. Even though She was the blessed mother She did not understand Him when He stayed behind as a child in the temple (Luke II. 50). Even though She is His blessed mother Jesus left Her later standing outside and, turning away from Her, said about His successors: 'Behold My mother and My brethren. For whosoever shall do the will of God, the same is My brother, and My sister, and mother' (A.V.). That his relatives thought Jesus mad is handed down in the same connexion (Mark III. 21). It is true that according to the Gospel of John Mary accompanies Jesus to the wedding in Cana, but there She was rejected by Him: 'Woman what have I to do with Thee?' (John II. 4). Thus the gospel shows us the blessed mother simultaneously as a woman troubled in faith, whose griefs are based not only in the suffering of her son but also on failure to understand His way. That Mary then, in spite of this trouble, stayed with the apostles after Jesus' resurrection with other women together in unanimity of faith was nothing other than divine grace.

The fact that the New Testament scriptures testify to both these things: Mary as the woman taken into service in a unique way and as the troubled woman, makes Her remembrance cherished and comforting. Thus She is an example of faith and a representation of the Church in Her earthly reality— namely of the Church which in this world is still on the way to the future perfection. In both things, in the selection as the mother of God's son and in the troubles of the suffering mother, Her life is an unforgettable hymn of praise of divine mercy.

5. For the rest one must not avoid the conclusions which result from this that all Churches have held to the Old Testament and understand the Church and Israel as one and the same people of God. Thus all Churches have in their Bible the prophetic books of the Old Testament. Prophetic preaching, however, reminded one not only of the covenant which God concluded for all time with Israel, of the act of selection by which God drew Israel to Himself out of endless compassion and made it His beloved bride. It also reminded one not only of the promises in which Israel must know itself secure. But it proclaimed judgement to Israel and the covenant, the selection, the promises were the reason for the unprecedented severity of the sermon of judgement. Even though loved by God, unified with God, Israel did not love God in return and did not give Him the honour due to him. It imagined itself to be at peace with God, but this confidence was shattered by the prophets. It was the false prophets who were proclaiming peace while the judgement was already beginning. Can the Church hold to the Old Testament and simultaneously speak of its unity with Christ with such confidence as if the prophetic reaching did not concern it?

In all these references nothing is said which all Churches would not theoretically know. But this knowledge is not existential. They know of God's struggle with Israel, but they are all inclined to lay claim to God's promises for themselves and to let God's judgements on Israel belong to the past. They know about Christ's struggle with the failure of his disciples and also of his mother to understand, but they are more or less all inclined to transfigure these forms and with them themselves. They know that Christ is the Lord who not only unites them with Himself but also commands and judges them, but they are more or less all inclined to equate his presence as saviour with their own circumstances. In their self-understanding they are too one-sidedly determined by the survey of their own history, but too little by their origin in the scandal that Jesus has been killed on the cross by the pious one of God's people. Finally they are too little determined by the end of their history, the coming of Christ as judge of Church and world. The doctrine of the Church finds itself presented in most dogmatics without a close connexion with the doctrine of the last things.

But where this knowledge becomes existential violent emotion arises. There the confidence and self-glory of the Church are shattered. There the outrage begins to burn in the hearts, which the Church through its disunity has inflicted on the Lord: they should proclaim the one saviour to the world but by their disunity they have obscured salvation from the world and made the message of divine peace untrustworthy. Where the Churches see themselves questioned by the Christ who has come and is coming repentance takes place which goes deeper than in the moral sphere only. For even with their dogmas and Church orders they are called to account and they cannot excuse themselves beforehand with the suggestion that this has all developed historically. There arises at the same time a longing for mercy, which goes farther than that they are satisfied with what God had given and is giving to each Church on its way. There arises the longing to share in all the gifts of grace wherever they are effected in Christendom. Communion with all believers becomes more important than the retaining of self-justification in isolation.

Where such violent emotion ensues there follow not only relaxed attitudes, rapprochements and a better understanding within the existing dogmatic and legal frontiers but the frontiers are broken through and the union of the divided becomes possible. For then it is no longer a question of one Church demanding a change of heart and return to the fold from the others but they will together be converted to the Lord and in the conversion to the Lord they will be converted to one another.

Is this a Utopia? Traditions seem too firmly ordained, too strong the protections, too obvious the frontiers. Must not chaos be the consequence if one sought to break through them?

There are certainly violent emotions which only bewilder and destroy. But there is also an emotion effected by the Holy Ghost which provides room for something new and which builds up by confronting man with the present reality of the living Christ. For everyone who looks more closely this pneumatic convulsion of Christendom has begun in our time. This is often clearer to laymen than to theologians. But even among them witnesses have stood up in all Churches who call for self-examination and new reflection. More strongly than ever one is beginning to perceive one's own guilt in the divisions and to speak of the church of sinners. More strongly than ever one is recognizing the common mission of the whole of Christendom in the world. It is still only a minority which is affected by this emotion. But everything depends upon the fact that the Churches as a whole let themselves be moved by it. If the Churches do not allow themselves to be moved by it then all their ecumenical efforts remain vain. For God is not satisfied with half-measures. He wants not only rapprochements between the divided Churches, but he wants unity.

Much will depend upon what opinion is expressed by the second Vatican Council on the relationship of Christ to the Roman Church and whether it resists those powers which would like to intensify the dogmatic statements about Mary and at the same time the self-glorification of the Roman Church.

4. Unity and Frontiers of the Church

It is of the greatest significance for the taking up of the ecumenical dialogue between divided Churches what ideas of unity and the frontiers of the Church those taking part in the discussion bring with them. For according to the narrowness or breadth of these ideas the discussion starts at the outset with a greater or lesser readiness to ask questions in the other Churches about the one Church of Jesus to which one is certain to belong as a member of one's own Church. Naturally when the ecumenical dialogue begins the question is always worked out how far the divided Churches have lived with one another or in opposition to one another in the past, whether for example the one has suppressed the other with force or has even tried to destroy it. More far-reaching, however, than these historical acts or even outrages are, above all, the fundamental effects of the dogmatic decisions in which one church has differentiated itself from the others. But above all it is decisive for all possibilities of a rapprochement what dogmatic decisions about the unity and the frontiers of the Church are put forward by those taking part in the discussion.

If we come to the New Testament with this question it is quite clear that the unity of the early Christian Church encompassed a great diversity of the confessional statements, the statements about the Church and the beginnings of Church order. The foundation of all communities is Jesus Christ, the crucified and risen, and he is this as the man witnessed by the Apostles, the eyewitnesses of His words and deeds, His suffering and especially His resurrection. But just as the handing down of the words and deeds of Jesus in the Gospels in consequence of the historical situation of the transmitting communities and in consequence of the theology of the evangelists already showed considerable differences, so still more the proclamation of the message of Christ into the different spheres of the Jewish, gnostic and hellenistic environment. The unity of the faith in Christ, baptism and communion did not manifest itself in the unity of the same formula of the creed and the same liturgical order in the act of baptism and the celebration of the Lord's Supper. Neither was there unity in the same order of the offices: neither a firm concept of the office nor the same definition of the relationship between office and free charismatic activities is found in the New Testament.

Even if in the first centuries an increasing consolidation of the formulas of the creed and the order of the liturgy and the offices ensued a great diversity is also characteristic of this time. Thus, for example, there is preserved for us a great abundance of old Church baptismal confessions, which at that time were recognized side by side in different eclesiastical provinces. The unity of the confession consisted not in one and the same formula but in the mutual recognition of the same content of the different formulas. This was correspondingly true of the variety in the liturgy and in Church orders. The basic structure of Church unity was that of the community in mutual recognition.

Only since the formation of the Church of the empire in the 4th century has this slowly changed under the influence of the principles of administration of the Roman empire. Now more and more the similarity of the formulas of the creed was seen to be necessary for the unity of the Church and there began to develop with the demand for uniformity in dogmatic statements as well as in the order of the liturgy and the offices a centralization which in the first instance was territorial. This process ensued in the different domains of the empire with very varying degrees of consistency but nowhere was it so logically followed through as in the domain of the patriarch of the West, the Bishop of Rome. The history of the Roman Church became in the centuries following the history of the increasing enforcement of a definite liturgy and ecclesiastical order of judgement and of the struggle for the papal central power over all other Church domains. At the same time no Church proclaimed further dogmas so widely as the Roman one and sought to give them currency with identical wording as necessary for salvation for the whole of Christendom and thus absolutely obligatory. That divisions in the Churches took place in this situation was obvious since neither the New Testament nor the primitive Church understanding of Church unity was uniform and centralizing.

In the face of all the divisions which have taken place in the course of Church history the Roman Church sees itself as the only Church in the true sense and thus absolutely as the one holy Catholic apostolic Church. This is true also *vis-à-vis* the Eastern Church. Over and above this, however, it denies to the Reformation Churches including the Anglican Churches that in their services of communion they receive the gift of the body and blood of Christ and refuses to recognize the authority of their ecclesiastical offices. It accordingly calls the Churches of the Reformation not Churches but only Christian communities if it does not term them even more reservedly as only Anglicanism, Calvinism, etc. From this assumption there results only the possibility of summoning the non-Roman

Y

Christians to return to the Roman Church. Strictly speaking it is thus not a question here of the union of divided Churches but of a subjection by which these other Christian communities first become Churches.

It is obvious that the other Churches reject this demand and indeed not only because they reject definite Roman dogmas on account of the lack of biblical foundation and polemical one-sidedness and perceive in the Roman centralization a far-reaching change in the early Christian and primitive Church community structure. Added to this is the fact that the subjection demanded of them would mean the denial of the fact that through the power of the Gospel and the gift of the sacraments they are already in Christ and are consequently already Churches.

The contrasts in the understanding of Church unity are so great and so rooted that a change appears possible only if such a far-reaching convulsion grips the Churches that even the historically developed foregone conclusions of their dogmatic and lawful cores are moved by it and the partitions are burst open by it. This agitation has so far taken hold of only a minority, but not the Churches in their entirety. In spite of this there are already beginnings which do not make it seem hopeless to take up the ecumenical dialogue on this theme. Even in the question of unity and of the frontiers of the Church the dialogue-situation is not fully recognized if one considers only the opposing dogmatic and legal positions of the Churches, however important they are. And indeed the question here is one not only of vague longings and hopes but of well-founded points of view. The following possibilities and points of departure must be considered:

1. It is a noteworthy fact that the Roman Church has not yet in the true sense interpreted its self-understanding in dogma, however shut off in may appear to be. Naturally, important preliminary decisions have in this respect entered into their other dogmas and also into their canonical law. But it still has no dogma in which it might dogmatically have defined in a real and strict sense the nature of the Church and with it its unity and boundaries. This is all the more astonishing when one considers that no Church has erected its doctrine into dogma so widely as the Roman church. But on this point

dogmatic decision is still outstanding. It is true that a dogmatic definition of the nature of the Church had been prepared for the first Vatican Council but the council did not come out in the question of the Churches about the infallibility of the Pope. Thus the Roman Church has today in the question of the unity and the frontiers of the Church still greater possibilities than in other questions which are already decided dogmatically, as for example the question of scripture and tradition. In questions already decided it sees only the possibility of new interpretations of the definitions considered to be final, a possibility which nevertheless should by no means be underestimated on the part of the other Churches. It is, however, true of the theme of the Church over and above this that its discussion still remains open in many respects. As the same proves true for most of the other Churches and as even the statements of the Protestant creeds are more statements about the characteristics of the Church than a comprehensive definition of its nature there still exists here in the whole of Christendom a place for ecumenical discussion which is not to be underestimated. The main reason for this particularly late development of dogmatic statements about the Church might be sought in the fact that the root of all dogmas is the creed and that the Church, in acknowledging its faith, looks away from itself to the triune God, whom it acknowledges.

2. Because the doctrine of the Church in significant respects is not yet fixed dogmatically the biblical exegetical work on this theme has greater possibilities of working itself out in Roman Catholic theology than on other themes which have already been decided by those in authority. With a noteworthy lack of prejudice Catholic bible scholarship has recently examined and worked out those New Testament facts which have played only a small part or none at all in the general Roman Catholic conscience. Of particular significance are the investigations into the relationship of the Church and the kingdom of God, which are becoming more clearly distinguished today than previously, the working out of the diversity of New Testament concepts and the connexions contained in them between Christ and the Church and between the Holy Ghost and the Church—and also the diversity of the beginnings of early Christian Church orders and in connexion with

that the diversity of the free charismatic services, that is the theme of the general priesthood of all believers. In these investigations there have been genuine encounters and many astonishing agreements with Protestant New Testament research. As in Catholic research facts emerge which were repressed in the Roman Catholic consciousness, so in Protestant research, for example, New Testament beginnings were discerned for the early Catholic understanding of the Church which had previously been overlooked.

Over and above scholarly biblical research new beginnings have come to light also in numerous Catholic systematic-theological publications on the Church, and indeed in connexion with the encyclical of Pius XII on the mystical body of Christ, the Church, and in the development of its ideas. In this encyclical the frontiers of the mystical body of Christ were completely equated with those of the Roman Church and only those baptized persons were acknowledged as members of the body of Christ who acknowledged the dogmas of the Roman Church and the sovereignty of the Pope. But— a further question was put—must not such statements be taken from tradition, according to which salvation is available already in certain undeserving cases where there is the wish for baptism in place of the receipt of baptism and likewise where there is the wish for the Church in place of lawful membership of the Roman Church? But if such acts of mercy of Christ are acknowledged outside the Roman Church must there not then also be talk of the Church and the communion of saints outside the frontiers of the Roman Church? Thus these Roman Catholic theologians hold fast to the identification of the Roman Church and the body of Christ according to the encyclical mentioned above, but teach at the same time that God's people or the communion of saints or even the Church extends further than the Roman Church. Thus even the old thesis that there is no salvation outside the Church is indeed portrayed for the Roman Church, but at the same time is extended to the receipt of salvation outside the Roman Church in a sometimes very astonishing manner and one which contradicts its historical meaning. There has doubtless been much activity here in the past few years which presses for clarification of the contradictions contained in these considerations and for new answers. It is true that in these extensions over the frontiers of the Roman Church the talk is above all of individual Christians, less of Christian communities, but even the question of the membership by non-Roman Christian communities of the Church is beginning to enter a new phase. Thus new hopeful beginnings for the Protestant-Catholic discussion have resulted and it seems, for example, that the solution of the old controversy of the visibility and invisibility of the Church is coming nearer today than in past centuries.

4. All this has not remained in the domain of abstract reflexions, but at the same time the Roman Church has set in motion an intensive attempt to investigate and understand the other Churches with new questionings. This had often been made too easy by comparing them only with the Roman Church and according as to whether in this comparison only legal or even dogmatic differences were to be ascertained, dividing them into schismatic and heretical communities, that is in those which separated from the Roman Church but have held to the same faith, and those which have fallen away not only from the Roman Church but also from faith. Today it has been perceived that this distinction is in no way sufficient to understand the nature of the other Churches. One no longer confines oneself to the affirmation of dogma and Church order and if need be to the liturgy of the other Churches, but endeavours to understand its spiritual life, its testimony and even its social-ethical effort in the world. Here too the Roman Church encounters the research work of the other Churches.

5. We must finally emphasize the newest beginnings of a shift in the Roman understanding of Church unity away from central uniformity in the direction of unity as a community in diversity. Here the matter has not stopped with theological judgements of a few theologians who have been concerned with New Testament and old Church research. Rather this displacement has made itself noticeable in the happenings of the council: already in the fact that Pope John XXIII convened a council at all and gave freedom for the formation of opinions and groups among the bishops to an unexpected degree—in communion with the bishops he wanted to lead the Church. Then in the great interest of the Pope in the fact that in the services held every morning at the beginning of the council

meetings the great variety of the liturgies and their languages made itself felt. These are only gentle shifts which have not yet had their outcome in legal Church definitions. We are also still very far from drawing from the conception of unity in diversity the necessary consequences for unity in a diversity of dogmatic statements. In spite of this we can say that the first signs of this are present, that the Roman Church and the Ecumenical Council of Churches are beginning to go up to one another in so far as in the Roman Church the dangers of uniform centralization and in the Ecumenical Council the opposite dangers of a lasting community without obligation are recognized.

The more clearly one sees all these fruitful new beginnings the more difficult appears the task which the theme of the Church places before the second Vatican Council. For however lively and hopeful these beginnings may be they are still for the present only beginnings. A Roman Catholic dogmatic council decision, however, claims immediately to be a final one. As the first Vatican Council decided from the prepared scheme on the Church only the theme of the infallibility of the Pope it is obvious that the second Vatican Council is filling with decisions the gaps which remained open then. But is this today possible, and in such a way that the ecumenical dialogue which is beginning is encouraged and not hindered by them? We must now bear in mind that the theme of the Church includes a large number of subsidiary themes which are of different theological difficulty and of different confessional range.

A dogmatic definition of the relationship of the bishops and the Pope has often been termed the most urgent of these. After the first Vatican Council the impression arose that the bishops might have lost their direct pastoral authority to the Pope and have become mere organs for carrying out the Papal will. Both in the more recent theological clarification of this question and in the collegial attitude of the Pope towards the bishops the presuppositions should be put forward so that decisions are made here and the community structure of the Church leadership is made visible.

Likewise particularly urgent is the repeated demand for the dogmatic clarification of the relationship between laymen and clergy, partly the stormy demand of those laymen participating at the preparations for the council or even at the council itself. Since a series of very noteworthy Roman Catholic works on the ecclesiastical position of laymen has appeared in the past few years and the ecclesiastical use of laymen of the highest position has been furthered by new questionings the presupposition should also be given here for bringing greater clarification to the question of the general priesthood of the faithful.

Incomparably more difficult, however, for this council could be the dogmatic definition of the unity and the frontiers of the Church. For the ecumenical impulses in the Roman Church are still too young for a new consensus already to be present in this question. At the same time the Church encyclical of Pius XII with its extremely narrow conception of the frontiers of the Church is still too near for something very different to be reduced to dogma. But must the unity of the Church be defined dogmatically now in any case? The Churches have lived for almost two thousand years without such a definition. Could one not wait until one can say of the Church by reason of the ecumenical experiences which are only now beginning that it includes all believers in Christ?

I must stop here. I have indicated some important themes of the second Vatican Council from the evangelical point of view. It is not possible to predict what the results of the council will be. It would be misleading to look only at the newly awakened powers which have come from biblical scholarship and the study of the old Church and are pressing for far-reaching reforms. Then the results could disappoint. But it would also be misleading to look only at the conservative powers, true though it is that one must reckon with them. For even if the results of the council were to lag behind what has been awakened in expectations within and without the Roman Church, it will have to be reckoned with that this new awakening cannot be undone. But in any case one can be certain that God will not leave the divided Churches in peace.

VI. THE RESURRECTION OF GOD'S PEOPLE

SERMON ON THE TEXT OF EZEKIEL XXXVII. 1–14[1]

ERE IS displayed to us a broad field strewn in every
direction by bleached human bones. It can no longer
be discerned which of these bones at one time belonged
to one and the same body. Was this a battlefield or a place
of execution, or was there here a cemetery where the earth
has been blown away from its burial-mounds by the storms?
Ezekiel's vision was far more gruesome than a site of death in
days of long ago. No, it was living human beings of his own
day and environment which he saw in this vision as dead
men's bones—men who breathe and eat and drink and marry
and work and play. And yet they are dead men, and indeed
decomposed, for they are men who have lost hope. Ezekiel
contemplated in this vision the reality of his people, of the Old
Testament Covenant people, in its dispersion, in part banished
to Babylon and in part miserable remnants in Jerusalem and
Palestine. What hope had this people lost? It was the hope of
again becoming united as the one people of God in the land
which God's promise had allocated to them.

We today can also be overtaken by this vision—as a
spectacle of the condition of Christendom. We are, to be sure,
alive and are intensively busy conducting services and instruct-
ing the youth. Our Churches run missionary activities and make
manifold incursions into the world. We regard these as actions
of the Holy Spirit and think that we are a new creation in
Christ, but amidst all this activity the vision of the field holding
dead men's bones overtakes us; for Christendom is not *one*
people. The Churches work alongside each other and against
each other. Again and again each speaks for itself and they are

[1] This Sermon was delivered in August, 1952, in the Chapel of the
World Council of Churches in the Château de Bossey at Geneva at the end
of the second session of the Commission for the preparation of the theme
for the World Council of Churches Conference at Evanston. Trsl. by
J. C. G. Greig.

all at cross-purposes. As a result of their disunity the Churches are repeatedly a hindrance to the salvation of the world. For on account of their disunity they refute the message of the sole Saviour and Lord of the world, under whom everything that is separated is one. Thus the Christians saunter along in life, out of touch and scattered like bones on the broad field of the earth, and to a great extent they have come to terms with this condition. Many have given up the hope that all who confess Christ should become members of one body and rise to join in common praise.

Ezekiel's vision was full of horror but the field of bones which is Christendom is still more appalling than that of the Old Testament people of God. For God has meanwhile saved His people in Jesus Christ from the dominion of death and has inaugurated a new Covenant through Him. God has poured out His Spirit upon all flesh at Pentecost and despite this we are not one. Is there anyone for whom in these circumstances the question can fail to arise whether we are in reality reborn and a new creation in Christ? But the new creation is a reality only as the community of the body of Christ which is *one* body; and the operation of the Holy Spirit means by its very nature the unity of the people of God as this people is gathered by the *one* Spirit of God.

Do you think these bones can again live? Thus God asks the prophet and so too He asks us.

In these days we have for the second time worked together on the theme of hope and our hope has been strengthened in this working together. Despite our origin in different Churches, lands and traditions we have become one community in which one has sustained the other by his testimony to the Christian hope and in which we have all then been able to express the one hope in Christ and even to fix it in writing, and to do this in common, not alongside each other or against each other, but with each other. In our midst we have in truth experienced something of the possibility of scattered bones again being knit together in one body and we all have good ground for thanking God for this.

But the question which God directs to us goes much further. It is concerned not only as in this place with a circle of twenty-five scholars but with the people of God as a whole; it is concerned with Christendom as a whole, the divisions and impotence of which we see so palpably before our eyes. Do you think that these bones can again live?

Ezekiel's answer says neither no nor yes. He answers, 'Lord thou knowest' and thereby he submits to God, recognizing him as the Lord who contrives everything and can do everything. God alone can raise the dead to life. Ezekiel's answer is thus for all its hesitancy not without hope.

But the decisive thing is that God is not content with such an answer either then or now. God constrains the one who hopes, takes him into service and makes him His instrument. He does not allow him to stand by waiting inactively as he says 'Lord thou knowest,' but sets him to work and makes him His mouthpiece and will accomplish His acts through him. Thus He sends the prophet and thus too He sends us after awakening hope in us and strengthening it.

What God lays upon us is so huge that He seems to be demanding nothing less than an absurd performance from man. We are to call upon those who do not hear, who have no ears, whose essential organs have long since mouldered away and crumbled into dust and ashes. We are to address dead and self-satisfied Christendom which has come to terms with living side by side in separated Churches 'You dry bones, hear the word of the Lord; thus speaks the Lord of these bones, behold I will put breath in you that you shall live. I will give you veins and will make flesh grow upon you and cover you with skin and give you breath that you may become alive once again and you will know that I am the Lord.' We are not to be talking *about* the dead—*about* those who have the mere semblance of life in them but in reality are dead: we are to address them. Is this not madness?

All God's words seem to us foolishness as long as we do not obey them in faith but we are to carry out this commission of God's and to believe that God's word is an active and life-giving word. By His word God at the same time gives the ability to hear and by His word he makes new organs effective. By the word God made the world and by the word God effects also the resurrection of the dead.

Even more astonishing is the continuation, 'Prophesy to the wind till they again become alive.' Who is meant by the wind? Is it the spirits of the dead which are again to return? No, it is the Spirit of God, the Spirit by which God gave life to the first man, the Spirit by which God inspired the prophets of the Old Testament, the Spirit which at Pentecost God poured out on all flesh. This Spirit of God is the God who makes alive Himself—the Lord. God orders us to call upon this Spirit in His name. There is not just a begging and beseeching in yearning uncertainty involved in this, there is a call made with assurance. Indeed it is almost a command laid upon us by God that we clothe Him in His Spirit. For it is God's will to implement the cry for His Spirit. However dubious many of our prayers may be the request for His Spirit is in any case well pleasing to Him. He wishes to give the Spirit to those who ask Him for it. His condescension is so great that He allows us in this certainty to call upon His Spirit, the third person of the Godhead Himself, and to expect from it what God has offered us and promised us.

Ezekiel did not only hear the commission but he also saw its fulfilment. The bones did come together again bone to its bone, and there grew veins and flesh upon them and breath came into them and they became alive again and stood up 'and it was a very great people'.

Let us disperse with this promise. The fulfilment of it is the body of Christ which rose from the grave and continues to grow as He unites in Himself believers from all peoples and ages—the body of Christ which fills the universe. Amen.